The
Feminist Possibilities
of Dramatic Realism

The
Feminist Possibilities
of Dramatic Realism

Patricia R. Schroeder

Madison • Teaneck
Fairleigh Dickinson University Press
London: Associated University Presses

Associated University Presses
440 Forsgate Drive
Cranbury, NJ 08512

Associated University Presses
16 Barter Street
London WC1A 2AH, England

Associated University Presses
P.O. Box 338, Port Credit
Mississauga, Ontario
Canada L5G 4L8

The paper used in this publication meets the requirements
of the American National Standard for Permanence of Paper
for Printed Library Materials Z39.48-1984.

Library of Congress Cataloging-in-Publication Data

Schroeder, Patricia R., 1951–
    The feminist possibilities of dramatic realism / Patricia R.
Schroeder.
        p.   cm.
    Includes bibliographical references and index.
    ISBN 0-8386-3677-2 (alk. paper)
    1. American drama—Women authors—History and criticism.
2. Feminism and literature—United States—History—20th century.
3. Women and literature—United States—History—20th century.
4. American drama—20th century—History and criticism.   5. Realism
in literature.   I. Title.
PS338.W6S37   1996
812'.5099287—dc20
                                                                95-50476
                                                                CIP

PRINTED IN THE UNITED STATES OF AMERICA

Contents

Preface   7
Acknowledgments   11

1. Realism and the Feminist Critique   15
2. Domestic Spaces, Women's Rights, and Realism:
   1910s–1930s   44
3. Remembering the Disremembered: Feminism,
   Realism, and the Harlem Renaissance   95
4. Refusing Containment   120
Conclusion: Appropriating the Master's Tools   149

Notes   159
Bibliography   167
Index   181

Preface

In the fall of 1991, as I began working on this book, I applied for an NEH fellowship. I was not surprised that my application was denied, since I knew that competition is keen and that the "F" word in my title might prove a red flag to the conservative granting agencies working under Lynn Cheyney and the Bush administration. What *did* surprise me, however, was the stated reason for the NEH's denial:

> There was a general feeling that your undertaking is of potential value to the field as well as to the humanities more generally. However, some of the reviewers were not convinced with your assessment of the feminist rejection of realism.

This report baffled me. In my proposal to the NEH, I had described the genesis of realistic drama, its central place in the development of American theater, and its ultimate rejection by feminist theater troupes and critics of the past three decades (topics I will explore in more detail in chapter 1). Central to my proposal was my thesis that realism need not be antithetical to feminist issues. I elaborated on this point by outlining some of the important feminist critiques of realism, explaining how I would refute them, and listing the American realist playwrights whom I see as feminists and whose works I would analyze to support my contentions. I appended a bibliography of over twenty-five critical works (the most I could squeeze onto my prescribed single page), nineteen of which (most of them books or collections of essays) comment directly on realism's deficiencies from a feminist viewpoint.

I recount this story here not because I feel snubbed by the NEH; given that only about one in ten proposals was funded that year, I did not expect their support of my project. What I did expect, however, was that they would be aware of feminist scholarship and its contributions to theoretical and dramaturgical debates, that they would have some understanding of the postmodern critique of realism (which embraces many theoretical and generic discourses in addition to feminism), and that a bibliography replete with titles like *Beyond Feminist Aesthetics, Beyond Naturalism, Performing Feminisms*, and

Feminist Practice and Poststructuralist Theory ought to convince even the uninitiated that the feminist (as well as poststructuralist) attacks on realism are a critical issue of some currency and concern.

Ironically, the NEH reviewers' negative response has indicated very clearly to me how much this study of realism's value to feminism needs to be undertaken. As a feminist, as well as a student and teacher of both American literature and modern drama, I am aware of the enormous complexity of the issues informing the debate over realism's compatibility with feminism. For example: while realism has dominated the mainstream American stage, the American theater also has a thriving experimental tradition; while contemporary feminists have rejected realism for a host of reasons that we should not dismiss lightly, and while realism does pose both textual and production problems for feminist playwrights and directors, these problems are not insurmountable, and realism is more varied and more potentially useful than many feminist theorists have recognized. Furthermore, American women playwrights, working under specific historical and social pressures, have often used realism as a tool of feminist expression. But despite these complexities, those engaged in the current critical debate over realism often take one of two rather extreme positions. On the one hand, many feminists attack realism, rejecting its referential power because it has so often been used as a tool of patriarchal oppression or to uphold the status quo. On the other hand, more traditional scholars tend to accept realism uncritically, overlooking the potential dangers of its representational strategies and its typically hierarchical methods of production.

Hence, this book.

I have focused my inquiry into the feminist possibilities of dramatic realism exclusively on American drama, primarily because dramatic realism has maintained its power throughout the twentieth century in the United States. While European theater has welcomed sweeping formal experimentation, mainstream theater in America has largely maintained its realistic framework (for economic as well as other reasons), adapting the inherited conventions rather than overthrowing them. Within this American theatrical context, a number of playwrights (many of them women) have expressed their feminist concerns (ranging from women's suffrage to reproductive freedom to women's conflicting social roles) in realistic dramas, their realism adapted in sometimes subversive ways that merit detailed examination from a feminist viewpoint. It is in this context where realism reigns that the sometimes subtle challenges to its authority can best be understood.

I have divided my discussion of feminism, realism, and American

drama into four chapters. The first chapter briefly outlines the historical development of realism and the modifications to the inherited
realist design that I see as typical of American realism. After thus
quickly setting the scene, in chapter 1 I examine in some detail the
evolving feminist critiques of realism, to which I respond with alternative theoretical positions. This chapter is intended primarily to
provide a theoretical framework for the discussions of plays and playwrights that follow in the succeeding chapters.

Chapters 2, 3, and 4 all explore the work of American playwrights
whom I see as feminist realists, working at different historical moments and in different cultural conditions. Chapter 2 looks at white
women working in mainstream American theater between 1900 and
1940, a time when feminist political activity went through an intense
growth cycle (building up to the passage of the Nineteenth Amendment in 1920) followed by a period of lamentable decline when the
vote failed to bring true political and social equality for women. The
women's plays of this period chart this cycle of growth and decline,
as playwrights like Rachel Crothers, Zona Gale, Marion Craig Wentworth, Charlotte Perkins Gilman, and Clare Boothe worked within
the inherited conventions of realism but often used them for feminist
ends. Their plays move from depicting the entrapment of women
in domestic spaces, to demonstrating the domestic consequences of
political choices and social movements, to parodying the conventions
of realism itself and of women's limited opportunities.

In Chapter 3 I examine the work of early twentieth-century
African-American women playwrights, who consciously worked in
multiple traditions and for multiple audiences. While I am aware that
this separate chapter may look like yet another ghetto for American
women of color, I believe the historical uniqueness of African-
American women's issues merits unique attention. In particular, I
examine in some detail the plays written during the Harlem Renaissance and through the 1930s, when playwrights such as Angelina
Weld Grimké, Georgia Douglas Johnson, Mary P. Burrill, and Shirley
Graham tackled controversial issues like lynching, demeaning sexual
and racial stereotypes, and reproductive choice in their realistic plays.
Their adherence to realism had much to do with their awareness of
a double audience (white and black) that looked on with different
expectations. Given this unique historical and theatrical context, their
plays deserve separate study.

Chapter 4 returns to a temporal rather than a racial grounding and
examines contemporary playwrights who adhere to the outlines of
realism but adapt them in experimental ways to express their feminist
concerns. While playwrights like Alice Childress, Marsha Norman,

Wendy Kesselman, and Barbara Lebow continue the interest in women's limited social roles and resultant split psyches begun by the playwrights discussed in Chapter 2, the intervening formal and social experiments of the 1960s offer them new ways both to use the strictures of realism and to expand its boundaries.

In all four chapters, I attempt to negotiate the dangerous waters of feminism's inclusions and exclusions with as much historical awareness as possible and with an attempt to de-center my own socially privileged positions as a white, middle-class, heterosexual academic. While this awkward invocation of my identities may seem like what Gayatri Spivak has called a "meaningless piety" (271), I feel it is crucial to situate myself in relation to the playwrights I discuss and to the historical conditions that led them to create realistic plays that depict, discuss, and protest the specific social and material conditions they saw and sometimes lived. For as much as I attempt to understand and respect the positions of theorists and playwrights whose work I discuss, my own subjectivity, howsoever acknowledged, will necessarily affect what I see and how I see it. I can only hope that by establishing specific historical contexts for the realistic plays I examine, I can bend the angle of my vision to see as the playwrights have seen, thereby avoiding what Susan Bennett has called the "tourist" or colonizing gaze (1993, 9). For while it is true that I have an agenda—to prove that realism can be an effective feminist tool—I honestly believe the playwrights whose work I examine would share that viewpoint.

Acknowledgments

I am grateful to Ursinus College for its continuing support of my research; to the Myrin Library staff—especially Joan Rhodes—for their always cheerful and expeditious help with my sometimes esoteric requests; to the Women and Theatre Program, which has provided both mental stimulation and encouragement; and to Richard G. Schroeder, who helped support me when the NEH wouldn't.

Earlier versions of some parts of this book have appeared elsewhere. Sections of chapter 3 have been published as "Transforming Images of Blackness: Dramatic Representation, Women Playwrights, and the Harlem Renaissance" in *Crucibles of Crisis: Theatrical Representation and Social Change,* edited by Janelle Reinelt (University of Michigan Press, forthcoming) and as "Remembering the Disremembered: Feminist Realists of the Harlem Renaissance" in *Realism and the American Dramatic Tradition,* edited by William W. Demastes (University of Alabama Press, forthcoming 1996). Parts of chapter 4 appeared as "Re-Reading Alice Childress" in *Staging Difference: Cultural Pluralism in American Theatre and Drama,* edited by Marc Maufort (Peter Lang, 1995) and as "Locked Behind the Proscenium: Feminist Strategies in *Getting Out* and *My Sister in This House,*" *Modern Drama* 32.1 (March 1989). The author gratefully acknowledges the publishers' permission to reprint.

This book is dedicated to the women who began and nurtured my lifelong interest in theater: to Susan Wickersham, who gave me my start in neighborhood plays by casting me as Bluebeard's wife; to Laura Wickersham, who took up where Susan left off and, being a visionary of cross-gender and cross-species casting, directed me as Dudley Dooright and Winnie the Pooh; to Mrs. Dowling, my first high school drama coach, who introduced me to the discipline of acting techniques and cast me as the male lead in several all-girl productions; to Jane Agostinelli, who gave me my first female role (outside my neighborhood) as Mrs. Marwood; to Joyce E. Henry, my former teacher and present colleague at Ursinus College, who has nurtured me in her many roles as a director, a peer reviewer of essays, and a fellow performer in feminist (and other) plays; to Gayle Austin,

11

J. Ellen Gainor, C. Dallett Hemphill, Joyce E. Henry, Margot A. Kelley, Kim Marra, Sandra Richards, and Jenny Spencer, who offered valuable suggestions on early drafts of this book; to all the members of the Women and Theatre Program, but especially past presidents Vivian M. Patraka, Jill Dolan, and Juli Burk, for their continuing encouragement of my work; and to Elizabeth M. Richards, my mother, who gave nine-year-old me a "Shirley Temple Theater" to play with, encouraged my script-writing and scene-designing efforts, and so initiated my love of theater.

The
Feminist Possibilities
of Dramatic Realism

1

Realism and the Feminist Critique

Recognizing Realism: The Case of Maria Irene Fornes

REALISM, as W. B. Worthen has recently argued, is "notoriously elusive" (1992, 14), difficult to define in terms of style or technique and difficult to locate in historical context. To illustrate this complex problem of definition and its impact on feminist studies of realistic plays, let me begin with a brief survey of the critical reception of Maria Irene Fornes. Author of more than two dozen works for the stage, recipient of numerous foundation grants and seven Obie awards (including one for Sustained Achievement in the Theater), Fornes has been a prominent playwright and director for more than two decades, and in the past ten years her work has begun to receive the critical recognition it merits. Yet critics and scholars seem at a loss about how to characterize her plays.

A number of critics locate Fornes within the traditions of realistic theater. For Bonnie Marranca, Fornes is writing "the finest realistic plays in this country" (29), using a "new realism" in which the characters exist in a linear temporal structure but avoid self-examination and declamation. For John G. Kuhn, Fornes's plays since 1967 have revealed a "fairly consistent if selective realism" (159), what Ross Wetzsteon calls "a kind of hyper-realism" (42). Jill Dolan likewise sees elements of realism in Fornes's work, claiming that the playwright overlays Brechtian techniques on "classic realist narratives" (1988, 110).

Other critics disagree, choosing instead to define Fornes's plays by the theatrical devices (as Dolan notes above) with which Fornes interrupts her realism. So for Judith L. Stephens, Fornes is a cultural feminist (a branch of feminism usually perceived as antithetical to realism, a subject I will return to later), because her "female characters . . . emphasize female bonding, nurturance, and unity" (1988, 62). Helene Keyssar agrees, arguing that the goal of Fornes's best work is "not the traditional self-recognition of one character, but a

15

collective and mutual acknowledgement of women by other women" (1985, 123–24).[1] Susan Sontag likewise minimizes the realism of Fornes's work, remarking "I am not convinced that Fornes's recent work is . . . a species of dramatic realism" (9). And W. B. Worthen takes this argument a step further, claiming that Fornes actually *repudiates* realism to explore "the ideological relation between theatrical and dramatic representation" (1989, 171).

Complicating this problem of the relative realism of Fornes's work is the feminist impulse often noted by critics, such as Stephens and Keyssar above. Among certain scholars, it has become a critical commonplace to discuss Fornes as a feminist: Gayle Austin describes her as a feminist "exemplar" in both form and content (1989, 76); Beverley Byers Pevitts sees Fornes as a feminist in sensibility, subject matter, characters, and dramatic structure (314); and Jill Dolan has called Fornes a materialist feminist "to a certain extent" in that "textual and performance interventions . . . undermine the tyranny of male narratives" in her work (1988, 101). Fornes herself, however, while claiming on the one hand that there is a female aesthetic ("How could there not be?" she says, "How could we, as women, have nothing in common?"—Betsko and Koenig, 163), has repeatedly refused to associate herself with the feminist movement.[2] Perhaps the best strategy for defining Fornes's plays is to agree with Janelle Reinelt, who argues that no single vocabulary "adequately captures" her theatrical style (1994, 136). Fornes offers, instead, a hybrid form, an adapted realism suitable for her sometimes feminist purposes.

I begin with the case of Maria Irene Fornes because it vividly illustrates many of the concerns central to my argument. First of all, what is realism? Must all the elements commonly attributed to realism be in evidence if a play is to be deemed realistic? Are there varieties of the form, perhaps "realisms"? What, furthermore, is feminist drama? Is it defined by content, theme, dramatic structure, staging techniques, production methods, performance styles? Is it necessarily experimental, necessarily antithetical to realism? Finally—and this is the central question that this book seeks to answer—can realism and feminism be compatible on stage?

The first problem made obvious by the reception of Fornes is defining exactly what stage realism is, and this struggle is certainly not unique to feminism. Realism does, however, have a definable purpose, a traceable history, and a shared set of conventions. The original purpose of realism was mimetic, or "the serious treatment of everyday reality . . . [embedded] in the general course of contemporary history" (Auerbach 491). That is, realism purports to reflect as closely as possible the offstage world of a particular time and place.

In realism's early years, realist plays focused on the upper-middle class social milieu of late nineteenth-century Europe—the here and now of its original practitioners—in order to depict societal problems and their impact on individuals. Realism thus privileges what Roland Barthes would call the "cultural" code of textual signification—that is, the social background of the action, or the offstage systems of knowledge to which the play continually refers—by emphasizing a specific cultural context.[3] It also rests upon what I will call the realistic contract, a compact between theater-maker and spectator that the play unfolding in a darkened auditorium is, in fact, a replica or analogue of lived experience outside the theater.

To create the action that would be played out before this illuminating social mirror, late-nineteenth-century realist playwrights also foregrounded what Barthes would call the "hermeneutic" code; that is, the articulation of a question that will be answered or a problem that will be explained, complete with suspense-generating delays in resolving the central enigma (17–19). Constructing the action according to this hermeneutic code (although not consciously using Barthes's terms, of course), playwrights of the era thus contrived a set of "realistic" stage techniques, including coherent, psychologically complex characters speaking ordinary language; a detailed set (usually but not inevitably a drawing room) separated from the audience by an imaginary fourth wall; and a causally structured, linear plot directed toward the resolution of a problem. These techniques, developed ostensibly for replicating offstage society and illustrating its impact on individuals, soon acquired the force of convention and were transplanted to the United States, where more than one hundred years later they still hold considerable influence in American theater. A realist play can thus be defined as one that reflects a specific social milieu in a particular era; that develops according to cause-and-effect sequences of actions; that ends with the resolution of some problem; that includes characters who react to the environment and action in complex and clearly motivated ways; and that attempts to convince the audience by all available theatrical means that the onstage action is, in fact, real (not fictitous) and occurring before them as they watch.

From its very inception, however, stage realism has evolved dynamically, as is suggested in the above comments from Jill Dolan, who recognizes that elements of realism can be combined with experimental techniques to create hybrid works that express hybrid visions. Marranca's description of Fornes's "new realism," like William Demastes's use of the same term to discuss playwrights like Marsha Norman and Charles Fuller, indicates that these critics, too, see stage realism as flexible and adaptable—more a terrain of inquiry familiar to spectators than a specific set of dramatic techniques. Furthermore, the codes of signification emphasized by realism are themselves evolving: cultural codes change as historical backgrounds shift, and the notions of linearity and causality underscored by the hermeneutic code are increasingly being challenged by deconstructive and postmodern formulations of meaning.[4] Clearly the realistic contract between audience and play can remain intact even as techniques evolve and conventions change.

In her illuminating study of realistic novels, Amy Kaplan argues that such modifications in using and understanding realism occur for two reasons: the aesthetic form itself changes through time, and critical reaction to the form changes according to the social conditions of the moment and the particular training of the critic (4–7). These twin processes seem to be at work in the development and reception of stage realism, too.

Changes in the aesthetic form itself are clearly illustrated by comparing the works of any two realist playwrights, say, for example, Henrik Ibsen and Arthur Miller. Both are seen as writers of conventional stage realism, and, in fact, Miller is often linked directly to Ibsen, by his own admission (21) as well as by critical comment. Yet Miller has imbued his stage world with expressionistic devices (like brother Ben materializing through a wall in *Death of A Salesman*), with narrative intrusions (like the comments by the lawyer Alfieri in *A View from the Bridge*), with lack of resolution (in *The Price*)—in short, he has consistently adapted the techniques of stage realism to suit his own designs and to reflect the selected aspects of offstage reality that interested him at the moment. Clearly this variety within realistic form is one reason why critics have such difficulty in labeling Fornes; as Ross Wetzsteon has remarked, her stylistic variety, her switching "from antic abstraction to a more three-dimensional realism" (44) has caused much critical confusion in responding to her oeuvre.

The second sort of changes that Kaplan notes—changes in critical reception—are also evident in reaction to Fornes. While all commentators agree that her playwriting style changes from play to play and that she uses both realistic and antimimetic elements, they cannot agree on whether that makes Fornes a realist, a "new realist," or not a realist at all. And this problem of recognizing realism becomes compounded by critical definitions, which often proceed by contrast; that is, critics define realism by differentiating it from either its antecedents, melodrama and the well-made play, or from its immediate descendent, naturalism. Examples abound of these attempts to define realism by contrast with closely related forms. For Lee Jacobus, then, realism is characterized by a frankness in treating potentially shocking subject material (unlike melodrama), but it can also include elements of fantasy (unlike naturalism) (365–66). William Demastes agrees that realism can contain fantastic elements and be mixed with other forms; for him, however, realism is defined by an empiricism that contrasts with naturalism's determinism (3–6). W. B. Worthen notes that naturalism uses the stage machinery of realism but adds "a sustaining ideological coherence" (1992, 6). And for Helene Keyssar, realism focuses on psychological revelation in private spaces whereas naturalism stresses behavior in a public environment (1985, 43).

Each of these definitions by contrast offers an important insight into the workings of realism, and such distinctions can be helpful in understanding what realism can and cannot do. In fact, one problem I see with the feminist critique of realism is that feminist critics do not always distinguish between realism and its related forms, leading Janelle Reinelt (for example), an otherwise astute and insightful commentator, to reject Pam Gems's *Camille* on the grounds of its realism, when her discussion clearly indicates that the "deadly pleasures" of her spectatorial complicity arise more from the play's melodramatic roots than its realistic elements (1989a, 102). Still, defining by negation has at least one serious drawback, since all such definitions tend to overlook one crucial point: the very cross-pollination between forms that makes such distinctions necessary ensures continual development and change within the forms themselves.

When definitions of realism move beyond this process of defining by contrast, they sometimes focus instead on locating a single distinguishing element out of the list of commonly recognized realistic techniques. John Gassner, for example, has suggested that the primary defining element of stage realism is the eavesdropping audience behind the imaginary fourth wall (26–27), a convincing analysis still accepted in much contemporary discussion of realism.[5] Another prime contender for the essence of realism is closure, the tendency of some realist texts to resolve plot complications in the last act, however simplistically or artificially.[6]

While these definitions have the advantage of accessing novelty— after all, a single defining element could conceivably be combined with many other elements, in many different ways—they pose a different problem: what of apparently realistic plays that violate the single defining principle? I have already mentioned the deviations from these realistic norms in Arthur Miller's plays, but even the more classic, turn-of-the-century realist playwrights offer exceptions to such single-element definitions of realism. From the slamming door out of Nora's doll house (leading where?) to George Bernard Shaw's famous last-act "discussions," realistic plays have left untied as many threads as they have neatly knotted, effectively eliminating closure as the sole determinant of a realistic text. Even the supremacy of the fourth wall has been challenged by plays that proceed realistically but include narrators who break the frame.

I do not offer these examples of inadequate definition to disparage the critics who proposed them; in fact, each definition contributes something significant to our understanding of realism and was constructed to clarify specific points in each writer's specific argument. Rather, these examples are meant to illustrate the difficulties of defining a form that has evolved continuously since it first appeared and to suggest, as Austin E. Quigley has noted, that we "bewilder ourselves unnecessarily when we struggle to find distinctive definitions of different kinds of drama on the basis of their realism or theatricality" (120). These differing definitions of realism, like the case of Maria Irene Fornes, reveal that while dramatic realism has a distinctive catalogue of attributes, the form is various and changes through time: "conventional" does not equal "monolithic."

I believe that this tendency to overstate realism's fixedness, to view it as a calcified set of immutable characteristics, is responsible for much of the feminist rejection of realism. As both Rita Felski and Sheila Stowell have argued, if realism is (in Felski's words) "a 'closed' form which imposes single and transparent meanings upon the reader" (157), how is it that critics, readers, directors, and spectators generate such highly contradictory readings of individual texts? In later chapters I will expand on this notion of realism's multiplicity, using contemporary feminist playwrights (other than the elusive Fornes) to illustrate the feminist potential of the realistic contract. However, feminist critics have raised other serious challenges to stage realism, and I do not intend to dismiss their arguments by equivocating about the definition of the term. Their reasons for repudiating realism take many forms—from a rejection of inherited tools of patriarchal oppression, to an insistence on creating a separate female aesthetics, to a sophisticated theoretical critique of realism's representational strategies. What I propose to do here, then, is investigate some key reasons for the feminist rejection of realism and explore the possibility that realism, while potentially dangerous from a feminist perspective, is not inescapably a tool that must be discarded.

Mimesis and Its Feminist Discontents

Like realism, feminist drama itself comes in many forms and from varying perspectives. Most commentators divide feminist drama into three major types, based on the political feminism with which each type is most closely allied. (And while these three categories do oversimplify a whole network of interconnected interests, they will provide an adequate shorthand here for distinguishing between broadly different kinds of feminist inquiry.) Thus we read about "liberal feminist" theater, which depicts female heroes in traditionally structured (often realistic) plays, allowing women's historically suppressed voices to be heard on stage; the "cultural (or radical) feminist" approach, which replaces linear dramatic structures with more fluid or circular forms, thought more accurately to reflect female experience (seen as both biologically and experientially different from male experience); and the "materialist feminist" approach, which disrupts linear narratives to expose the cultural construction of seemingly natural roles like gender, race, and class and to emphasize the material conditions that promote various oppressions.[7]

Since the heart of a liberal feminist agenda is to demonstrate that women are equal to men, a liberal feminist playwright would have no qualms about using realism, which can record historical events (and showcase female role models) or show a female character succeeding in traditionally male occupations and endeavors. For other feminists, however, this use of realism to depict female heroes merely replicates the existing hierarchical model of success without questioning the sources and uses of power. Susan Bassnett-McGuire has noted that plays about autonomous women sometimes mirror the paradigm of the "great man," which is by nature both sexist and elitist (449–53). Michelene Wandor has likewise observed that a play can be written by a woman, focus on women's experiences, have an all-female cast, and still fail to challenge the antifeminist notions of biological determinism, cultural inferiority, and gender-based oppression (1986, 131).[8]

As these comments on liberal feminism suggest, different cultural and materialist feminists challenge different elements of the realistic project. Nonetheless, virtually all their various objections stem from a shared discomfort with the central notion of mimesis, with the very idea that art can imitate nature—or, in this context, that realistic performance can mirror offstage reality and still be of value to feminists. Whose reality is reflected? By what mechanisms? For whose eyes? Questions like these form the crux of most feminist interrogations of realism. As we shall see, in some cases the feminist critique assumes that realism's representational strategies falsify female experience. In others, realism is seen as too mimetic—that is, too closely allied with oppressive offstage reality to be useful as a feminist tool of resistance. Yet other theorists fault realism for not being mimetic enough, for failing to depict accurately the social construction of gender and other naturalized roles. Whatever the perspective of the particular critic, the issue of mimesis is central to all feminist critiques of realism and will provide a useful organizing strategy for evaluating their specific and sometimes overlapping concerns.

Cultural Feminism: Replacing a False Mimesis

Cultural feminism (as philosophy and theatrical practice) first appeared widely in the 1960s, as part of the social upheavals that included (among other important phenomena like antiwar protests and the Civil Rights movement) the simultaneous flowerings of the women's movement and experimental theater. Positing a separate female culture, based on women's shared biological and historical experiences, with norms and values (such as nurturing and bonding) opposed to the dominant or "male" culture, cultural feminists seek to create both a society and a dramatic form that repudiate patriarchy and the status quo.[9] As Josephine Donovan has explained, cultural feminism stresses "the identification of women as a separate community, a separate culture, with its own customs, its own epistemology, and, once articulated, its own aesthetics and ethics" (100).

In attempting to create a separate female theatrical practice, cultural feminists often work in groups, forming feminist theater collectives in which shows can be scripted collaboratively (often in avant-garde styles) and produced by the ensemble.[10] Other cultural feminists prefer to work individually, writing plays or one-woman shows about women's experiences in forms developed to express what they see as a uniquely female vision. Whatever method of writing, performing, or producing theater they choose, however, cultural feminists are united in their goal of providing an alternative forum for representing women's lives—emphasizing issues like female sexuality (both heterosexual and lesbian), mother-daughter bonds, or women's social inequality—in newly created "female" formats.

Since cultural feminists focus on the female body as the primary site of a woman's identity, it is not surprising that a major premise behind their rejection of realism is that it reflects male bodily experience. Nancy S. Reinhardt has explained the objection succinctly:

> the structure of traditional Western drama, an "imitation of an action," is linear, leading through conflict and tension to a major climax and resolution. . . . One could even say that this aggressive build-up, sudden big climax, and cathartic resolution suggests specifically the male *sexual* response. (35–37)

Playwright Anne Commire agrees, describing "the male climax" of a realistic play in violent physical terms, like "a gun going off or a punch in the nose" (Betsko and Koenig, 90). The traditional "male" dramatic structure is furthermore based on individual self-recognition, not the collective awareness that many cultural feminists prefer to celebrate; and its linear plot and language are thought incapable of reflecting women's ways of knowing, which many cultural feminists see as more fluid, circular, or instinctive. [11]

If one allows these assumptions about gender differences, rejecting realism and developing separate "female" mimetic forms becomes an imperative. One important project of cultural feminists, then, has been to recognize and develop a separate female aesthetic that would more accurately express what they see as the unique experiences of women, and feminist theater scholars have studied these developments in an attempt to define a feminist aesthetic for the theater. [12] Linda Walsh Jenkins, for example, emphasizes the centrality of women's relationships to each other; for her, a feminist play depicts those shared experiences in imagery and settings traditionally familiar to women (such as a kitchen) and in language that tends to be inclusive and circular (9–11). Helene Keyssar insists that women's plays replace traditional recognition scenes with conventions of role transformation, arguing that such transformations "emphasize the commonality of the stories told and . . . refuse the old hierarchies of the theatre" (1985, 90). Rosemary Curb, too, has defined a "woman-conscious" theater as one that unravels women's collective imagination in a multidimensional, psychic replay of myth and history (1985, 302–3).

What all these formal experiments have in common is an acceptance of mimesis—the notion that theater can accurately reflect off-stage existence—but a rejection of realism as an inherited male form, a mimesis false to female experience. For cultural feminists, the mimesis of realism was designed to reflect specifically and only male experience. To accede to realism's demands is to accept the images of a distorting mirror and so to disfigure oneself; survival as women depends on replacing the mirror, on allowing (in Jill Dolan's image) "women's hands [to] hold the mirror up to nature [and] to reflect women spectators in its glass" (1988, 84). Rejecting realism is not a rejection of the mirror itself, but of the mirror framed and (up)held by the father.

The cultural feminist undertaking, both in general and in the theater, has been critiqued extensively by materialist feminists in recent years (even though materialist feminists, too, have their own reasons for dismissing realism, which I will explore later). Their general arguments are helpful in indicating where the cultural feminist rejection of realism goes astray or overstates its case.

The most obvious problem in cultural feminist thinking is its essentialism, which offers twin propositions: that "male" and "female" are innate oppositional qualities rather than social constructs, and that women's interests are both unchanging and universal. To many observers, this belief in essential and universal female difference—even superiority—really just inverts the bipolar, patriarchal model that cultural feminists otherwise protest, replicating hegemonic thinking in a feminist context.[13] Furthermore, defining male and female as opposites, thus positing biological sex as the primary determinant of identity, elides the enormous differences among women. Placing this anti-essentialist argument in a theatrical context, Michelene Wandor has noted:

> there is not much to be gained from assuming that drama is per se some kind of "male form," and that when women write, they write in a totally different form which has never been invented before and which is common to women. Emotional, aesthetic, and structural styles are very varied among women writers. (1986, 184)

As a result of this understanding of the dangers of essentialism, numerous scholars have criticized the cultural feminist agendas (theatrical and political), arguing from materialist, African-American, lesbian, and other diverse points of view what Lynda Hart pointed out at the 1992 Women and Theatre Conference: that race, gender, class, and sexuality cannot be theorized separately.[14] Once one follows this logic and overturns the assumption that biology is the sole determinant of identity, the impetus for dismissing realism as an inherently male form of mimesis disappears.

Even if one accepts the notion that "male" and "female" are unchanging, innate attributes, the notion that stage realism is by definition male must be called into question. Most dramatic forms are, in fact, inherited from male playwrights of earlier ages, since women historically had little access to theater practice. Those cultural feminists who object to realism as "male" sometimes replace it with expressionistic devices or choral chanting, both of which were also originally designed by male playwrights and used for decidedly unfeminist purposes. Furthermore, if one sees identity as constructed by the particular historical moment one lives in (as materialist feminists do), it becomes difficult to sort out which aspects of that culture are "male" and which are "female," and doing so can create new sorts of limitations for feminist playwrights.

The philosophical problem of essentialism, however, is not the only blind spot in the cultural feminist critique of realism. Much of this attitude stems, I believe, from the historical context that originated the cultural feminist movement, or at least gave it momentum. In the ferment of the 1960s, discarding tradition seemed crucial. Furthermore, because feminists and theater practitioners were equally engaged in the counterculture revolution, the simultaneity of the two movements has made them seem inextricably linked. In fact, while much important experimental feminist theater was created during this period, there is no direct and inevitable connection between formal experimentation and feminism; as Teresa L. Ebert contends, "Mimesis . . . is neither reactionary nor liberating *in and of itself,* nor is antimimesis subversive *in and of itself*" (103). Rita Felski has likewise argued this point:

> An exploration of avant-garde form can constitute an important part of an oppositional women's culture; but the fragmentation and subversion of patterns of meaning do not in themselves bear any relationship to a feminist position . . . (32)

If it is an essentialist stance to assume that traditional forms of drama are innately "male," it is surely no less so to assume that experimental forms are automatically "female" or inevitably subvert the patriarchal status quo. Ultimately, the attempt to define oneself or one's theatrical practice in oppositional terms—female is not male, feminist is not realist—is still to depend on the dominant perspective as a starting point for self-identity; alterity does not necessarily equal sedition.[15] Surely it is the purpose to which a form is put, its use within an ideological context at a specific historical moment, that determines its effectiveness as a feminist challenge.[16]

Finally, however, the problem with the cultural feminist critique of realism comes back to the vexed issue of mimesis. While rejecting the mimesis of realism as a false reflection of female experience, cultural feminists merely replace realistic mimesis with mimesis of a contradictory, "female" sort. Materialist feminists take the argument against realism a step further, arguing that mimesis itself—the attempt to reflect offstage reality—is what must be discarded in a feminist rejection of realism.

Materialist Feminism and "The Prison-House" of Realism

"Materialist feminism" is not a unified body of thought. Rather, materialist feminist theorists and critics of drama come from a variety of academic disciplines (theater, language, philosophy, anthropology, and so on), use diverse analytic tools, and disagree on many points of definition and interpretation. What they share, however, is a commitment to understanding the cultural construction of "truth"—the way material conditions such as economic status, class background, gender, race, ethnicity, and sexual orientation combine and recombine to construct individual identity and shape what we call reality. As a result of this attention to the constructedness of social roles and categories, materialist feminists use a variety of poststructuralist analytic techniques that presuppose identity as shifting and reality as contingent, subject always to the historical and material contexts of their production.

Given these notions of identity as fluid and reality as provisional, some materialist feminists reject realism for its apparently faithful depiction of a stable offstage world—for presenting a mere construct and passing it off as normative "Truth." Other materialist feminists complain, conversely, that to be useful theater should depict the social construction and constructedness of that normative vision, which mimetic realism historically does not (and presumably cannot) do. While the list of these critics' specific accusations against realism is lengthy and varied, the charges can all be seen as variants of these two contradictory categories: mimesis that works too well or mimesis that fails. Let us examine them in turn and in some detail.

Overly Successful Mimesis

Materialist feminist critics do not assume that plays and other cultural artifacts can actually reflect history mimetically. As Judith Newton has explained it, "Since we live within myths and narratives about history, there can in fact *be* no reflections of it. Literature, rather, draws upon various ideological productions of history or discourses about history to make its own production" (xxiii). One of their major complaints about realism, therefore, is that it purports to mirror an objective offstage reality which in fact does not exist independent of its stage representation. For these materialist feminists, realism belies the fact that "meaning is always *produced;* it is never simply expressed" (Williams 1977, 166).

The actual content of a realistic play, then, becomes a site for contestation, since realist playwrights pass off as actual what they have in fact constructed. In looking at the history of stage realism, many feminist critics have rightly observed that realism has most often focused on the interactions of traditional Western families, thereby presenting a theatrical version of the exclusionary "family values" idealized by the Republican party during the 1992 presidential campaign. Within these family dramas, women are typically depicted as domestic servants or as obstacles to male fulfillment—in short, they are appendages to a plot that spotlights male crisis. As Sue-Ellen Case has forcefully argued:

> Realism, in its focus on the domestic sphere and the family unit, reifies the male as sexual subject and the female as the sexual "Other." The portrayal of female characters within the family unit—with their confinement to the domestic setting, their dependence on the husband, their often defeatist, determinist view of the opportunities for change—makes realism a "prisonhouse of art" for women, both in their representation on stage and in the female actor's preparation and production of such roles. (1988, 124)

Within the picture-frame set of the family living room that characterizes realistic plays, women are erased as desiring subjects, lesbians are invisible or "moralized against" (Dolan 1990, 44), and plots maintain a melodramatic family focus that "naturalizes an asymmetrical relation between the sexes within marriage and the family" (Patraka 1989, 129).

Clearly this representation of women's place within traditional family structures is an ideological construct designed to uphold a patriarchal status quo. Realism, however, masks this ideology as objective truth, mediating between offstage reality and theatrical production but pretending not to. As a host of materialist feminist critics have pointed out, this operation validates the norms and values of the dominant culture and reifies the unequal power relations between genders.[17] Realism therefore functions as a instrument of dominant ideology, rendering it problematic for feminists committed to social change. This position has been ably summed up by Elin Diamond, who notes that Bertolt Brecht also rejected realism for its covert ideology. Diamond notes: "Realism disgusted Brecht not only because it dissimulates its conventions but because it is hegemonic: by copying the surface details of the world it offers the illusion of lived experience, even as it marks off only one version of that experience" (1988, 87).

This mystification of authorial ideology is compounded for materialist feminist critics of realism by the operations at the other end of the theatrical continuum: that is, by the role of the spectator implied by realistic performance. Like the author, the spectator is invisible, sheltered by the darkness on the audience side of the proscenium arch, assumed to be a passive consumer of the theatrical product.[18] Poststructuralist reception theories have increasingly identified the audience as central to the construction of meaning, crucial to "the circuitous process, the clandestine interchange, by which the meaning of the *mise-en-scène* is produced" (Koppen 382). However, spectatorial contributions to the theatrical process remain largely unremarked upon and unaccounted for in realistic theater.

This passive and invisible spectator sometimes imagined as inevitably predicated by the realistic contract poses numerous problems for materialist feminist critics. Foremost among these problems is the tyranny of "the male gaze"—that is, the assumption that the invisible spectator is complicit in the patriarchal ideological biases of stage realism, that the spectacle is designed precisely for a male viewer to identify with and for his eyes voyeuristically to devour.[19] For if women are constructed as "other" to the central male characters of a realistic play, they are likely to be viewed as alien or consumable "other" to the concealed spectator of a realistic performance, regardless of the spectator's gender.

This criticism of realism's implied spectator assumes that audiences remain naive to the representational apparatuses of realism, which are, as we saw above, covert. Yet the fact that realism hides its theatricality does not necessarily mean that spectators are unaware of it. Semiotic studies of theater have amply demonstrated that theater is by definition polyvocal, "offering a polyphony of competing and overlapping signs that belong to many systems" (Alter 93) and to which a single spectator can respond in conflicting ways.[20] So, for instance, we can be emotionally affected by the pain of the suicidal character Jessie in Marsha Norman's *'night, Mother* while simultaneously recognizing that Kathy Bates is giving a powerful performance of that role. The same is true of set design. As Sheila Stowell has pointed out:

> One of the paradoxes of stage realism at its most extreme is that its material exuberance encourages audiences to admire the painstaking business of its illusion making. Accordingly, audiences who applauded the Trafalgar Square set of Elizabeth Robins's *Votes for Women!* (1907) were appreciating the virtuosity (i.e., the artificiality) of a tableau. They would not, one presumes, have gone to Trafalgar Square to applaud the "real" thing. (1992a, 85)

The notion that an audience lacks competence to distinguish between onstage and offstage worlds is, I think, exaggerated. Were it otherwise, we would all be like Jonathan, the country bumpkin in Royall Tyler's *The Contrast* (1787), who thought he was peering into a neighbor's house and never even knew he was in a theater.[21] The audience at a theatrical event is a collection of diverse spectators, not some "monolithic tabula rasa" (Stowell 1992a, 82) under an author's spell.[22]

In fact, this whole three-pronged attack on realism's excessive mimesis—that the content is patriarchal, that the author's ideology remains obscure, and that the audience is a collection of unwitting co-conspirators, dupes of the realistic process—seems to me to be based on a series of overinclusive premises. First, while the traditional subject matter of realism has been the domestic situation, it does not necessarily follow that this need always be the case; realistic plays take place in courtrooms (Miller's *The Crucible*), in prison camps (Sherman's *Bent*)—in short, in a variety of locations that do not necessarily highlight family interactions. But even when the setting is domestic, a playwright can use the form to *criticize* the social norms it depicts as well as to uphold them. In the hands of its turn-of-the-century practitioners, for example, realism was often intended to challenge the normalcy of the restrictive stage world it portrayed.[23] More recently, "new realists" like David Rabe and Sam Shepard have used realism to challenge the naturalistic world view, "to disrupt the surface appearance of everyday reality in order to explore more subjective levels of existence—not just the social dynamics of the eternally troubled American family, or the pathological psyches of individual characters, but more deeply still, 'the non-rational impulses of a mythos.'"[24] And in the hands of a feminist playwright, the strictures of stage realism can work to emphasize the entrapment of women in those very social and domestic settings realism was originally designed to portray. One can think of Arlie in Marsha Norman's *Getting Out*, whose realistically portrayed domestic situation parallels very closely the prison life from which she has just been released. It would be foolish to overlook the political efficacy of realism's referential power when used to illustrate the entrapment of women in prescribed social roles. Sheila Stowell has cogently summarized the overgeneralization I am trying to correct; she argues that while stage realism *can* be used to depict an overly fated world, "realist theatre does not *necessarily* present a coherent or unassailable view of society" (1992a, 82).

As for the author's potentially covert ideology and the audience's uncritical complicity with it, the complex processes of producing and attending a play both intervene in that ideology, mandating that "the meanings derived from any one performance will vary endlessly" (Dolan 1988, 121). Moreover, while audience reception is "a potent and active force in creating significance," it is no less so in response to non-realistic texts (Stowell 1992a, 83). Overt theatricality is no guarantee that an audience will maintain critical objectivity, as Bertolt

Brecht discovered to his dismay when early audiences took Mother Courage to be a model of adaptive survival instead of the crass capitalist opportunist he evidently intended (and not even covertly!) to create.

In fact, this assumption that audience response to a realistic production will be predictable, uncritical, and unvaried ignores entirely the material conditions of production. In what space is the play being presented? How did the audience arrive there? From what socioeconomic brackets do they come? How much do the tickets cost? Is the neighborhood safe? Are the seats comfortable? All these factors will contribute to a spectator's response to a theatrical event, even if s/he succumbs somewhat to the comforting blanket of darkness that protects the audience during a (realistic) performance. Furthermore, to presuppose the audience's tacit agreement with the ideology being presented (covertly or otherwise) is to discount the diversity of individual audience members as well as the multiple identity positions (race, class, gender, and so on) within each individual spectator— what Susan Bennett has called the under-investigated "inevitable tension in the spectator's position" (1990, 85). Given the materialist feminist emphases on material conditions and shifting identities, I find this creation of an unthinking and undefined monolithic spectator a serious logical contradiction.

Materialist feminists have done us an invaluable service in pointing out the potential pitfalls of succumbing uncritically to the hermeneutic pleasures of a realistic performance—of accepting too readily the constructed truths of mimesis. However, many materialist feminists themselves advocate "reading against the grain"; they suggest resisting the implications of a traditional text by noticing the ways the text constructs gender and gender relations and by refusing to accept the apparently patriarchal assumptions that a play can pass off as universal truth.[25] While it is true that the realistic play does not *invite* a resistant reading in that it maintains its illusory seamlessness and generally pays no attention to the eavesdropping audience, it nonetheless does not *prevent* a viewer from challenging its premises or refusing to be moved.

In sum, the argument that realism succeeds too well in its mimetic project to be of value in promoting feminist visions is certainly true of some realistic texts, at some historical periods, and in some spectatorial contexts. However, it is not necessarily accurate that realistic texts are by definition sexist, that authors conceal their political beliefs, or that audiences fail to read the multiple systems of signification produced by a realistic performance. As we shall see later in this chapter, the mimetic power of stage realism offers distinct advantages in promoting feminist agendas, advantages that may offset the potential dangers of the realistic contract.

Inadequate Mimesis

Another sort of materialist feminist argument against realistic theater focuses not on content or reception, but on the apparatus of dramatic realism itself—its representational machinery. Like the cultural feminist argument discussed earlier, this approach to criticizing realism presupposes that realistic mimesis falsifies everyday experience. However, from the materialist feminist point of view, the falsehood is not in the exclusion of uniquely "female" experience (a concept most materialist feminists would reject as essentialist and universalizing), but in realism's failure to depict experience as multivalent and continually under construction. In order to understand this important and increasingly frequent critique of realism, it will be necessary to review briefly a few of the poststructuralist premises on which it is founded.

For a poststructuralist, signification itself is unstable, since it is based on signs that are momentary and conventional, with no fixed meaning or inevitable referent. In the case of theatrical signification, where sign systems are always multiple (including such diverse and overlapping codes as the words of the text, the actors' bodies, the lighting, the blocking, and so on), the issues of *how* meaning is produced and *whose* meaning is produced become very slippery. A crucial question for these materialist feminists, then, is "Whose interests are served in this representation?"[26] Using a variety of analytic tools (ranging from psychoanalytic theory to semiotics to deconstruction and beyond), a materialist feminist with poststructuralist training will focus on unveiling two things: the operations of power hierarchies that lie hidden beneath the premises of theatrical representation, and the operations of the representation itself. To these thinkers, realism is dangerous because it presumes falsely to mirror a stable world rather than a provisional offstage reality; for them, true mimesis would reflect the process of construction instead of an ostensibly finished construct.

A corollary to the poststructuralists' agenda of revealing the instability of representation is their emphasis on replacing the liberal humanist concept of a coherent individual with the notion of a human *subject*, a shifting nexus of temporary identity formations, always in the process of becoming. As Jane Gallop and Carolyn Burke have explained this distinction, "The 'self' implies a center, a potentially autonomous individual; the 'subject' is a place in language, a signifier that is already alienated in an intersubjective network" (106). This notion of shifting subjectivity becomes crucial in a feminist context, where it undermines the notion of gender as a stable referent and so denaturalizes traditional gender roles. For many materialist feminists, gender is a performative act, not a natural expression of bipolar biological differences.[27] So Judith Butler describes gender as "an identity tenuously constructed in time—an identity instituted through *a stylized repetition of acts*" based on individual performances of an inherited script (1988, 519). Because of these inherited cultural constraints, gender (like other identity locations, such as race or sexual orientation) is seen as "a relative point of convergence among culturally and historically specific sets of relations" (1990a, 10).

For feminist theater practitioners, this notion of gender has profound implications for the representation of women. By disguising its representational strategies (that is, its theatricality) behind a deceptive facade of illusory linear narrative, orthodox stage realism also conceals the social machinery by which gender is constituted, performed, and politicized, positing "woman" as a coherent and stable entity rather than a contextual performance. Realistic mimesis thus becomes inherently a misrepresentation. As Jill Dolan has explained, "If feminism points out that representation does not construct women as subjects, and also views coherent identity as a myth, a feminist mimesis is extremely difficult to theorize" (1988, 96).

The mimesis these materialist feminists see as falsely representing women also depicts a dangerously oversimplified offstage world. By emphasizing qualities like causality, coherence, and closure, realism produces a seamless illusion instead of reflecting the contingencies and fabrications that constitute contemporary notions of "reality." Seen from this perspective, the problem with realism is not that it succeeds too well at replicating a repressive offstage world and so gulls the spectator (as the first materialist feminist critique would have it); the problem is, rather, that realism fails to account for shifting identity, incoherence, and the layers of meaning in everyday experience, thereby failing to replicate the offstage world at all. Because it camouflages constructedness (both its own and society's at large), it reflects a single exaggerated image instead of a hall of mirrors.

The solution for these materialist feminists, then, is to discard realism and replace it with dramatic forms designed to reveal the gaps and omissions within the apparently seamless world presented on the realistic stage. As Jeanie Forte has argued, such a text would be subversive by nature; it "would not provide the detached viewpoint, the illusion of seamlessness, the narrative closure, but instead would open up the negotiation of meaning to contradictions, circularity, multiple viewpoints" (1989, 117).

Catherine Belsey's influential essay "Constructing the Subject: Deconstructing the Text" (1985) has laid much of the foundation for this argument. In this oft-quoted piece, Belsey invokes Barthes and the hermeneutic code to argue that formal realism (whether in fiction or on stage) performs the work of capitalist ideology in representing a world of consistent subjects who originate meaning and action. For Belsey,

> Classic realism.is characterized by "illusionism," narrative which leads to "closure," and a "hierarchy of discourses" which establishes the "truth" of the story. . . . Classic realist narrative, as Barthes demonstrates in S/Z, turns on the creation of an enigma through the precipitation of disorder which throws into disarray the conventional cultural and signifying systems. . . . But the story moves inevitably towards closure which is also disclosure, the dissolution of enigma through the re-establishment of order, recognizable as a reinstatement or a development of the order which is understood to have preceded the events of the story itself. (53)

A number of materialist feminists (and other poststructuralists as well) have cited Belsey prominently in their arguments for abandoning realism.[28] In particular, they share Belsey's insistence that "the gap between the ideological project [of a realist text] and the specifically literary form" creates inevitable "incoherences, omissions, absences and transgressions" within the text (56–57). For these thinkers, therefore, realism presents a false mimesis, the apparent reflection of an intelligible world order that is only "masquerading as coherence in the interests of the social relations generated by and necessary to" the workings of conservative ideology (46). As Belsey describes the apparently obvious "truth" of a realistic performance: "If it is true . . . it is not the whole truth" (46).

Many of these arguments against realism, however, rest on only the first half of Belsey's germinal essay. In fact, while pointing out the dangers of realism's partial truths and selective mimesis, Belsey does insist on a certain amount of agency within the spectator, who is capable of resisting conventional readings of a text. She says, "It is important to reiterate, of course, that this process [of readers' uncritically accepting realism's coherence] is not inevitable, in the sense that texts do not determine like fate the ways in which they *must* be read" (53). Furthermore, she goes on to argue *not* that realism must be dismissed as a tool of oppressive ideology, but that critics must find ways of responding to realist texts (and, presumably, performances) that reveal the texts' constructedness. Her argument is not so much that realism must be discarded, but that we must find decon-structive ways to read and view it. For Belsey, realist texts always already contain the seeds of their own deconstruction:

> The object of the critic, then, is to seek not the unity of the work, but the multiplicity and diversity of its possible meanings, its incompleteness, the omissions which it displays but cannot describe, and above all its contradictions. In its absences, and in the collisions between its divergent meanings, the text implicitly criticizes its own ideology; it contains within itself the critique of its own values, in the sense that it is available for a new process of production of meaning by the reader [or spectator], and in this process it can provide a knowledge of the limits of ideological reproduction. (57)

As Belsey goes on to note, by discarding a realistic work as inherently unacceptable, a critic effectively censors not only the work's distorted claims to mimesis, but also the inevitable elements within it that collide with dominant ideology; in effect, this critic discards the baby with the bathwater. "To deconstruct the text, on the other hand, is to open it . . . to reveal the partiality (in both senses) of the ideology inscribed in the text" (58). Once again, the value of resistant reading, of reading an ostensibly coherent text as fractured and contradictory, seems to outweigh the benefits of simply rejecting the form.

A number of other feminist critics follow Belsey's potentially pro-ductive agenda for deconstructively reading and viewing realism. While these critics recognize that realism presents a false mimesis in that it fails to reflect the mechanisms of its production, they suggest that discarding the form on these grounds alone may be an overreac-tion. Teresa Ebert, for example, notes realism's link to ideological representations, but cautions against simply discarding realism in favor of innovative or deconstructive forms. She argues that "antireal-ism and experimental avant-garde writing are equally historically de-termined and just as much ideological apparatuses as mimesis—antirepresentationalism can be used as easily to conserve and rese-cure patriarchy as to contest it" (105). Furthermore, Maria Irene Fornes has criticized the materialist feminist notion that realism's closure is deadly for women, arguing that "The way a play ends is not the statement of the play!" (Wetzsteon 45). And Judith Butler has shrewdly observed (albeit in a different context) that "strategies always have meanings that exceed the purposes for which they are intended" (1990a, 4).

In this discussion of the feminist critiques of realism, I have tried to make two things clear. First, feminists do have real and serious

reasons for mistrusting realism. It has traditionally been used to uphold an oppressive status quo, to normalize misogynist ideologies, to
falsely document the existence of an ideologically dangerous offstage
world. More recently, it has been found to offer visions of stability
where none exist and to dissimulate the processes of its own construction. It is simultaneously too mimetic and not mimetic enough.

However—and this is my second point—to label a dramatic form
as inherently repressive and politically inefficacious is to confuse a
tool with its potential uses. Who among us has never hammered a
nail with the end of a heavy stapling gun, or pried open a bottle cap
with a penknife? While such tools were not designed expressly for
these alternative tasks and therefore may not be the most efficient
implements for such purposes, they *are* readily available and they *do*
get the job done. Butler's point that strategies always have meanings
that exceed the purposes for which they are intended cannot, I think,
be overstated. Moreover, many feminists implicitly accept this premise when they champion, say, Brechtian theatrical techniques (like
alienation and *gestus*) as useful methods of feminist disruption, even
though this is surely not the purpose for which Brecht designed
them.[29]

Thus far, I have argued for restoring realism only in a negative
sense—that is, I have attempted to refute those critics who insist on
dismantling it, hoping to demonstrate the overgeneralizations and
overreactions embedded in their sometimes convincing arguments.
At this point, I plan to go a step further, to explore the *positive*
contributions to feminist undertakings that realism can potentially
make. Elin Diamond, in an attempt to theorize a feminist mimesis,
summarizes her purpose in this way:

> Why make this effort to recuperate mimesis? Because it tends, I think,
> to recuperate us. It is better perhaps to acknowledge certain mimetic
> desires, to militate for the complex, the *different* referents we want to
> see, even as we work to dismantle the mechanisms of patriarchal model-
> ing. (1989, 62)

While realism is obviously not identical to mimesis, Diamond's justification of her project echoes my own. Recuperating realism is more
than a nostalgic maneuver designed to retain a semblance of classical
order or escape into hermeneutic pleasure; it is an attempt to show
how an old tool can be put to powerful new uses.

Re-evaluating Realism

Given the preceding discussion of the feminist critiques of stage
realism, one might ask with some justification, "What good can real-

ism do?" Since it is tainted by a history of repressive uses and retains potentially dangerous representational strategies, why bother to recover it? After all, a wide variety of plays are being written today from a distinctly feminist viewpoint and in methods designed expressly for feminist purposes. In addition, performance art, overt theatricality, and parody are all thriving in feminist circles, and all are frequently championed as inherently subversive and therefore more useful than realism from a feminist viewpoint.[30] Given the plethora of theatrical alternatives to stage realism, why resurrect it at all?

A number of critics have provided partial answers to this question, signaling their intentions with cleverly alliterative titles and arguments. So Sheila Stowell has rehabilitated realism, Michael Vanden Heuvel has ransacked it, Amy Kaplan has resituated and restored it, William Demastes has reestablished it. The source of this apparently irresistible alliterative impulse is embedded in the prefix "re" that coincides with the first syllable of "realism," a prefix that invites us to do anew—in this case, to re-think realism. In so doing, we can discover a number of reasons, both old and new, to reevaluate stage realism and recover it for feminist purposes.

The first reason to reevaluate realism is simple: realism was created not only to reflect social conditions but also to comment on them. As Amy Kaplan notes, "The realists do not naturalize the social world to make it seem immutable or organic, but, like contemporary reformers, they engage in an enormous act of construction to organize, re-form, and control the social world" (10). Even given our postmodern suspicion of mimesis and our awareness that all art creates a reality it cannot simply reflect, realism can invoke analogues (if not exact replicas) of offstage conditions and demonstrate the social consequences of oppression.

As we saw in the first section of this chapter, realism was originally designed to subvert the status quo in both social context and theatrical practice. In terms of social commentary, turn-of-the-century realistic plays shifted away from "formulaic comedies and melodramas *set* in a given milieu to dramas *about* a given milieu or about a social or psychological problem that it produced" (Murphy 95). Common among these social subjects were politics, gender relations, women's suffrage, divorce, women's economic dependence on men, and changing class distinctions. In the preface to his *Plays Unpleasant*, George Bernard Shaw explained that the dramatic impulse behind his realistic plays was "to force the spectator to face unpleasant facts . . . [and] social horrors" (xxix). His Victorian audiences, accustomed to the easy entertainment of melodrama and the simplistic morality of the well-made play, found realistic plays disturbing because they challenged established social practices. Witness, for example, the public outcry over the ending to Ibsen's *A Doll's House,* a controversy that generated the publication of several revised endings in England as well as a revised first production in Germany.[31] Realism was clearly used by even its earliest practitioners as a form of social protest, an antidote to the mindless entertainment usually offered up at the theaters of its time. It is a rather cruel irony that this "progressive force exposing the conditions of an industrial society" is now seen by some as only "a conservative force" complicit with the hierarchies of power (A. Kaplan, 1).

In fact, realism *can* still serve this progressive function, especially if imported to a feminist context. It can still depict social inequality, protest unequal conditions, and show the deleterious effects of sexism, racism, and economic limitations. As Sheila Stowell has argued:

> Theatricalizing workrooms, drapers' establishments, law offices and (yes) drawing-rooms can have the effect of making visible traditionally invisible processes of capitalist production, exposing the usually hidden workings of an oppressive system, such staged revelations calling into question existing ideology's "naturalized" view of the world, each one a call to action. (1992a, 85)

This view of realism goes somewhat beyond the maligned liberal feminist assertion that presenting female heroes on a realistic stage can make women newly visible. From Stowell's point of view, realism can expose the construction and manipulation of power hierarchies as well. It can fulfill the social function of art, as described by Raymond Williams, by showing "the real grounds of the inclusions and exclusions, the styles and ways of seeing, that specific conventions embody and ratify" (1977, 173). Taken a step further in a feminist direction, such a dramatization of power hierarchies within a specific context might also be used to reveal the cultural construction of traditional gender roles as a man-made tool invented by those who wield the power.

While the content of stage realism can thus still be subversive, it is probably true that in terms of stagecraft the form has lost its power to shock. Moreover, consistent characters with comprehensible motivation may look just as contrived to us as the fiendish villains and unsullied heroines of melodrama did to early realists like Ibsen and Strindberg. However, an audience's familiarity with realistic conventions can actually be an advantage in presenting radical content. Just as Victorian audiences were comfortable with melodrama and farce, mainstream audiences in the postmodern era have been prepared by television and Hollywood cinema to respond to conventional realism.[32] Stage realism can use that familiarity to attract wide audiences, then upend conventional expectations by presenting explosive content. A feminist playwright might thus specifically choose realism as a political strategy designed to have wide popular appeal. As Rita Felski has argued, since *all* discursive positions are constructed and therefore ideological, the choice of style or form becomes one of relative merit in a particular context. For her, realism foregrounds the message rather than the medium—what she calls the "semantic" rather than the "formal and self-reflexive" component—and is thus an appropriate choice for contemporary women writers proposing a feminist political agenda for a diverse popular audience (79).

Conversely, a more avant-garde production style can confuse or offend those audiences who might benefit most from seeing the world through a feminist lens. As Susan Bassnett-McGuire has pointed out, experimental feminist theater troupes sometimes find themselves unable to progress beyond their own "closed circle," playing to like-minded audiences, "trapped by their own . . . outward-directed attacks on existing structures" (459–60). Even the redoubtable Fornes has admitted that her plays fail to reach wide audiences not because of shocking or outrageous content, but because of her experiments in dramatic form (Betsko and Koenig 164–65). Clearly, the advantages of creating alternative dramatic structures to reflect feminist visions must be balanced against the political value of attracting spectators.

A second reason to consider stage realism as appropriate for feminist interests is its long stage history. While realism (as we saw earlier) cannot simply reflect the here-and-now it attempts to replicate, it can and does provide us with a history of *representation*—of how women were expected to look and behave or how they were imagined in the specific historical circumstances of a play's production. If, as Chris Weedon suggests, we begin "to look at fictional [or dramatic] form as an historically produced discursive construct effective in different ways in different contexts" (172), it becomes clear that realistic texts have something to tell us about the social construction of gender at different periods of history—even (or especially) during those periods when such construction was denied or untheorized. Looked at this way, the history of stage realism becomes an important record of ideological discursive practices within specific historical moments.

Feminist theater historians are quite aware of this point, of course, and have complained at times that the insistence on dismissing traditional dramatic forms amounts to a rejection of women's literary history and a dismissal of their own important revisionary work. At the 1989 Women and Theatre Conference in New York, Kendall, a specialist in eighteenth-century drama and a pioneer at recovering women's lost plays, argued this point in an all-conference discussion session. At the ATHE Conference that same summer, scholar and theater reviewer Elinor Fuchs commented (in response to a paper of mine) that the materialist feminist demand to abandon realism is on a collision course with the interest in reviving women's populist literature, which often uses realism to scrutinize the material conditions that limit access to power. And students of African-American women's drama, as I will explain further in chapter 3, have argued that realism was crucial to the early twentieth-century African-American agendas of counteracting demeaning stage stereotypes and recovering lost history. Examined from these perspectives, the rejection of realism might seem both counterproductive and elitist, an ahistorical enterprise with damaging and distorting consequences.

Teresa Ebert, in attempting to create a feminist postmodern theory of mimesis, has convincingly argued this point about the value of representational history. In her view, shared by the materialist feminists discussed earlier, representation does not reflect an extradiscursive "real" but is, rather, "the ideological *production* of 'reality'" (105). Yet Ebert, unlike those feminists who simply repudiate realism, sees some value in exploring potentially or traditionally repressive forms. Like Belsey, she argues that we need new ways to read and view realistic productions, although she differs from Belsey by focusing on the hidden workings of power hierarchies within a text rather than on its internal incoherencies. She writes: "the political economy of representation should be sought *not* in the slippages of signifying systems but in examining how certain forms of representation preserve and render natural the interests of certain classes and gender" (105). She advocates, in other words, preserving the history of realistic representation in order to analyze how representation creates, traces, and/or reifies social inequities.

Combining Belsey's understanding of the inevitable transgressions within a realistic text with Ebert's interest in the material context of production provides us with a third reason to reevaluate realism. As Fredric Jameson has noted, an individual text is polyvocal, containing both a hegemonic and an oppositional voice (85–86). Working within a feminist context, a number of literary critics have echoed Jameson's observation, noting that women's texts tend to tell two stories: that of the dominant society that restricts women (the material text that interests Ebert) and that of the psychic repercussions that women experience as a result of those social pressures (the disrupted text that Belsey's approach reveals). So Elaine Showalter, working to recuperate nineteenth-century women's texts for contemporary feminist analysis, speaks of women's fiction as "a double-voiced discourse, containing a 'dominant' and a 'muted' story, what Gilbert and Gubar call a 'palimpsest'" (266). Stage realism, like the realist fiction described by these critics, inevitably tells this double story, and can thus prove valuable for feminist purposes.[33]

Working consciously in this "palimpsestic" or double-voiced form, a feminist playwright might use a picture-frame stage and the causal structure of formal realism to illustrate the social restrictions placed on female characters. Within this linear stage world, however, she could insert experimental techniques (such as scenes presented out of sequence, mime, music heard by some characters and not others, and so on) that would express the psychological rifts within those female characters, making the characters' interior reality available to the audience despite the proscenium divide between them. In this way, a suitably modified stage realism could depict not only the social consequences of injustice, but also the psychic reverberations.

Certainly American playwrights, feminist and otherwise, have long used expressionistic devices in their otherwise realistically structured plays to illustrate the psychological effects of social restrictions. Witness Blanche DuBois's internalized polka music and gun shot in Tennessee Williams's *A Streetcar Named Desire* (1947), the falling leaves seen only by Willy Loman in Arthur Miller's *Death of a Salesman* (1949), or the symbolic pantomime scenes in Wendy Kesselman's *My Sister in This House* (1982).[34] Even Alice Gerstenberg's *Overtones* (1913), sometimes described as a classic expressionist text because it splits its main characters into social and primitive selves, takes place in a familiar drawing room where the women's realistic conversation turns on issues of financial stability and dependency on men.[35] Marsha Norman's *Getting Out* (which I will discuss in detail in a later chapter) is perhaps the best recent example of this hybrid form (although Gayle Austin makes a good case for Fornes's *Fefu and Her Friends*—see "Madwoman" 77–81). In *Getting Out* (1978), Norman uses the proscenium arch of the realistic stage (which depicts her protagonist's apartment) to echo structurally the prison catwalk of the character's past and so reinforce the idea that life outside a literal prison is still a type of confinement for women who lack economic opportunities. Yet within this doubled proscenium arch, Norman (like Gerstenberg) splits her protagonist in two, using past and present avatars of a single "rehabilitated" ex-convict to suggest the continuing psychic disturbance the character suffers.[36] These examples all suggest that the "dark doubles" created by nineteenth-century women novelists who simultaneously identified with and revised "the self-definitions patriarchal culture [had] imposed on them" (Gilbert and

Gubar 1979, 79) are also accessible through stage realism. Since realism was designed to depict social boundaries, it can graphically represent the patriarchal cultural model that women are taught to
internalize; since it is a flexible dramatic tool with a long history of
adaptation, it can expand to contain a shifting or fragmented protagonist, a subject-in-process constructed by her own desires as well as
by social conditioning.

A detractor might argue, of course, that the "suitably modified"
realism I am describing here is actually not realism at all. To these
critics I would respond that realism has always been in the process
of development, that the plays I describe in the previous paragraph
all take place in a private living space behind an imaginary fourth
wall (a classic definition of realism, as we saw earlier in this chapter),
and that all dramatic conventions change through time. Furthermore,
as I demonstrated earlier with the varied critical reception of Maria
Irene Fornes, I am not alone in recognizing realism's adaptability.
William Demastes and Bonnie Marranca have both described a "new
realism" that partakes of realistic conventions but moves beyond
them; William Worthen has defined a "critical realism" that avoids
the "duplication of patriarchal subjection in the theater" (1992, 183);
Rita Felski posits a "subjective" realism, "centered upon the experi-
encing consciousness" that can incorporate "the depiction of dreams,
fantasies, flights of the imagination as part of its conception of the
real" (82); Sheila Stowell and Amy Kaplan both argued convincingly
that realism is not the monolith that critics with limited historical
awareness sometimes mistakenly perceive. As Enoch Brater has recently asserted, "The possibilities we now find in that elusive term
realism . . . are really quite different from those stable qualities we
were once told were there. Context is everything" (1990, 300). And
in the context of feminism, the mutability of realism can be a valuable asset.

One final reason to reevaluate realism has nothing to do with realism itself—its representational strategies or its history—but everything to do with feminism. Realism itself is *not* an ideology but an
aesthetic structure. While it is true that this structure (like all discursive models) is implicated in the political ideologies that led to its
construction, the structure itself is not the equivalent of patriarchal
oppression. Sheila Stowell, for instance, has noted that "while genres
or styles . . . may not be politically neutral, they are capable of presenting a range of ideological positions" (1992a, 87). Judith Stephens
concurs, noting about realism specifically that "the development of
dramatic character through traditional linear form is not necessarily
a patriarchal structure but an artistic structure" (1985, 20). Recogniz-

ing that the aesthetic conventions of realism are "easily sacrificed to patriarchal and popular attitudes," Stephens nonetheless insists that the form can be used to defy those same attitudes. And as Judith Butler has argued in a different context, "to operate within the matrix of power is not the same as to replicate uncritically relations of domination. It offers the possibility of a repetition of the law which is not its consolidation, but its displacement" (1990a, 30).

As I see it, the danger for feminists in entirely rejecting an aesthetic strategy—*any* aesthetic strategy—is that we risk reproducing the hegemony we object to in traditional patriarchal discourse. This issue of a hierarchy of discourse is debated increasingly in feminist circles as we struggle to assess literary merit, theatrical effectiveness, and political value in ways that do not denigrate the multiplicity of feminist work or assert our own monopolies on truth.[37] So literary critic Nina Baym has written that contemporary feminist theory is "permeated with musts and shoulds" and laments, "I've been here before" (166–67). Playwright Joan Holden has complained that the concept of a female or feminist aesthetic, originally designed as a defense against traditional critics, is beginning to create a tyranny of its own (Stephens 1985, 8–9). Painter and writer Pat Mainardi agrees, claiming that "women must be free to explore the entire range of art possibilities. We who have been labelled, stereotyped, and gerrymandered out of the very definition of art must be free to define art, not pick up the crumbs from The Men's table" (Leavitt 10).

Surely the issue at stake for feminists is, as critic Jeanie Forte notes, empowerment (1989, 125), and this empowerment of women theater practitioners can come only if all options are open for them to explore. In fact, the variety of available theatrical forms is one of the strengths of the contemporary theater, and feminists can use this variety to their advantage. To deny women playwrights this freedom, to insist that their plays are inadequate unless they adhere to a particular ideological stance within feminism or that they take shape in a certain prescribed dramatic form, is to create a feminist literary canon which, like more traditional canons, would become "self-referential and self-reinforcing, a touchstone system" (Gardiner 114). Such thinking restricts rather than enables feminist playwrights, and seems to me much more dangerous than the prospect of reviving traditional dramatic forms.

If we endorse the goal of empowerment for women, and if we accept that feminism is and must be polyvocal and evolving, then it seems crucial to me that we recognize realism as one of many inherited tools at a feminist artist's disposal. British socialist playwright John McGrath, noted for his work in bringing theater to working-class audiences, has recognized the problems of using mainstream theater for political ends, but nonetheless sees its value as an instrument of change. Focusing on the production hierarchies of traditional plays, he writes:

> The process, the building, the wage structure, the publicity machine, the free interval drinks budget, all these can turn opposition into novelty. But it could be short-sighted to deny the value of trying. This challenge to the dominance of bourgeois ideology on its own ground is important; it creates allies for the movement and is a weapon to use, and we are not in a position to throw any weapon away. (46)

Feminists, too, are in no position to discard the equipment at their disposal, to overlook any tool of resistance, even one—like realism—inherited from the fathers who may have used it against us. Audre Lorde has argued that the master's tools will never dismantle the master's house (98), but when a sledge hammer is lying in the back yard, I say "Use it."

2

Domestic Spaces, Women's Rights, and Realism, 1910s–1930s

No Ibsens or Shaws: Feminism, Realism, and Historical Context

WRITING in the journal *Forum* in 1914, theater critic and playwright Florence Kiper surveyed the previous New York theater season from, in her words, "the feminist viewpoint." Her comments on women's social position at the time and on then-current stage conventions can reveal much to those of us now studying early twentieth-century feminist drama. The first insight of importance to contemporary feminists is Kiper's insistence on the centrality of the so-called "woman question" to society as a whole. Seen from our vantage point almost a century later, Kiper writes with seeming prescience about the class and gender struggles that characterized her era, much as they do our own:

> the woman movement is undoubtedly, if perhaps the class-consciousness in the labor struggle be excepted, the one most important tendency of the century. It is important because it deals not with a limited and selected class of society, but with the very fundamentals of society—the relation of the sexes and consequently the next generation. Race-suicide, the double standard of morals, the taints of heredity, these are not side issues, but of relevancy to all of national existence. (921–22)

A second important insight—one that we contemporary feminists might even take as an admonishment in our current struggle to recognize and respect the multiplicity of feminist viewpoints—is Kiper's understanding of the variety within the women's movement. For her, the "woman movement" included investigation "of the meaning of the growing divorce 'evil,' of the suffrage agitation, of women in the professions, of young girls in industry, of the sudden awakening of the sheltered woman to a knowledge of prostitution and venereal diseases" (921). In short, for Kiper the women's movement demanded attention to a wide and varied array of social, political, and economic controversies.

In terms of my discussion of feminism's compatibility with stage realism, however, Kiper's explicit linking of the two is her most important message to 1990s scholars. In the same paragraph in which she asserts the pivotal position of the women's movement in social discourse, Kiper laments the lack of socially aware realist and naturalist playwrights to engage the topic in the American theater:

> We have at present no Ibsens, Shaws, Björnsons, Strindbergs, Brieuxs. . . . Almost none of our clever writers for the stage are bringing to these vital themes [i.e., those women's issues noted above] a conscious philosophy or an informed understanding. (921)

By directly correlating these prominent realist and naturalist playwrights with the stage representation of women's issues, Kiper suggests that in her era, realism was not only suitable for feminist exploration of social issues, but virtually equivalent to it.

Kiper's direct association of feminism with realism in 1914 illustrates vividly some of the blind spots in contemporary feminist drama criticism that I delineated in chapter 1. The most obvious problem suggested by analyzing Kiper's review is our sometime tendency to engage women's texts (as well as their performances and political activism) from our own perspectives rather than from those of the historical period under scrutiny, and so trivialize or oversimplify what to women of the era were complex feminist issues. As Kiper saw clearly, during the 1910s the women's movement was extraordinarily diverse, and it evolved rapidly just before and just after the passage of the Nineteenth Amendment. Many women's plays of this period actually chart the changes and developments within feminism, illustrating Rita Felski's point that "the political value of literary texts from the standpoint of feminism can be determined only by an investigation of their social functions and effects in relation to the interests of women in a particular historical context" (2). A very brief survey of feminism in this historical context—the decades before and after the vote was won—will help frame my discussion of feminist realism during this era.

In the 1910s, during the peak of the women's suffrage movement, the women's movement in general encompassed a wide assortment of diverse women's groups. Topics as seemingly unconnected as food preservation, the double standard of morality, the education of women, divorce and alimony, child labor laws, popular images of women, lynching, and taxation without representation were all crucial items on various feminist agendas (Friedl 11). What obscures this diversity from our 1990s perspective is the impressive consolidation of these various women's groups into the movement for women's suffrage. Believing that problems from contaminated milk to prostitution could be remedied if women were allowed to vote, diverse factions of women collaborated in the campaign for women's suffrage, building coalition (as historian Nancy Cott has noted) by acknowledging that "women had variant and perhaps clashing loyalties" (156). After the passage of the Nineteenth Amendment, however, these conflicting loyalties within the women's movement reemerged. Lacking a common agenda such as the one suffrage had provided, the feminist community became painfully fragmented (Chafe 43–49; Cott 156; Lebsock 54–55).

In the 1920s, then, while the hedonistic flapper replaced the dedicated suffragist as the New Woman portrayed in popular culture, the women's movement faltered. Many younger women, assuming that the battle for equality had been won with the vote, returned (after a period of sexual liberation emblematized by the flapper) to domesticity, eschewing education and careers in favor of more traditional roles as wives and mothers (Chafe 100–106; Pruette 131–32). Those feminists who remained active in public life split into at least two competing factions, notably the National Women's Party, a militant group that introduced the Equal Rights Amendment in 1923, and the League of Women Voters, a more conservative group with a wide-ranging reform agenda and an insistence on using "respectable" tactics (Becker 223; O'Neill 273–77). By the mid-1930s, hostilities among the competing factions had undermined the possibility of any unified feminist agenda (Chafe 58).

Feminist plays from all three decades illustrate these changes and schisms. In the 1910s, many plays depicted feminists overlooking the differences among them—what today we would call the competing identity positions of race, class, sexual orientation, age, education, and so on—in order to promote female solidarity and achieve their goal of voting rights. In the twenties and thirties the plays changed tone, often lamenting the decline of political feminism, depicting the losses and reversions that attended the return to domestic roles, and detailing the sobering effects of women's hostility to other women (Kolb 152–58; Sutherland 325–26). A theoretical perspective that ignores this historical context might not see these plays as written "from the feminist viewpoint," thereby unfairly diminishing the work of these early feminist playwrights.

Such an ahistorical perspective on women's issues is compounded, in many current theoretical formulations, by an ahistorical perspective on stage realism—another point suggested by Kiper's remarks. For many early twentieth-century playwrights, realism was an important theatrical innovation designed expressly for the serious exploration of complex social issues. As W. B. Worthen has argued, "the first generation of realistic playwrights often adopted a critical posture toward the pieties of the middle-class audience whose attitudes were embodied in the 'realistic' vision of the world" (1993, 373). Sheila Stowell, in her examination of English suffrage plays, concurs, noting that during the woman suffrage era realism was "championed as a means of challenging the ideological assumptions embedded in melodrama and the well-made play" (1992b, 5). Realism was thus designed from its inception to critique social injustices rather than merely to replicate them in an unexamined way, and women playwrights and reformers were quick to put it to that use.

In addition to its innate critical function, realism offered women playwrights the mimetic potential (illusory though it might be, as we saw in chapter 1) to articulate their own experience of social realities, experience that often conflicted with the stereotypes imposed by society at large as well as by conventional theatrical representation. Sharon Friedman explains realism's appeal for early twentieth-century feminists in just such terms, arguing that with the advent of realism in the United States,

> the insistence upon truth, the goal of verisimilitude, the "desire to get closer to the fact" . . . [became] the dominant chord in American drama, and women playwrights did not hesitate to portray issues [such as the New Woman and the wife's revolt] that drew upon the "facts" of their lives as women. (74)

Using this built-in power to reconstruct social and dramatic discourse, many early twentieth-century feminist playwrights constructed their own versions of the way things were, asserting a counterclaim to the dominant male picture and illustrating its shortcomings.

Many feminist playwrights of the period went beyond simply exploiting realism's mimetic power, however, and included theatrical innovations within their realist plays, adapting the dramatic form passed down to them by Ibsen and his contemporaries in order to express their feminist concerns. As J. Ellen Gainor has pointed out, realism arrived on the American stage simultaneously with other, "experimental" genres like expressionism and symbolism. Since playwrights in the United States were not necessarily conversant with the theoretical underpinnings of these European dramatic movements (which sometimes posited each mode as a rejection of or commentary on another), they were free to intermingle them, and frequently did so.[1] Beginning with Strindberg's *A Dream Play* (1902) and escalating their efforts after the New York success of the German expressionists in the early 1920s, American playwrights characteristically embedded antimimetic techniques within their otherwise realistic plays. In the hands of feminist playwrights, expressionistic techniques could be used within realist productions to indicate the repression suffered by female characters (such as the split characters in Alice Gerstenberg's *Overtones*, for example) or to illustrate the contrast between social restrictions (depicted realistically) and personal freedom (depicted expressionistically)—a contrast I explore more fully in my discussion of Rachel Crothers's *Mary the Third*. In sum, when contemporary feminist critics dismiss realism as limiting for feminists, they reveal an oversimplified understanding of realism's flexibility as well as a lack of historical awareness about the development of the genre in the United States.

Although Florence Kiper was justified in her lament that few American playwrights (especially during the 1913 Broadway season she described) were seriously exploring women's issues in realistic social dramas, a number of feminist playwrights working in Kiper's era were beginning to use realism for that purpose. In this chapter, I explore some of these plays by women, focusing on the varying feminist uses those playwrights found for realism.

The most obvious use of realism for these early twentieth-century dramatists (and, to date, the most frequently studied manifestation of early feminist realism) is to depict the entrapment of women within domestic roles. Whether in service to their parents, to a husband, or to widespread social expectations, turn-of-the-century women often found the household a place of severe confinement. Contemporary feminist critics like Sue-Ellen Case are quite correct in noting that realism's family focus posits woman as a dependent sexual "other" (1988, 124); what such criticism sometimes overlooks, however, is the protest agenda of many such depictions.

While the conventions of realism (especially the fourth-wall set and the everyday characters) do emphasize the domestic world, a number of plays from the 1910s move beyond it, focusing on the relationship between the individual household and larger social issues. Indeed, in many of these plays domestic decisions are shown to have widespread political consequences. Conversely, the home, often touted during these decades as a place of protection and security for women, is often revealed in these women's dramas to be infected by the very social ills it ostensibly prevents.

In addition to portraying the penetration of private spaces by external social forces, some feminist playwrights of the period depicted the movement of women out of that private world and into public life. While such plays do suggest that women have choices and opportunities beyond the domestic sphere, they also unflinchingly depict the economic hardships and personal struggles inevitably faced by independent women of the period. Finally, after the passage of the Nineteenth Amendment in 1920, feminist playwrights used realism to depict the decline of the women's movement and to confirm women's attendant losses.

While theater historians may note apparently idiosyncratic oversights in my selection of plays to discuss, it is not my intention to offer an exhaustive survey of women playwrights of the period, to trace the development of realism in America, nor to assess the career achievements of individual writers. Rather, I have selected a number of plays, interesting in their own right, that demonstrate the potential of realism for feminists of the era and that illustrate its various uses. Furthermore, I have deliberately chosen to emphasize those women's plays that have not frequently been studied (thereby omitting detailed analysis of sometimes relevant but more frequently scrutinized works by playwrights like Susan Glaspell and Lillian Hellman) in an attempt to bring the work of these overlooked early feminists to light. For while Florence Kiper was correct in noting that the United States in 1914 had produced no playwright with the international stature, social consciousness, and realist agenda of Ibsen and Shaw, she also predicted the imminent emergence of the feminist playwrights whose work I discuss here. She wrote:

> It will require some skill to project dramatically the domestic problems of every day, of the prosaic majority, the tragi–comedies of warring temperament within the bond of family. The vital playwright, however, can and will render these themes of more interest to us than the occasional lady-with-a-past or the flippant "indiscretions" of high society (925).

Let us then turn to the American dramatic scene in the 1910s, where from Broadway to the little theaters of Greenwich Village, feminist realists were depicting the "domestic problems of every day" as women adjusted to and contributed to a rapidly changing social milieu.

Domestic Confinements

In their germinal study of nineteenth-century women writers, literary critics Sandra M. Gilbert and Susan Gubar note the preponderance of stories of enclosure and escape in women's novels of the period. According to Gilbert and Gubar, these women writers added a new dimension to the common nineteenth-century tradition of prison stories written by men (Poe, Byron, Dickens, and so on), a dimension not readily apparent to the male publishing hierarchy. As Gilbert and Gubar explain this difference:

> [M]ale metaphors of imprisonment . . . may have very different aesthetic functions and philosophical messages in different male literary works. . . . Women authors, however, reflect the literal reality of their own confinement in the constraints they depict. . . . Recording their own distinctively female experience, they are secretly working through and within the conventions of literary texts to define their own lives. (1979, 87)

This comment offers two important insights into the literary productions discussed by Gilbert and Gubar. First, it suggests that nineteenth-century women writers were not creating the romanticized stories of escape and adventure that their male counterparts constructed, but depicting the specific forms of social, familial, economic, and political restrictions that women routinely faced in their daily lives. As Gilbert and Gubar go on to note, many of the most important and enduring women's novels of the period focus on "what women writers tend to see as their parallel confinements in texts, houses, and maternal female bodies" (89). Second, their observation about these writers' use of prevailing literary conventions suggests that these conventions provided women writers with a way to insert their voices, their viewpoints, and their experiences as an oppressed class into the dominant discourse. Thus, the very act of artistically rendering images of their own imprisonment provided these women writers some escape from it, their ostensibly conventional texts thereby becoming subversive feminist activities.

In the early decades of the twentieth century, a parallel strategy emerged in a number of plays by American women. These playwrights used the restricted drawing-room world of the realistic stage to depict women characters trapped in the limiting roles imposed by their families and husbands and sustained by inherited social norms. Their feminist goal was twofold: to depict and so protest women's entrapment in inherited roles; and to use realism, that recently arrived vehicle for critiquing social conventions, as a means of insinuating their voices into the raging controversy over women's rights.

It is important to remember that (despite the contrary protestations of some materialist feminists, noted in chapter 1), depicting a repressive reality is not the same as endorsing it; such a depiction can also be used to expose the unjust power relations that make it possible. This subversive use of realism's mimetic power was an especially powerful tool in the United States in the early twentieth century, when (as we saw in the preceding section) realism was seen as a theatrical and literary innovation uniquely suited for social commentary. Amy Kaplan has explained this use of realism as an act of rebellion and reform in the works of American realist novelists of the early twentieth century; her description applies equally well to women's realistic plays of domestic entrapment from the same period. Noting that representation—even realistic representation—is a construct, an ideological discursive practice by which writers actively create and criticize the formations of their culture, Kaplan describes the reform agenda of early American realists:

> The realists do not naturalize the social world to make it seem immutable or organic, but, like contemporary reformers, they engage in an enormous act of construction to organize, re-form, and control the social world. . . . Furthermore, by containing the threats of social change, realistic narratives also register those desires which undermine the closure of containment. (10)

In their plays of domestic entrapment, a number of women playwrights of the era followed this pattern, recording power inequities within the nuclear family and registering the contrary desires of often thwarted female characters who engage the audience's sympathies. While this mimetic use of realism to protest women's social restrictions could certainly be misused or co-opted, it offered an important first step for women playwrights seeking to expose the unjust social and familial power hierarchies that inhibited female self-fulfillment in the 1910s.

A brief but particularly direct example of a playwright's use of realism to depict both a woman's entrapment and her contrary desires is Edna Ferber's one-act play *The Eldest*, first performed by the Provincetown Players as part of their 1919–20 season. The focus of the play is Rose, a forty-year-old woman who lives with her parents and much younger siblings, all of whom treat her with extreme disrespect, expecting her servitude and offering nothing but complaints in return. Through the course of the play we learn that Rose has been tending her invalid mother and fulfilling her family's daily domestic needs for fifteen years, having broken off a romantic attachment with Henry Selz (whose yellowed letters she still treasures) to do so.

On the day depicted in the play, Rose has spent her time marketing, scrubbing floors, cooking supper, baking a pie, taking messages, and acceding to her whining mother's every request (including frequent demands for hot water bottles on a day all the other characters find stifling). Rose's entrapment in this endless round of drudgery is suggested by the realistic set of the play. Most obviously, the set reveals the extent to which Rose is overburdened. As the evening meal is about to begin, her ladder and scrub pail are evident on stage, with dining chairs still piled on top of the table as the family members arrive home from work, complaining about the state of the room and clamoring for their supper. In addition, Rose moves about the stage from interior space to interior space, entering and exiting only through the doors to her mother's sickroom and the kitchen. Her father and siblings, in contrast, use only the other two doors, one leading to individual bedrooms (places of privacy) and one to the outside world. Rose alone is confined to common domestic spaces.

The action of the play illustrates Rose's confinement as well. After hurriedly gulping down the meal Rose has prepared, her father and siblings all depart, each with a hurtful or inconsiderate remark directed at Rose. When Rose suggests that her father could visit with his ailing wife instead of leaving Rose alone to care for her, Pa retorts, "I been slaving all day. I guess I got the right to a little amusement! A man works his fingers to the bone for his family and then his own daughter nags him!" (72). Her brother Al, after refusing to help Rose put away her stepladder (exclaiming, "What d'you think I am! The janitor!"—69), borrows the last of her household money to go on a date. Finally, her pretty, flighty younger sister Floss announces that she has a theater date with Henry Selz (who has seen her that day at her department store job and mistaken her for the Rose of fifteen years before), and chides Rose for not having ironed the dress she intends to wear. The play ends with Rose sitting alone at the littered supper table, destroying Henry's letters before she resignedly resumes her round of toil.

This short play clearly depicts the entrapment of women in inherited domestic roles and suggests some of the reasons for it. As the eldest, Rose was expected to care for her sickly mother, an activity that prevented her from marrying the man she loved or from obtaining gainful employment outside the home. Yet after fifteen years of loyal service, Rose has become a nonentity to her father and siblings (all of whom work outside the home and therefore have some economic freedom—witness the new hat Floss splurges on while Rose is chastised for her allocation of household funds), earning no independent income and no respect from those for whom she toils. The play suggests that as long as domestic work remains an unpaid service exacted from female family members, neither household work nor the women who perform it will be respected by society at large.

Despite its vivid depiction of what women suffered when forced into unchosen and unpaid domestic service, when seen from a postmodern feminist perspective, *The Eldest* might also seem to illustrate some of the problems contemporary feminists see as endemic to realism. Most obviously, the play posits Rose as a victim with no choices, thereby suggesting a form of biological determinism that is not very helpful for feminists hoping to incite social change. Furthermore, a sympathetic spectator might be led to lament Rose's fate, believing (as Rose seems to) that if only she could have married Henry in her youth, her life would have been happier. Marriage is therefore presumed to be a solution, while it was equally likely to have been a variation on the same domestic trap. These factors do partially undermine Ferber's otherwise chilling use of realism to portray the domestic imprisonment of women. As Judith Stephens has noted about Zona Gale's *Miss Lulu Bett*, however, the fact that realism was "easily sacrificed to patriarchal and popular attitudes" should not encourage us to condemn the aesthetic form itself, only to scrutinize its uses very carefully (1985, 20).

In fact, Ferber's play may simply illustrate the "critical doublebind" that Penny Boumelha sees in some feminist critiques of realism. For Boumelha, some feminists reject the closure of realism "not simply as representing but reproducing—enforcing, even—the impoverished opportunities that the social order afforded actual historical women of the middle class" (85). However, these same feminists also view fantasy or romance (which might offer alternatives) as "unworthy and evasive." This paradox establishes "a critical double-bind . . . by which all novels [and plays!] written before the contemporary expansion of both women's opportunities and feminist theory must be judged and found wanting" (85). In Ferber's play, this doublybinding critique would reject the depiction of Rose's restricted opportunities on the one hand and denounce her thwarted romantic longings on the other. In fact, what the play does is document a common social problem for unmarried women and define Rose as a desiring subject, thereby using realism to attack two issues of feminist concern.

A play that offers a similarly serious depiction of a woman's familial entrapment while sidestepping the potential pitfalls of determinism and romanticism is *Miss Lulu Bett*, the Zona Gale play mentioned above (first performed in 1920). Like *The Eldest*, *Miss Lulu Bett* depicts an unmarried woman's domestic enslavement to her unappreciative and demanding family. However, it differs from *The Eldest* in that it critically examines the plight of the other women in the household and ends with the suggestion that autonomy and self-direction, not marriage, may offer the only escape from enforced domestic roles. In these ways, *Miss Lulu Bett* offers a realistic depiction of household confinement without suggesting victimization or marriage as the only alternatives.

Gale's three-act play focuses on the title character, who, in the first act, is in a situation of domestic entrapment similar to Rose's. Lulu's plight may be even worse, however, in that she performs all the household work for someone else's family, her labor the price paid so that both she and her mother can exist as dependents to her sister Ina's husband Dwight. The family mythology has defined Lulu as not "strong enough to work" (91), thereby emphasizing both Lulu's dependency and the belief that performing all the household duties for four adults and two children does not constitute "work." This devaluing of Lulu's contribution to the family permits Dwight and Ina to see Lulu as a faceless drone, not as a person with desires and aspirations of her own. They criticize everything she does, from the crispness of the bread she toasts for them to her purchase of flowers to brighten their table (at which she rarely gets to sit). Although Lulu owns nothing but what they provide her, including a wardrobe of Ina's cast-off clothes, they complain about Lulu's appearance, finding Lulu's presence in front of company to be an embarrassment (90). Dwight's kindhearted brother Ninian sums up Lulu's plight when he tells her, "They make a slavey of you. Regular slavey. Damned shame *I* call it" (103).

Like *The Eldest*, *Miss Lulu Bett* uses the realistic set to emphasize the protagonist's restrictions. Act 1, in which Lulu functions solely as a household servant, takes place in the family dining room, an enclosed space which Lulu enters and exits from the kitchen while the rest of the family sit and eat. At the end of act 1, however, Lulu marries Ninian, and the scene thereafter shifts to a side porch of Dwight's house. This space, attached to the house but with fewer confining walls, parallels Lulu's partial break from Dwight's family. After traveling briefly with Ninian, Lulu has seen something of the world and has been recognized as an individual instead of a mere functionary filling a role. Unfortunately, when Ninian confesses that he lost touch with his first wife fifteen years previously and does not know for certain if she is dead (and, therefore, if his marriage to Lulu is legal), Lulu feels she must return to Dwight and Ina's home. At this point, however, she is, like the porch, attached to the household but not entirely confined by it, and she begins to assert herself against Dwight and Ina, keeping their daughter's secrets from them, appropriating a dress of Ina's without permission, and reading Dwight's letter from Ninian despite Dwight's express order not to. This movement to an exterior space thus symbolizes Lulu's emerging consciousness of her own identity and desires, desires that cannot be contained within the walls of Dwight's house.

In Gale's original script, Lulu's desires also exceeded the boundaries of realistic closure, an important innovation in an otherwise realistic play (Barlow xxiv). In that original ending, Ninian's first wife is found to be alive, thus invalidating Lulu's marriage. Rather than marrying Cornish (another suitor) or maintaining her position in Dwight's household, however, Lulu chooses a life of uncertain independence. Refusing to let Cornish explain her decision to Dwight and Ina, Lulu insists on speaking for herself. Furthermore, she leaves town alone to seek employment, needing, as she says, "to see out of my own eyes. For the first time in my life" (161). The play thus originally concluded with Lulu's escaping her lifelong imprisonment but without any resolution of her economic or social problems. Like the shift in set, then, the original ending of Gale's play indicates the rebellion of Lulu's desires against the forces of oppression, forces represented, in part, by the realistic set and resisted by Lulu's refusal of containment.

Unfortunately, this open ending caused so much controversy in the original 1920 production that the author felt compelled to change it to ensure the play's successful run. In the revised ending, Ninian's first wife turns out to be dead, and he returns to rescue Lulu from her life of drudgery in Dwight and Ina's house. While Cynthia Sutherland sees this change as Gale's capitulation to public opinion—in her view, an example of women choosing increasingly to act as mediators rather than revolutionaries in the women's movement of the 1920s (324–25)—Cynthia Cole notes astutely that both versions retain Lulu's basic evolution as she strives to define herself rather than merely accept Dwight and Ina's definition of her (119–20). The merit of Cole's interpretation is further suggested by other elements in Gale's realistic text, elements hinting that domestic entrapment was common among women of the era and suggesting some of the social and economic forces that sustained it.[2]

The primary reason women accepted roles like Lulu's within Dwight's family was economic necessity, a condition Lulu recognizes and laments on several occasions. First she discusses the problem with Ninian, revealing her awareness of her plight as just one example of a widespread social condition. She says: "I can't do any other work—that's the trouble—women like me can't do any other work" (103). Later, she makes a similar remark to Cornish, explaining her desire for independence and the economic difficulties that prevent her from achieving it. She tells him that although she is a locally renowned cook, "I can't earn anything. I'd like to earn something" (131). Lulu's perceptions of her limited earning power accurately reflect the conditions of the time. Despite the political gains women apparently achieved with the passage of the Nineteenth Amendment in 1920 (the year of *Miss Lulu's* premiere), political rights did not bring economic equality. As historian William Chafe has noted, almost all the women who joined the labor force in the 1920s were motivated by economic need (most of them being poor African-American and immigrant women working in sweatshops), yet they were treated on the job as marginal employees whose primary responsibilities—and chief sources of support—were in the home (78). While clerical opportunities for refined, middle-class, white women were expanding, uneducated women like Lulu rarely had the chance to "earn something" and so support themselves.

Given these economic limitations, marriage might seem to be the most desirable option a working-class woman had to ensure her financial support. Yet Gale's play emphatically suggests otherwise, even given the revised ending in which Lulu is reunited with Ninian. Close scrutiny of the other female characters reveals the strictures placed on *all* women within the traditional patriarchal family, even if those women were not primarily responsible for domestic work. Lulu's mother, for example, states outright that marriage offers no better alternative to Lulu's position. When Ninian asks Mrs. Bett if Lulu wouldn't be better off married, Mrs. Bett replies: "Wouldn't make much difference. Why look at me. A husband, six children, four of 'em under the sod with him. And sometimes I feel as though nothin' more had happened to me than has happened to Lulie. . . . Only she ain't had the pain" (107).

In Ina, the female head of the household, we see the clearest example of how limiting marriage could be, especially to women married to petty tyrants like Dwight. Despite his contradictions and repeated sexist remarks, Ina follows her husband's lead in all actions, accepting his every notion, no matter how illogical or insulting. In everything from the proper preparation of potatoes to the value of family life, Ina echoes Dwight's remarks with her own "That's what I always think." When Dwight attempts to coerce Lulu's obedience with a family vote, Ina mindlessly follows his lead, consolidating his power and making a mockery of the democratic process. (This voting scene might also be read as a worried comment on women's suffrage, suggesting that married women voters would simply double their husband's vote and influence.) In short, Ina is a cipher, a useless woman literally unable to boil water without Lulu's directions or to conceive a thought without Dwight's instructions; she is yet another victim of Dwight's manipulation, even as she practices the same arts on the other, less powerful members of her household. As Cole has explained it, the play

> is a study of the power relationships within the nuclear family. Indeed, the play constitutes a devastating portrait of the male autocrat who holds absolute power in ways both petty and profound and the hierarchy that forms among the female family members based on each one's relationship and usefulness to him. (116)

Given a social reality in which most women lived as economic dependents of possibly despotic men, some form of entrapment for women was virtually inevitable. And while Gale's play does focus on a domestic world where women are "others" with little possibility for self-fulfillment or even self-definition, *Miss Lulu Bett* uses the conventions of realism to criticize those limitations and to suggest some of the widespread cultural conditions that create and sustain them. In this way, the play makes a strong political statement regarding the rights of women. Some materialist feminist critics have argued that realism is without value for feminist dramatists because it is incapable of exploring individual dilemmas in terms of a broad social context.[3] *Miss Lulu Bett*'s attention to historical context, social convention, and women's economic realities challenges the universal applicability of this dismissal.

Another play that does an exemplary job of using a realistic format to interweave private predicaments, social pressures, and public policy is Marion Craig Wentworth's one-act play *War Brides* (1915). The play takes place in "a room in a peasant's cottage in a war-ridden country" (3). Expanding the realistic set of this cottage parlor is an open upstage door, through which the audience sees women performing all varieties of farm labor. The stage directions emphasize that this is a world of women, "aristocrats and peasants side by side," working together to gather the harvest while also completing all the daily domestic chores. In the opening dialogue between nineteen-year-old Amelia and her mother, the reason for this single-gender society becomes clear: the village men (including Amelia's three grown brothers) are all at war, leaving behind a community of women and boys, guarded by transient garrisons of soldiers.

The action of the play focuses on the government's recruitment of war brides (that is, women who would wed soldiers about to leave for the battlefront), the government hoping this scheme will stem the tide of depopulation set in motion by the war.[4] Amelia has received a proposal from one Hans Hoffman, a "handsome lieutenant" whom she barely knows but whom her mother deems an exceptionally good catch by virtue of his appearance and his rank. Amelia has refused his proposal, not only because she doesn't know him but also because she wants to join the Red Cross and work as a nurse. The debates about Amelia's marrying Hoffman form much of the play.

Arguing for the marriage is Hoffman himself, who claims it is Amelia's duty to marry him. He enters their house to press his case, claiming "Pretty girls like you should marry. The priests and the generals have commanded it. It's for the fatherland. . . . It's your patriotic duty, Amelia" (19). Hoffman thus brings with him the visible symbol of his uniform and the authority of both church and state, male hierarchies of power that (like the more subtle but equally coercive Dwight in *Miss Lulu*) impose their will on female subjects. Indeed, the women of the community have accepted the logic of this arrangement, indicating how easily women can be indoctrinated into the sexist economies of their cultures. Amelia's neighbor Minna, for example, enters proudly, flashing her iron wedding band (symbol of a war bride), extolling the excitement of the group ceremony ("It was fun—just like a theater"—21) and the widow's pension she will receive should her new husband die in battle. She also delights in her good fortune at escaping life as an "old maid," reveling in the fame and glory she expects to win as a war bride. In addition to Minna, Amelia's mother (identified in the stage directions only as "the Mother") accepts without question the government's plan for its women because, for her, producing an heir should be a woman's highest priority. In discussing the pregnancy of her resident daughter-in-law Hedwig, the Mother says, "I tell you I must have that child, Amelia! I cannot live else" (14).

Hedwig herself, however, is Amelia's strongest supporter in refusing Hoffman's proposal. For Hedwig, hurried weddings deny the sanctity of the marriage bond; the widow's pension is a bribe; a war bride is a "breeding-machine" (31); and the excitement of a theatrical ceremony does not make up for the hardships a single mother will endure, both during childbirth and in raising her child alone. As the play progresses, Hedwig is discovered attempting to subvert the government's plan by discouraging potential war brides; these activities make her, in the soldiers' eyes, guilty of treason. Nonetheless, Hedwig sees her endeavors as the only way to stop a war in which she has had no say and for which she must suffer much. She attacks Hoffman with these words:

Are we women never to get up out of the dust? You never asked us if we wanted this war, yet you ask us to gather in the crops, cut the wood, keep the world going, drudge and slave, and wait, and agonize, lose our all, and go on bearing more men—and more—to be shot down! If we breed men for you, why don't you let us say what is to become of them? (33)

Later, when a captain comes to imprison Hedwig for treason, she exclaims:

If we can bring forth the men for the nation, we can sit with you in your councils and shape the destiny of the nation, and say whether it is to war or peace we give the sons we bear. . . . Laugh, Herr Captain, but the day will come; and then there will be no more war. (54–55)

At the end of the play, after Hedwig discovers that her husband is dead and that she will be incarcerated, she shoots herself, her suicide part of her plan that the women of the nation refuse to bear children until the war is ended.

While the action, set, character development, and closure of this short play certainly define it as a realist text (and the accompanying photographs reveal the original production to have been in the realist mode as well, the "cottage" room resembling a neat American farm parlor set behind an imaginary fourth wall), the play clearly has metaphoric elements that emphasize its feminist goals. In terms of depicting entrapment, the play shows the relegation of women to the domestic world, here expanded somewhat to include all the labor and responsibility of farm management as well as child care and routine household chores. To Hedwig, the work they do indicates women's importance; she says to the captain, "Look out in those fields. Who cleared them, and plucked the vineyards clean? You think we are left at home because we are weak. Ah, no; we are strong. That is why" (58). Yet when she dares to protest this government-enforced detention of women without their consent, she is threatened with literal incarceration—the logical extension of the life she already leads.

War Brides goes well beyond this depiction of domestic entrapment, however, in its multiple analogies to urgent feminist issues of its time. In Amelia's disparaged aspiration to work for the Red Cross rather than marry, we see the pressures on women of the 1910s to eschew personal ambitions and careers for the sake of family stability and continuity. In Hedwig's convincing the village women not to be war brides, we see the value of women's subversive measures and a call to grassroots political activism for women of the day. In Hedwig's protest that women should have some say in creating government policy, we see an invitation for women to work for women's suffrage.

In Hedwig's allegation that if women worked in government we would have fewer wars (her logic being that women would not willingly send their sons to be killed, as all of the Mother's are in *War Brides*), we see the strong antiwar sentiments that colored many feminist activities of the time (despite what a 1990s perspective might perceive as an oversimplified, biologically based argument). And in Hedwig's suicide, we see the frustration and loss that inevitably accrue when women are powerless to influence their own fates. Hedwig, at least, has determined hers.

In *War Brides*, then, Wentworth went beyond the conventional depictions of women as domestic "others" to explore some of the cultural and political causes of their limited opportunities. While the play's disturbing antiwar protest was clearly a large part of Wentworth's agenda in 1915, the play also approximates the situation of women everywhere who were trapped in traditional roles. The female characters of Wentworth's play are engaged in an endless round of unpaid work, intimidated by government policy and social norms to value the production of male heirs as their highest religious and patriotic duty, afforded no voice in the government policies that controlled their destinies; in short, the women of *War Brides* are themselves besieged. By incorporating these public issues into the private and domestic realities of her characters, Wentworth shows realism to be an effective method for expressing the feminist concerns of her era.

Permeating Domestic Boundaries

As the example of *War Brides* makes clear, realism could be used not only to depict the deadening effects of domestic enslavement for women, but also to show how social convention, government intervention, and religious repression create and support those domestic conditions. A number of other plays from this era move in a different direction to dramatize a similar interpenetration of public and private spheres. These plays focus not only on the private suffering engendered by public attitudes and events but also on the power of women to reach beyond their domestic spaces to influence social norms and shape public policy. In these plays, the domestic space is seen as a potential base of power inextricably connected to the public domain.

Using the domestic setting, ordinary characters, and cause-and-effect plots of stage realism, feminist playwrights challenged a variety of social conventions regarding these intertwined worlds. Some tried to show the home itself as something other than a place where women were safe from harm, thereby debunking the patriarchal myth that domestic space was a protective cocoon necessary to women's survival. Some illustrated that women, while apparently isolated within domestic spaces, had the power to stimulate social change when they banded together in common cause. By thus expanding realism's domestic borders, these playwrights were able to show that the boundaries of the private world were not unassailable and that enclosure therein did not preclude the exercise of social and political influence.

One prolific playwright of this era who consistently addressed such topics is Rachel Crothers, a once neglected dramatist whose work has recently attracted much attention from feminist critics and theater historians.[5] Like Florence Kiper (who admired Crothers's work), Crothers saw women's issues as central to her era and appreciated realism—what she called "the highest form of dramatic writing" (1928, 126)—as a vehicle for exploring those issues. Crothers was attuned to the extraordinary changes occurring in women's roles in the early decades of the twentieth century and saw in these changes the truest barometer of social transformation. In 1912, Crothers told an interviewer:

> Most of the great modern plays are studies of women. I suppose it is because women are in themselves more dramatic than men, more changing, and a more significant note of the hour in which they live. If you want to see the signs of the times, watch women. Their evolution is the most important thing in modern life. (Cited in Gottlieb 1975, 71)

From a postmodern perspective, one might dismiss the essentialism of Crothers's assumption that women are innately more mercurial than men. But despite her rationale, her point—that women's social "evolution" accurately reflects changes in modern society—is borne out in her long and successful career. Crothers consistently created women characters who struggled to define themselves as individuals against a backdrop of traditional heterosexual relationships, rigid social expectations, and economic barriers to independence. Since each of her plays is concerned with, in her words, "a social attitude toward women at the moment I wrote it" (cited in Sutherland 319), her plays register the changes in the feminist movement during the course of her career, from female careerism and political activism in the 1910s to disillusionment in the 1920s and 1930s.[6] While some contemporary scholars find her later plays (predominantly social comedies) somewhat disappointing from a feminist point of view,[7] her early problem plays "challenge relations between the sexes on a personal as well as public level" (Gottlieb 1979, 150). One early play that vividly dramatizes the connections between private spaces, public discourse, and women's ability to effect social change is Crothers's *Ourselves* (1913).

The play concerns a wealthy socialite, Beatrice Barrington, who has recently become interested in moral reform work. The play opens as Beatrice visits a girl's reformatory, hoping to hire a young "fallen" woman as a personal secretary and so assist in the girl's reformation. The first act of the play takes place in the parlor of this reform home, a room which approximates the protected domestic space of patriarchal mythology but which turns out to represent quite different realities to the young women who reside there. It is obvious from the opening stage directions that the drawing room offers no emotional solace to the girls who live in the house. The drawing room is described as "conventional," even "comfortable," but also "unhomelike, with rather a forlorn air" (1.1).[8] For the girls, the room represents not safety but unwelcome restrictions to their freedom. As Miss Carew, the reform home manager, explains to Beatrice:

> When a girl's been on the loose in any way, she's free—and when you take away her liberty and her old associates—the excitement, the companionship—everything she's used to—and shut her up and try to teach her something else, of course she's bored to death—*bored*. Why shouldn't she be? (1.3)

Miss Carew's sympathetic assessment is supported by several of the young women whom Beatrice interviews. When Beatrice asks Lena, a Swedish immigrant who longs for a career as a manicurist, whether she wouldn't rather "be in a good home where [she'd] be protected and do house work," Lena replies, "Oh, I couldn't do no house-work. It's too lonely. You god shut up all day" (1.14). Later in act 1 we learn from Kitty, another inmate, that the girls remain at Miss Carew's only to avoid more stringent incarceration. As Kitty says, "You can run away easy enough if you want to—but you get the worst of it if you do. If you get pinched again you get *longer* time in a *worse* place" (1.21). For the young women, residing at Miss Carew's reform "home" is simple imprisonment—the easiest way of doing time.

Perhaps the girls all see the domestic setting as a type of prison because most of them have never experienced it as anything else. In discussing the reasons young girls end up on the street, Miss Carew cites poverty as one major factor. She tells Beatrice that "a girl born on Fifth Avenue has a better chance of keeping straight than the one on Avenue A, because she has everything to protect her—and the other everything to pull her down" (1.13). The kind of "protection" that both Beatrice and Miss Carew assume as desirable and normative does not, in fact, exist for women from indigent families. Lena, for example, describes her husband's turning her out to streetwalk. When Beatrice asks how her husband could force her into prostitution if she didn't want to go, Lena replies, "he say if I try to get away he kill me—and he shoot me in the shoulder to show me" (1.16). Later in the play we learn from Molly that the myth of domestic protection conceals parental abuses as well. In talking to Wilson, Beatrice's compassionate housekeeper, Molly reveals conditions of her childhood that she never mentioned to Beatrice:

> I never told her there was nine of us living in three rooms. I never told her we had a boarder, an Italian, and my mother tried to throw me in with his board. . . . I got wise and got out—found a job—but you can't live on three dollars a week. What was there for me to do—will you tell me—but what I *did* do? (2.19)

Given these past histories and present realities, then, it is no wonder that the many residents who crowd Miss Carew's drawing room find the home to be a place of confinement, boredom, and isolation, despite their numbers. While they are not household drones to manipulative family members (as were the middle-class Rose and Lulu), these young women from impoverished families find no comfort in a residence where their freedom of choice is limited and their access to the outside world severely curtailed. Furthermore, their varied experiences of abuse expose the idealized picture of domestic protection as a widespread social fabrication. For these women, the domestic setting has never offered a safe haven from harm, but rather a springboard to it.

One might assume that the problems faced by the reform home inmates are those of class more than gender, that at least wealthy women like Beatrice live in homes that shield women from social ills. Acts 2 and 3, however, which take place in Beatrice's elegant drawing room, show that even those domestic spaces protected by money and prestige cannot be counted on to safeguard the women who live there. It is not merely that Miss Carew's parlor is, in fact, only a quasi-private space, inhabited by numerous unrelated individuals and accessible to reformers and government agents. The issue at stake in this play is that *no* domestic space is impervious to the penetration of crimes against women; in fact, the domestic setting is a vital component in the perpetuation of those crimes.

That domestic spaces are really not separable from widespread social problems becomes abundantly clear after Beatrice brings Molly home to become her secretary. Beatrice herself has laudable goals in trying to reform Molly, a process which she views as the first step in setting up her own reform home in the country, which Molly could then manage. From her point of view, if only a girl like Molly could experience domestic life as it ought to be, she'd work to achieve it for herself. As Beatrice tells Molly when she hires her: "You've been down all your life—but you didn't put yourself there. I want to let you see the other side—then if you want to go back, you're free to choose. But it's not fair for you never to see the other side" (1.27). Unfortunately, Molly enters Beatrice's home only to fall prey to Beatrice's profligate brother Bob, who seduces her with protestations of love and then abandons her when his wife, Irene, discovers the affair. From this plot line, it becomes clear that the ideal of protecting women in domestic spaces is created and maintained only for the wealthy class, and even then the shelter is less to provide women with protection than to ensure their blindness to men's deceptions and to social hypocrisy. This point is made explicitly (albeit unwittingly) by Beatrice's fiancé Collin, who claims that Beatrice's moral reform work "is not a woman's job. It only makes you unhappy finding out disagreeable things. I can't bear to have you touch it" (2.22). For Collin, then—who is a rather sympathetic character, at least compared to Bob—women should stay out of public life and avoid reform work because they are best off not knowing that things like prostitution, venereal disease, and poverty exist—even when the men in their lives perpetuate them.

After the first act in Miss Carew's parlor, the double standard of morality becomes the primary theme of the play, as the characters endlessly debate the issue of men's animal nature and women's responsibility to curb it. For critic Lois Gottlieb, the attention to this issue dates the play, limiting its interest for contemporary feminist readers (1979, 69). At the time of the play's first production, however, the double standard of morality (which, you may remember, Florence Kiper mentioned as an integral facet of the "woman question") was central to much feminist debate. Much of the late-nineteenth-century feminist movement emerged from women's reform groups, temperance organizations, and other religious and welfare-minded women's clubs. For these women, before the pleasure-seeking flapper emerged to complain that sexual freedom should be available to both sexes, eliminating the double standard did not mean promiscuity for all, but moral restraint for all (Kolb 153).

But even given the play's perhaps outmoded emphasis on conventional morality, *Ourselves* can be seen as offering a version of a materialist feminist critique: it examines the interaction of economic forces, domestic arrangements, gender roles, and human sexuality in order

2: DOMESTIC SPACES, WOMEN'S RIGHTS, AND REALISM

to interrogate the status quo. The play might even be seen as a Foucaultian genealogical critique, which, in the words of Judith Butler:

> investigates the political stakes in designating as an *origin* and *cause* those identity categories that are in fact the *effects* of institutions, practices, discourses with multiple and diffuse points of origin. The task of this inquiry is to center on—and decenter—such defining institutions: phallogocentrism and compulsory heterosexuality. (1990a, viii–ix).

In terms of Crothers's play, Molly's status as a "fallen woman," for instance, is depicted as the result of poverty, male exploitation, family structure, and lack of opportunities for self-support, not of her promiscuous female nature or innately criminal heart. Meanwhile, the play reveals that the myth of domestic security has been created by upper-class men to consolidate their power over women of all classes.

It is in Beatrice herself, however, that the play's feminist critique of social institutions emerges most clearly and where possibilities for personal and societal change are most obviously suggested. From the opening moments of the play, Beatrice is a strong advocate for individual responsibility. Her goal in hiring a reform home inmate (as is made clear by her speech to Molly, quoted above) is to give the girl a chance to experience a better life than prostitution and then to choose it for herself. And Beatrice's social work extends beyond the simple hiring of one girl. She is also active in promoting a series of lectures on social reform. As we learn from Molly, who is busy addressing invitations to an upcoming meeting, the next lecture will be delivered by Dr. Von Flexner on "the moral responsibility of the individual toward society" (2.26).

Beatrice's faith in individual accountability is most evident in her second-act conversation with Irene, her sister-in-law, about the double standard of morality. For Irene, reforming one girl is simply a waste of time, since there will always be another to take her place on the street. Furthermore, Irene sees sexual promiscuity as innate to men, and, in fact, even desirable; she claims that men are more "animal" than women and that women prefer them so, that "so long as a man is decent about his affairs a woman can't complain. I say it's the way things are. So why eat your heart out about it" (2.3). Irene is sure that her husband Bob will never do "anything common or scandalous" (2.4), such scandal being the only thing she fears.

Beatrice sees Irene's attitude as rather scandalous in itself. For her, it is a woman's responsibility to reject the sexual status quo, to demand equal fidelity from both marriage partners. Having seen for herself the conditions faced by the women in Miss Carew's reform home, Beatrice has accepted her own accountability for the existence of prostitution and the double standard. As she tells Irene: "[Now] that I understand the horrors of what we call the social evil—I know that good women are *terribly* to blame for it all—because of our indifference to the whole thing. It's we—*we ourselves* who are responsible for conditions—*ourselves*" (2.4). For Beatrice, the apathy of "protected" women to the conditions faced by "fallen" ones helps maintain the sexual status quo and its attendant health and economic problems.

At this point in the play, however, Beatrice feels responsible for "the social evil" only in the abstract. It is not until she is confronted by Bob's affair with Molly that she learns the importance of female solidarity across class lines. At first, Beatrice reacts instinctively to protect her family and her position, and blames Molly, the former prostitute, for the affair. In an echo of Irene's position, Molly, the true victim, tries to explain her motives and simultaneously protect Bob, crying: "He—don't blame him. . . . A man can't help it. . . . Oh, honest, Miss Barrington, I wouldn't have done it but I love him. He's so different from the others" (3.15). At this point Beatrice reacts only in anger, unfairly blaming Molly for the seduction and herself for bringing Molly home. As the crisis reaches its crescendo, with Beatrice, Irene, and Bob all assigning blame in different ways, Molly reminds them—and us—that domestic spaces are inextricably linked to "the social evil" they were ostensibly designed to combat, and that blame must be shared by all. As she exits the premises at Beatrice's insistence, Molly rebukes Beatrice and Irene:

> I don't know what you call good and bad—the way you see it—all I want is to get out. You happen to find out one little thing and act like this when it's too late? Are you blind as bats? Don't you live in this world? Don't you know what's going on? If you feel like this about it, why don't you stop it? If this is the worst thing your men can do why do you let 'em? Why do you stand fer it—and there wouldn't *be* any of us. (3.19)

In this speech, Molly stresses that women of all classes are victimized by the double standard, but only upper-class women have the power to change it.

In the final act of the play, Beatrice recognizes—belatedly—her complicity in Molly's victimization. When the characters undergo another confrontation in Bob's studio—where Molly has gone seeking shelter, only to be turned out again—Beatrice accepts her responsibility for Molly's plight. In a show of support for Molly, whom Bob has just described to his wife (in Molly's presence) as "nothing per-

2: DOMESTIC SPACES, WOMEN'S RIGHTS, AND REALISM 67

sonal," as not "someone I could be in love with," and as someone who "doesn't *exist* so far as you and I are concerned" (4.7), Beatrice accepts her role in Molly's fall. When Bob blames the affair on Beatrice, who, after all, hired Molly, Beatrice retorts: "There's only *one* thing to blame me for—and that's for driving that girl out of the house—for not defending her before you all—and telling her *then* that I *did not* hold her responsible for all that's happened—but *you* entirely" (4.10). In this way, Beatrice reveals that she has learned two important feminist lessons: that personal accountability is not equally distributed among all individuals but is mediated by other factors (in Molly's case, by factors such as class, age, and isolation); and that women of all classes must work together to create social change.

As a result of Beatrice's support, Molly's faith in herself is restored. While she agrees to return to Miss Carew's to spend the night, she insists on leaving the next morning to make her own way in the world. Rejecting the domestic world that has caused her repeatedly to come to grief, Molly asserts, "I can't stay shut up no more. I want to stand on my own feet. I want to be alone and feel safe. I want to trust *myself*" (4.10). The play thus ends with Molly's feeling empowered as an individual and important as part of a female network, although one wonders about her chances for self-actualization given the economic realities she must face and the emotional wounds she has endured.

Despite the inconclusiveness of the ending, however, and the didactic discussions of morality, the play forces audiences to confront a number of serious feminist issues relevant both in 1913 and to feminist debate today. The play suggests that women and men are not innately different in their desires (a point the newly aware Irene makes clearly to Bob); that women who blindly accept male protection and class privilege are actually complicit in the perpetuation of social problems from which they are only apparently immune; that domestic confinements protect male rather than female interests; and that female solidarity is necessary to promote widespread social change. As Gottlieb has noted, in this play

Crothers is concerned to free poor women from the confines of social prisons, and to free all women from the domination of "a man's standpoint," which consigns lower-class women like Molly to a category of "irrelevant" sex objects and consigns "good" women to hypocritical pretense and silent suffering. (1979, 68)

In *Ourselves*, Crothers powerfully asserts the interconnectedness of private and public spheres and challenges women to investigate the consequences—both public and private—of accepting social privilege.

Many of Crothers's plays besides *Ourselves* deal with these same issues—the double standard, women's activism in the reform movement, the necessity for female solidarity across class lines—with *A Man's World* (which I discuss later in a different context) being perhaps the best-known example.[9] But Crothers was not alone among female playwrights of the era in realistically depicting the inevitable interpenetration of the domestic sphere and the public world. Another play insisting that the personal is the political is Charlotte Perkins Gilman's 1911 suffrage play, *Something to Vote For*.

Something to Vote For, as its title suggests, is unabashed suffragist propaganda, a form of agitprop not unlike much 1960s feminist drama, as Sheila Stowell has observed.[10] Gilman's play is notable, however, for its connection of milk standards—an issue many "Antis" (that is, women against suffrage) would have regarded as strictly a domestic matter—with overtly political issues like government corruption and women's suffrage.[11]

The play takes place at a Women's Club meeting attended by the town's leading socialites. As the play begins, the women are unanimous in their anti-suffrage stance. In fact, when Dr. Strong, a new member from Colorado (which had already passed a woman suffrage bill), raises the issue of suffrage, the club meeting loses all pretense of order as the established members shout out all the traditional rhetoric against women's suffrage. Their complaints quickly summarize anti-suffrage sentiment: the suffrage movement is designed to break up the home, which is woman's true place; women are unfit for politics, as they "haven't the mind for it"; and, finally, women's real power is through indirect influence on their husbands and on social norms (151–52). For these clubwomen, gathered to hear public officials speak on the dangers of impure milk without recognizing the issue's connections to Progressive reform, "political issues continued to be dissociated from personal lives in which an equator divided the world of human activity marking 'homemaking' and 'breadwinning' as hemispheres" (Sutherland 320).

Gilman's realist play, however, demonstrates the inseparability of the personal from the political. The setting alone reveals this point: the club meeting (a public event) takes place in the parlor (a private space) of the club president, Mrs. Carroll, who has opened her home for the occasion.[12] The parlor furniture has been replaced by rows of chairs for the club members and a platform and table for the speakers, indicating that domestic spaces overlap with public concerns. As Janelle Reinelt has remarked (albeit in the context of professional wrestling—a very different sort of performance), "The transformation of traditionally private experience into public spectacle helps transform notions of individual problems into social ones" (1986, 160). In the privately constructed public forum that is her set, then, Gilman offers audiences a way to see how political events shape and are shaped by domestic choices, thereby making a feminist political statement of her own.   -

The action of the play also supports the notion, suggested by the set, that women relegated to domestic roles are neither immune to nor unable to affect public policy. Early in the play Mr. Billings, the head of the Milk Trust, notes that it is unusual for Mrs. Carroll to interest herself in public affairs, to which she replies that "milk is really a domestic matter" (150). As the play progresses, however, she learns to see this distinction as fallacious. The plot focuses on the conflict between Dr. Strong, the suffragist pure-milk advocate, and Mr. Billings, chief local supplier of milk products. Mr. Billings has agreed to have his milk tested for purity at the club meeting and has brought along a sample bottle of his best grade of milk. Dr. Strong, with the aid of the milk inspector who is to perform the test, substitutes a different bottle of milk, this one also produced by Mr. Billings but purchased at the local market. After Dr. Strong presents information on the direct link between infant mortality and impure milk, and after Mrs. O'Shane, a working-class woman whose only child has died from tainted milk, speaks movingly to the wealthy socialites, the milk fails the inspector's test for purity. Once it is disclosed that Billings has attempted to bribe the milk inspector to falsify the test results, the women rise up against the forces of power and patriarchy, having realized that public decisions (like the election of milk inspectors) have direct repercussions on family health.

By the end of the play, the women come to see that without the vote, their "influence" is a myth—something the action of the play has already demonstrated to the audience. At the outset, Mr. Billings flatters Mrs. Carroll on her ability to sway social opinion. He tells her: "Look at the way you swing this club! And those are the society lights—all the other women follow. And the men are yours to command anyhow! I tell you such influence as yours has Woman Suffrage beat to a standstill!" (150). Later, however, when the women are off-stage and Mr. Billings tries to bribe the milk inspector, Billings reveals his true feelings about women's influence by describing the meeting as "a foolish hen-party" (156). Once his milk is shown to be tainted, however, the women band together and decide to exert *true* influence by working for the vote. In Mrs. Carroll's final speech to the club members, she rallies them with this cry for direct public action and sisterhood:

> You [Billings] said this club could carry the town; that we women could do whatever we wanted to here—with our "influence"! Now we see what our "influence" amounts to! Rich or poor, we are all helpless together unless we wake up to the danger and protect ourselves. That's what the ballot is for, ladies—to protect our homes! To protect our children! To protect the children of the poor! I'm willing to vote now! . . . I've got something to vote for! (161)

In Mrs. Carroll's transformation (sudden though it may be), we see the dawning awareness of a new feminist consciousness to certain political truths. Like Beatrice Barrington of Crothers's *Ourselves*, Mrs. Carroll comes to recognize that women have a responsibility to band together across class lines to improve domestic conditions through political action. And just as Beatrice learns that the domestic protection of women is a patriarchal myth designed to conceal widespread social wrongs, Mrs. Carroll discovers that the notion of woman's indirect influence is also a patriarchal fabrication intended to placate women while it fortifies male power and privilege. By using a realistic set and cause-and-effect logic, Gilman underscored "what suffragists had been arguing all along: There was political significance to what women did at home" (Lebsock 53). But she also took the issue of public/private interaction in the opposite direction, demonstrating that women needed to wield political clout because public decisions affected their daily lives.

Domestic Departures and Communities of Women

While Gilman and others were using realism to convince traditional, family-oriented women that they could work for suffrage without becoming "unwomanly," other playwrights were portraying women who had already moved outside the domestic sphere. This depiction of single women pursuing careers and creating alternatives to patriarchal living arrangements reflects a social trend of the 1900s and 1910s. As historian William Chafe has observed, at the end of the nineteenth century, "half the graduates of the best women's colleges remained single, and they constituted the core of female professional workers" (111). These career women faced a number of social problems that sound distressingly familiar to 1990s feminists: hostility to women working outside the home (especially from men competing for their jobs), lack of role models in other than traditionally female fields such as teaching and nursing, disparagement of female aspirations, malicious rumors about independent women's private lives, and the apparent need (predicated on the accepted division of labor and child-rearing duties along gender lines) to choose between marriage and a career (Chafe 107–11). So while female playwrights of the era were eager to depict autonomous working women with interests beyond the domestic, as working women themselves they recognized the potentially paralyzing problems such women faced. As playwright Martha Morton observed in an interview, "Woman is going out into the world and helping to do the world's work, and adapting herself to the new condition hurts" (in Patterson 128).

A number of playwrights writing between 1900 and 1920 explored these sometimes hurtful adaptations in their realistic plays, documenting the personal and professional problems faced by career women and protesting social conditions that interfered with women's pursuit of economic independence. By their very existence these plays counter the criticism that realism was limited to portraying (and therefore reifying) the domestic world of the patriarchal nuclear family. The feminist plays I have chosen to explore in this section show the conflicts between and within individual working women, conflicts created by social mores and internalized by the women characters of these realistic plays. In this way, these plays show that female identity is, at least in part, culturally constructed. Furthermore, they delineate the problems that arise when the forces of convention or individual desires conflict with a woman's wish for autonomy. These plays reveal that realism could be used in theater (as well as in fiction) to depict "what women could realistically expect to attain and at what cost" when they moved outside traditional domestic spheres (Gilbert and Gubar 1987, 80).

Two rather similar plays that use realism to explore the plight of the career woman are Rachel Crothers's *A Man's World* (1909, pub. 1915) and Marion Craig Wentworth's *The Flower Shop* (1912). Both plays focus on independent women with satisfying work to do, and both emphasize the central character's connections with a community of women who exhibit various stages of feminist awareness. Both plays explore the economic and social forces that propel women into marriage, and both depict women in conflict with the men they love when it comes to balancing a home and a career. However, the similarities between the plays end at their conclusions, as the two central characters find different ways to reconcile their romantic attachments with their feminist ideals.

A Man's World takes place primarily in the apartment of Frank Ware, a female novelist and social reform worker who lives with her small adopted son, Kiddie. While Frank's drawing room is conventionally appointed and focused on the domestic, it certainly offers a counterpoint to the male-dominated living spaces inhabited by, say, Gale's Lulu Bett or Ferber's Rose. Frank's parlor is located in a rooming house occupied by an assortment of struggling artists, musicians, and writers, male and female, who each occupy a private space but who nonetheless move rather freely from one room to another. The extent to which Frank's bohemian drawing room differs from that of a traditional patriarchal family is illustrated vividly in the first act, when Frank arrives home from work to find a group of male friends entertaining Kiddie—that is, engaging in child-care activities traditionally associated with women. As Frank flops onto a chair, the men gather to wait on her, offering her food, stoking her fire, and helping her off with her gloves. Lois Gottlieb has noted that this scene *reverses* the patriarchal norm in which the male breadwinner enters a domestic space expecting service from the subservient women who work within the domestic space (as do most of Frank's artist friends) and whom he supports (Gottlieb 1979, 40–41). Yet despite the fact that she is the only one of the group who is financially successful, Frank asserts no authority; she is simply depicted, as the stage directions clarify, as an equal, exuding "the frank abandon of being one of them—strong, free, unafraid" (10).

Unlike most of the other inhabitants of her building, Frank takes her work outside her home: she not only publishes critically acclaimed novels about the exploitation of impoverished women, she also is deeply involved in setting up a "girls' club" for former prostitutes. While Frank may write in her apartment (her exact writing habits are never made clear), her work in both publishing and social reform extends her influence beyond the domestic scope. As Sharon Friedman has argued:

> Through her social welfare activity and her writing, Frank makes these private grievances [i.e., unequal sexual relations and men's exploitation of women] a matter of public concern, and in the process gives herself a platform. As social housekeeper, mother to destitute girls, Frank makes maternity her career outside the home. (78)

Frank's life work is therefore the inverse of that we have seen in other plays of this period. Rather than showing us the impact of social concerns on the home, Crothers has created a feminist-activist protagonist who takes the values of home and care and attempts to infuse them into society at large.

Margaret Kendall of Wentworth's *The Flower Shop* is a similar character: an independent career woman (formerly an opera star, currently a shop owner) with an interest in social reform and in building community with other women. The setting of Wentworth's play, however, moves out of domestic spaces entirely and into the flower shop of the title, an enterprise owned and managed by Margaret. While the set is realistic in its functioning doors and its attention to detail, it depicts a public space controlled by Margaret and populated with her staff, her customers, and occasionally her women's group, which holds its meetings in the shop. Margaret's social work differs from Frank's however, in that she is attempting to enlighten women of her own upper-middle class as to the dangers of being financially dependent on men. For Margaret, economic freedom is the greatest freedom of all, the one on which all other liberties depend. As she tells a friend, "I shall always be my own mistress because I have my own work, my own pocket-book" (23). For her, many of the members of her women's club—her "followers"—"seem like a lot of frightened slaves . . . and the husbands masters and owners by right of the household purse" (20). Perhaps Margaret's work to "abolish" this form of domestic slavery is not so different from Frank's work with "fallen" East Side women after all, since Margaret views marriage based on financial dependence as just another form of prostitution (91).

Building communities of women for their mutual support is thus important to both Frank and Margaret. Frank defends her rooming-house arrangement against a detractor as "Rather good for me . . . The house is filled with independent women who are making their own living" (24); she also experiences great satisfaction in her reform work with poor girls. Margaret likewise is dedicated to her "followers," claiming that the interests of a family (were she to have one) would not make her forget "the *other women*, their helplessness and their needs" (62). Yet both plays do an excellent job of depicting the differences among the varied women each independent protagonist encounters. As Doris Abramson has noted about *A Man's World*, not all the women characters are at the same level of emancipation, so the play illustrates a moment of historical transition. Each female character has to make decisions between new freedoms and old customs and prejudices (61).

In *A Man's World*, this transitional moment for women is perhaps best reflected in the character of Clara, an aspiring miniaturist from a wealthy family who (as one of the other artists describes her) would "like to tiptoe through bohemia, but she's afraid of her petticoats" (17). While Clara admires everything about Frank, from her self-sufficiency to her generosity and kindness, she herself is without marketable skills and feels "absolutely superfluous" (52). Complaining about the double standard that relegates unmarried women to "old maid" status, Clara asserts: "If I were a man—the most insignificant little runt of a man—I could persuade some woman to marry me—and could have a home and children and hustle for my living—and life would mean something" (53). But Clara is not the only counterpoint to Frank. Leone, a singer, while more independent and also more talented than Clara, also rails about the unfair position of women who must depend on men for financial support and social position. Her response to the problem, however, is a self-centered acceptance of the status quo. She tells Frank:

> Men are pigs of course. They take all they can get and don't give any more than they have to. It's a man's world—that's the size of it. What's the use of knocking your head against things you can't change? I never believed before that you really meant all this helping women business. What's the use? (57)

Despite these women's differences (from each other and from her), Frank responds to both of them with sympathy and support. While Frank herself values autonomy and fosters sisterhood, she realizes that not all women would or could make the choices she has made. As she tells Clara, who accuses her of believing "in women taking care of themselves": "I believe in women doing what they're most fitted for. You should have married, Clara, when you were a young girl—and been taken care of all your life" (52). Given this backdrop of social reform work and varying states of feminist consciousness, Crothers's play avoids being a polemic about the gender antagonisms it realistically depicts (Gottlieb 1979, 45), focusing instead on the complex network of environmental forces complicating women's choices.

The Flower Shop also depicts the various conflicts faced by women, both the New Woman and her more traditional sisters, during this transitional historical period. In Wentworth's play, these differences emerge most clearly in the discussions about marriage in which Margaret's staff frequently engage. For Polly, young and pretty and enamored of her beau, a traditional marriage offers the utmost happiness. Noting that "It is a man's *place* to provide for the women he loves" (27), Polly proclaims that she wants "a real *old-fashioned* marriage," in which she will quit her job, devote her time to caring for the household, and never feel uncomfortable asking her husband for money (94–95). Lena, another shop worker, sees marriage not as a romantic adventure but as an opportunity to rest from toil. Like Crothers's Clara, Lena is aging, unmarried, and alone. She sees marriage to a decent carpenter whom she does not love as "a good chance" to achieve financial security, to avoid lifelong loneliness, and to have a child, which she wants desperately. These experiences with other women, while they do not change Margaret's ultimate choices for herself, do allow her to see (as Frank does) that not all women have the fortitude or the training to face daily economic demands and a solitary life. Both these plays, then, document the difficult choices and limited options women faced in the early twentieth century, thus providing a tapestried background against which to evaluate the actions and decisions of the central characters.

Against this background, Frank and Margaret look all the more courageous in overcoming the many obstacles to their freedom. For Frank, most of these obstacles are placed in her way by social convention and public opinion. The strength of these forces against an independent woman are made clear in the very first scene, when Frank's male friends are discussing her book in her absence. First they read aloud from a glowing review, which finds Frank's novel especially impressive in its "strength and scope" now that she has been revealed to be a woman. This brings them to wonder where she finds her material—that is, what man is ghostwriting for her. Their gossip then moves to her love life, and they wonder about the exact nature of her relationship with Malcolm Gaskell, whether they are, in fact, lovers, and whether he is the man supplying her material (7–8). That Frank's alleged friends have such doubts about her veracity and ability suggests the wave of hostile criticism and innuendo faced by women active in public life.[13]

Frank's problems in maintaining her autonomy are compounded by her love for Gaskell, a successful newspaper man and a staunch supporter of the gender-divided status quo. He disparages her book as "clever as the deuce" but not "big" (23); he asserts that "Women are meant only to be loved—and men have got to take care of them" (25); he protests that her settlement work is "disagreeable" (26); and he summarizes proper relations between men and women this way: "Man sets the standard for woman. He knows she's better than he is and he demands that she be—and if she isn't she's got to suffer for it" (23). In addition to his belittling of Frank's work and beliefs, he insists that she reveal her entire history (especially how she came to adopt Kiddie), while insisting that she has no need to know his. It may seem unlikely that the independent Frank could actually fall in love with such a man. That she does suggests two things: that independent women have as much a need for love as traditional women do; and that, as products of the social system they are trying to reform, women like Frank have nonetheless internalized much of their patriarchal culture. As Florence Kiper noted in the 1914 review with which I began this chapter:

> [Frank] is a type of the modern feminist. And the conflict of the drama is waged not so much without as within her own nature, a conflict between individual emotion and social conviction. What many of our writers for the stage have missed in their objective drama that uses the new woman for protagonist is a glimpse of that tumultuous battlefield, her own soul, where meet the warring forces of impulse and theory, of the old and the new conceptions of egotism and altruism. (928)

The conclusion of the play indicates exactly how painful this conflict between "impulse and theory" is for Frank and how much she is willing to pay for her feminist ideals. Just after Frank reveals to Gaskell that she reciprocates his love, they discover the secret of Kiddie's parentage: Gaskell is actually Kiddie's father and, therefore, a man Frank has long hated for abandoning the boy's biological mother. When Gaskell refuses to admit any responsibility for the affair, Frank refuses his marriage proposal. In a reversal of Nora's slamming the door to Ibsen's *Doll's House,* Gaskell leaves Frank's apartment, closing the door behind him.

While the door may be shut on Gaskell's relationship with Frank, the debate between the New Woman and the traditional man, and thus the issues of the double standard and equality for women, are left open at the end of the play (Murphy 97). The play thus beautifully illustrates Kiper's point about the New Woman's inner conflicts. Because the play ends, as Kiper describes it, with "no sentimentalism, no attempt to gloss over the situation with the pet American dramatic platitude that love makes right all things" (928), we are left inspired that Frank has stood up for her principles but saddened that her stand has cost her emotional fulfillment. In short, Crothers's realistic treatment of an increasingly common predicament of the era, combined with the varied background characters and with her innovative refusal to provide an easy solution, forces an audience to feel something of the losses women face when their feminist ideals collide with their very human hunger for love.

In *The Flower Shop,* Wentworth does an even more thorough job of depicting the "warring impulses" within career women of the day. Her task is made easier because Margaret has already rejected her version of Malcolm Gaskell, the extremely chauvinistic William Ramsey who years before had wanted Margaret to renounce her career as an opera singer in order to marry him. Her current problems are twofold: the first involves helping her old friend Louise, also a former opera star and now married to Ramsey, to return to her career over

her husband's objections; the second concerns reconciling her insistence on financial independence with her deep love for Stephen Hartwell, who is currently running for a judgeship under much public
scrutiny.

When the wealthy Hartwell first proposes, he simply assumes that
Margaret will give up her flower shop. Once she convinces him of
the absolute necessity, for her, of maintaining a separate income and
therefore her own business, he capitulates, realizing that "It is easy
to be romantic . . .—set woman on a pedestal as a saint for devotion
and all that,—it is harder to help her live her own life, but perhaps
after all that is the most genuine devotion—real chivalry in the end"
(113). Given his public position, however, it soon becomes clear to
Margaret that her independence may cost him both the support of
his traditional family and the judgeship he seeks. Her conflict, then,
is internal—her desire for autonomy versus her love for Hartwell—
but includes public repercussions for the man she loves.

In act 3, as she waits in the darkened flower shop to hear if Hartwell
has found some way to reconcile their love and his public interests,
and as Polly and Lena come in separately to tell her of their wedding
plans, Margaret vacillates in agony. While the play as a whole suffers
even more than *A Man's World* from improbable coincidences, this
scene of Margaret's turmoil brilliantly encapsulates the "tumultuous
battlefield" within themselves that independent women of the era
suffered. First Margaret thinks of her "followers," lamenting that she
cannot give up her business without disappointing them. Then,
haunted by the dance music filtering in from across the street and
tormented by the sensuous fragrance of the flowers surrounding her,
she surrenders to her emotions and desires, feeling that she cannot
bear losing Hartwell's love. Margaret cries out: "Is this what it is to
be merely a woman—no will—no head—all heart—nothing but
heart, with a cry in it that will not be stilled. *I want him*. . . . Ah,
my sisters, I have understood your needs—now I know your tempta-
tion" (98). Just as she decides to send for Hartwell and renounce
her flower shop, however, Louise returns with the news that she has
abandoned her plans to return to the opera for fear of losing her
husband's love. Louise's lack of persistence reinvigorates Margaret's
own, and she vows to "renounce the sweetness" in order to promote
the new order she envisions between women and men.

Unlike *A Man's World*, however, *The Flower Shop* ends with a
conventional reconciliation. It seems Hartwell's publicity director has
found a way to avoid "the woman question" during his campaign, so
Hartwell and Margaret are free to marry under their original agreement. This forced closure does falsely simplify the complex issues

raised by the play and obviate the question for the audience. However, Hartwell's resolve to stand by Margaret no matter what the cost suggests a more positive vision for social reform than the one Crothers envisioned in *A Man's World*. Margaret's happy ending suggests that men as well as women can suffer from sexist public criticism, that some men are willing to support women's autonomy, and that hetero-sexual love is not necessarily a cage designed to restrain women and regulate their activities. It also vividly portrays the conflicts and ago-nies that career women faced in trying to lead full emotional lives.

Unfortunately, the obstacles to emotional fulfillment that career women of the 1910s faced did not diminish quickly. Twenty years later, in a 1935 essay on the relationship between biological sex and career achievement, anthropologist Margaret Mead addressed the cultural sources of the problems faced by Margaret and Frank and by countless heterosexual women like them. Describing the differ-ences in socialization between boys and girls, Mead observed:

> So the boy is taught to achieve, the girl to prove that she doesn't achieve, will never achieve. The same threat hangs over the unachieving boy and the achieving girl, the threat that he or she will never be chosen by a member of the opposite sex. . . . For a woman to succeed in a field defined as male, she must not only compete with men in a difficult and exacting occupation but work under the knowledge that with every suc-cess she gains, as a lawyer or a businesswoman, she loses, as a woman, her chance for the kind of love she wants. (302–3)

In these plays of women at work, both Crothers and Wentworth dra-matize this conflict between career ambition and the desire for love that working women of the early twentieth century faced. Using a realistic set, everyday characters, increasingly common situations, and the linear logic of realism, the plays accurately depict and protest the barriers to achievement faced by women of the 1910s. By using realism in this way, these playwrights made the new and sometimes radically revised ideas about gender roles and gender relations more accessible to theatergoers of their era, inviting audiences to see that these changes were a part of everyday reality.[14]

But the plays are not focused entirely on the stumbling blocks to self-fulfillment—the public ridicule, the pressures to conform (both external and internal), the economic strains, the threat of lost love—that were part of this everyday reality for working women of the period. Both Frank and Margaret receive great personal satisfaction from supporting themselves financially and from their work on behalf of other women. According to Cynthia Cole, this focus on women helping women was not unusual in women's plays from 1909 to 1920.

Cole's research shows that "[d]efining, creating, and asserting the pre-eminence of communities and thus finding the source of their power become the primary challenge for the characters in these plays" (49–50), who thus defy the prevailing discourse that would isolate women in individual domestic spaces and so disempower them. Rachel Crothers also commented on the importance of women's working together, which (as we have seen in the cases of *Ourselves* and *A Man's World*) is a recurring theme in her plays. Emphasizing the extent to which other women theater artists had helped advance her playwriting career, Crothers told an interviewer:

> When I look back on it, I realize it is to 3 women that I owe my freedom . . . Carlotta Nielson, who liked my play; Mrs. Wheatcroft, who asked me to be coach; and Maxine Elliott, who let me in on the professional work. For a woman it is best to look to women for help; women are more daring, they are glad to take the most extraordinary chances. (Cited in Gottlieb 1979, 146).

Given that the decade 1910 to 1920 encompassed the height of the movement for women's suffrage, this emphasis on female solidarity in plays from that period can be seen as a direct and positive comment on actual historical conditions. After 1920, however, as the factions within the suffrage movement began to polarize, women's realistic plays began to reflect a very different reality.

Transforming the Structures: Formal Experiment and Parody

After the passage of the Nineteenth Amendment in 1920, the women's movement in the United States seemed to deflate. Historians of 1920s feminism explain this loss of political energy in various ways.[15] William L. O'Neill claims that the organizers of the suffrage movement were themselves to blame, partly because they failed to see that suffrage was the only issue holding diverse groups of women together and partly because they were overly emotional zealots who "oversold the vote" (273).[16] For Susan Becker, the clash between the social reform-minded feminists and the more radical supporters of the Equal Rights Amendment suggested that women were unable "to reach consensus on the meaning of equality after suffrage was won" (223). William H. Chafe argues that preexisting social structures created insurmountable barriers to women's emancipation and thus were more to blame than factionalism for the apparent decline in political feminism (43–49). And while Nancy F. Cott has recently argued convincingly that feminism did not fail at all in the 1920s, the consensus among historians seems to be that "A strong feminist movement existed with women organized around a wide variety of social issues in 1920. By 1929, women's groups were disorganized, fragmented, and unable to agree on the best way to change their status in society" (Jensen 199).[17]

With this loss of concentrated political vigor came changes in women's options and choices. Unlike the career-minded Frank Ware and Margaret Kendall in the plays discussed above, in the 1920s most adolescent girls preferred marriage to a career (Pruette 131–32), as did most college-educated women (Chafe 111). The number of women professionals did increase during the 1920s, but career women were still largely restricted to traditionally "female occupations" that commanded lower wages. In New York, for example, there were more than 63,000 female teachers and 21,000 nurses by the end of the 1920s, but only 11 engineers and 7 investment bankers (Chafe 100; O'Neill 304–6). In the workplace, women did not receive the same treatment as men, and their job titles were often listed differently from those of men performing the same work. Evidently voting rights brought few advances in economic and social equality.

As the achievement of winning the vote began to pale in importance, the dedicated suffragist was replaced in popular iconography by the pleasure-seeking flapper—a "New Woman" of a very different ilk. These young women of the 1920s may have thought themselves individualists, but their interests were more hedonistic than career-oriented, focusing on sexual liberation rather than on political or economic equality. Lacking the seriousness of purpose or the idealism of the suffragists, these young women both rebelled against convention and mocked the earlier generation of feminists for their middle-class moral stance (Sutherland 326). As a result of their declining interest in political reform and their limited opportunities for economic independence, women of the 1920s returned increasingly to the domestic ideal, opting for a conventional marriage after "a more liberated courtship" (Kolb 158) and avoiding public political activity. As Chafe has observed about this apparent decline in visible feminist activism, "Nothing did more to eviscerate feminism of the radical potential than this popular tendency to equate 'freedom' with the life-style of the flapper" (106). And while women were perhaps able to smoke, drink, swear, and have affairs, they were still expected to be wives and mothers; sexual freedom did not effect structural change in the gender distribution of social and domestic roles.

Not surprisingly, these changes in women's attitudes and the lack of progress in their options for economic and political equality were reflected in feminist plays of the period. While critics sometimes see the plays that record these failures to advance as a retreat from feminism on the part of the playwrights, this is not necessarily the case; some of these plays simply record the continuing dearth of opportunities for women and depict the new sets of conflicts brought about by changing social norms (Friedman 72). Furthermore, these playwrights' formal experiments with realistic conventions—experiments ranging from embedded expressionistic scenes to comic parodies of social norms—can be seen as offering alternative responses to the breakdown of feminism.

One good example of such a play is Rachel Crothers's *Mary the Third* (1923). While Crothers's post-World War I plays are often viewed more as social comedies than as problem plays (Gottlieb 1979, 146), in *Mary the Third* Crothers provides an incisive portrayal of the flapper's retreat into marriage. Along the way, Crothers suggests that marital relationships are inherently limiting for women, a problem that can be solved only by radical changes in the structure of the institution. Of particular interest for a feminist analysis of twentieth-century realism are the technical innovations Crothers incorporates into her realistic framework to illustrate the difficulties of effecting such structural change.

The play revolves around Mary Hollister (the Mary III of the title), a twenty-year-old flapper who lives in a household with her mother (Mary II), father, brother, and grandmother (Mary I). The plot concerns Mary's intention to go on an unchaperoned camping trip with a group of friends, male and female, so they can get to know one another outside conventional society and so choose marriage partners more wisely. As Mary explains the scheme to her horrified mother and grandmother, "People don't *know* each other before they're married. That's why most marriages are merely disappointing experiments instead of lifetime mating. That's why the experimenting ought to be done *before* marriage" (29). The theme of the play, then, is modern marriage, with Crothers using the three generations of Marys to illustrate both the changes and the continuities within women's expectations of married life.

Of special interest in this play is Crothers's alternation of realistic scenes with antimimetic ones, evidence that Crothers was attuned to the recent European experiments with dramatic form (such as surrealism and expressionism) that had recently appeared on the New York stage. In Crothers's hands, however, the techniques take on particular significance by being embedded within, and so contrasting with, the traditional realism of her plot and setting. In *Mary the Third*, traditional realism depicts the limitations of conventional life, while illusory moments of freedom and romance take place in a world apart.

The play begins with a two-part prologue on a nearly bare stage, the set consisting only of a spotlighted, center-stage sofa surrounded by a pool of darkness and by dark curtains instead of walls. On this sofa, detached from time and place, Mary I and then Mary II sit to receive their marriage proposals. In 1870, Mary I is clearly revealed as an exploiter. Through her conversation with William, the man she prefers, we learn that she had previously broken off her relationship with William because another suitor had more money. Now that William has become a financial success himself, Mary manipulates him into breaking his engagement to his current fiancée, Lucy, in order to marry her. Marriage is thus depicted as a financial transaction, prettified by the illusion of romantic love. At this point, however, William and perhaps even Mary believe that their union will flourish because, as Mary tells him, "There has never been a love as great as this" (9). For the audience, however, money is at the heart of this relationship, which is obviously based on calculation and deceit. Later in the play we see that Mary I is actually *proud* of her manipulations. She tells Mary III:

> You oughten't to let 'em [men] *ever* see how smart you are. Why I had my way about everything on earth. The madder your grandfather got the more I cried and the softer I was. I just twisted him round my finger— like that. And he thought I was right under his thumb. (89)

In 1897 Mary II also faces the dilemma of choosing between two suitors, but she is truly torn between her idealistic soul-mate, Richard, and the practical, dashing Robert. Eventually Mary II chooses Robert, and they vow to make their love "the most wonderful love that ever was in the world" (16). Clearly the sofa, surrounded only by curtains, is a zone of fantasy and romantic dreams, where protestations of eternal love and promises of unchanging devotion are unmediated by the demands of everyday reality. In each case, however, the Mary in question chooses the man more likely to become a stable provider. As Cynthia Cole has noted, both Marys manipulate their suitors, but neither one can realistically choose *not* to marry:

> both must base their decisions on economic grounds since, once married, they become dependent on the man's ability and willingness to provide for them. As a result, the woman is put in the position of "trapping a man" of sufficient resources. But this cold-blooded and pragmatic approach is veiled by the ideology of romantic love that obscures the materialistic basis of marriage for women. (155)

Crothers's prologue, therefore, with its isolated sofa and repetitive action, represents the ungrounded, unrealistic, romantic expectations with which both women and men gloss over the economic realities of the marriage contract. Furthermore, the repetition of the action through two generations, combined with the doubling of the actors (with the same two men playing the suitors and the same young woman playing both Marys), suggests that neither gender relations nor marriage as an institution change much over time.

The main action of the play—that is, the plot surrounding Mary III's camping expedition—begins in act 1, which focuses on the very real world of conventional structures and traditional domestic arrangements that all three Marys now inhabit. The set illustrates this return to the workaday world, since the action takes place in the family's comfortable drawing-room, "the conventional room of a conventional success—filled with a certain amount of beauty and comfort produced by money rather than individual taste" (19). Obviously Mary II's financial transaction has paid off in prosperity if not in emotional fulfillment, a contrast suggested by the dark draperies of the prologue that remain in place to form the walls of this otherwise realistic set. Evidently romance, if it continues to exist within the institution of marriage, is pushed to the fringes of the everyday world and broken up by the set-in frames of doors and windows.

Before Mary III makes her first entrance, we meet her mother and grandmother in their 1922 avatars and learn what leading conventional lives has done to each of them. Mother is clearly dissatisfied with her life, bored with the card parties that form her social world and stifled by her subservient role in Robert's household. When Granny reminds her that Robert is successful and has "put [her] in this beautiful house," Mother replies "He certainly did *put* me in it" (25), implying that she had no choice. But Mother also recognizes her personal dissatisfaction as endemic to modern married life, a common condition for wives of the day. When Granny reminds her that her husband is a good provider, saying "As men go, he's a very fine man. You're a very fortunate woman," Mary II replies: "As women go, I suppose I am" (24). Granny has been shaped by convention in a different way: she advocates hypocrisy instead of rebellion against convention (Mary's reaction) or weary acceptance of it (Mother's response). Chastising Mother for her ennui, Granny says: "You're a happy woman. If not, you should be ashamed of yourself. When I was your age, it was the fashion to be happy. Women loved their husbands and appreciated their blessings. Or if they didn't they didn't air it from the house-tops" (25). Act 1, then, uses the detailed set, the expository dialogue, and the linear plot development of realism to focus on the conventional. In contrast to the free zone of possibility suggested in the separate vignettes of the prologue, act 1 emphasizes the hierarchical interactions of the nuclear family, the power of the breadwinning patriarch to define the lives of his dependents, and the pervasive societal assumptions about proper behavior for wives.

Since Mary III is currently in a period of rebellion against such convention, several of her key scenes are played outside this setting of domestic restriction—or at least played with the lights so dimmed that the furniture disappears. Like her mother, Mary III is torn between two suitors, the idealistic Hal and the more conventional Lynn; like her mother, she eventually chooses the more pragmatic of the two. All three of these young characters were played in the original production by the actors who performed the prologue, indicating from the outset that Mary is probably doomed to reenact her foremothers' choices, regardless of her current mutiny. And indeed, late in act 1 both Hal and Lynn enter separately to sit on the sofa with Mary and declare their eternal devotion. With the lamp next to the sofa providing the only illumination on these scenes, "the rest of the room is in shadow—with the same effect as in the scenes in the prologue" (37). This very telling staging effect suggests that for Mary III, like the Marys before her, the choice of a mate depends on creating the illusion of romance to obscure the reality of married women's dependency on their husbands.

This same effect is recreated in act 2, scene 1, the only scene (other than the prologue) to take place outside the family home. In this scene Mary, Hal, and Lynn are in a roadster, facing the audience on an otherwise darkened stage, speeding through the night to their campsite, free of the trappings of convention represented by the Hollister living room. Exhilarated by the lack of restriction, Mary revels in her freedom, explaining to the men:

> I was never so alive before. Isn't it glorious to know nothing can stop us! We're free! I feel as if we were part of the wind and sky. . . . This is the way everything always ought to be—going with all we've got and nobody saying *"don't."* (52)

In fact, Mary's rebellion never does take her very far, since she soon aborts the camping scheme out of respect for her mother's feelings. Before she makes that choice, however, Mary experiences a moment of abandon, a fleeting escape from convention that she will probably never be able to recapture. Once she returns to her father's home, replete with parental injunctions about her behavior and the economic realities of daily life, Mary succumbs to social pressures and accepts Lynn's marriage proposal. It is only when she is outside the patriarchal domain or at least oblivious to its intrusions that Mary can make free choices. By setting all but three brief scenes within that domestic trap, Crothers illustrates the difficulty of women's bucking convention or achieving true independence. The ending, then, in which Mary agrees to marry Lynn, is not the conventional comic resolution some critics thought they saw,[18] but an ironic comment on the formidable persistence of social institutions (Barlow xvi).

Mary's capitulation to traditional marriage, however, is somewhat perplexing in light of what she learns about her parents' marriage after her short-lived trip. Returning home in the middle of the night, she discovers her brother Bobby looking for her. Mary tries to explain to Bobby that she returned for the sake of her family. "I began to think about Mother and Father somehow. They're narrow and old-fashioned, but they're *good*," she tells him (67). In Mary's analysis, her parents are naive and uninteresting, sheltered by their love for each other and by their shared family ideals, and while Mary finds these ideals quaint, she is unwilling to shatter them.

The truth Mary discovers when she hears her parents quarreling shatters all of *her* notions about her "happy" family. Mary II accuses Robert of being domineering to her and the children, of being "hard" and "pig-headed"; he counters by blaming her for not controlling the children, for being "weak" and "sloppy" (70–71). Mary II admittedly regrets that she married Robert and describes their entire marriage as "a failure—a jogging along—letting out the worst side of ourselves for the other to live with" (72). Robert counters with the assertion that he could never "count on" her, that she "isn't *there*" (72). Horrified at overhearing this honest quarrel, Mary renounces her decision to uphold the "happy home" that she now sees was all a sham. When her father accuses her of destroying "everything your Mother and I have held up to you as right—all our standards—the sanctity of the home," Mary replies, "I came home for that and found it was a joke" (76).

Mary's response to learning the truth of her parents' unhappiness with their superficially successful marriage is to encourage her mother to seek a divorce. When she discovers that her mother has no separate source of income and therefore cannot divorce Robert, who supports both Mary II and Mary I, the youngest Mary is horrified, claiming that such dependence is "disreputable. . . . It's *buying* things with *you*" (91). Mary III has different plans for herself:

I shall *have* my own money. I shall live with a man because I love him and only as long as I love him. I shall be able to take care of myself *and* my children if necessary. Anything else gives the man a horrible advantage, of course. It makes the woman a kept woman. (92)

And yet, despite her new awareness that marriage is "a disgusting sordid business affair" (98) and the fact that she has no apparent means of self-support, Mary III accepts Lynn's proposal, planning (in a direct echo of Mary II's speech in the prologue) to "make it the most wonderful love that ever was in this world" (105). Like her mother and grandmother before her, Mary III capitulates to the romantic fantasy that *her* marriage will be a unique exception to the ordinary, a forward-looking alternative to the traditional norm, even as she follows the pattern set in place by all the Marys who came before her.

In *Mary the Third*, then, Crothers shows us how difficult structural change is in a convention-bound world. Mary's capitulation at the end is *not* Crothers's rejection of feminism and the New Woman, but a realistic look at the pressures to conform that snare us all. Mary snatches at freedom when she can escape the patriarchal walls of her family, but loyalty to her upbringing—and the fact that she is, despite her ideals, in part *constructed* by that upbringing—takes her back. Furthermore, Mary III is not a brilliant, independent heroine with talents and maturity, as are Frank of *A Man's World* or Margaret of *The Flower Shop*. Rather, she is an average, likable young woman with a utopian vision and little practical sense. As Mary II describes her to Robert, "She's thinking nearer the truth then *we* ever did. She's got something dangerous and ridiculous in *one* hand and something big and real in the other" (93). By presenting the conflict between the warring contents of Mary's two hands, Crothers is documenting a transitional moment in women's history, the moment when women begin to look beyond the conventional yet still find it impossible to overcome. And by dramatizing that moment in the contrast between the fluidity of experimentation and the solidity of stage realism, Crothers anticipates the modifications to dramatic form that characterize feminist realist plays written after 1960, as we shall see in chapter 4.

Mary III's decision to follow the traditional path of matrimony (even if she does not realize that this is what she's doing) illustrates one common phenomenon of the 1920s, when the women's movement suffered a loss of momentum. But there were also other ramifications of the changes in the women's movement. In particular, women who had been willing to build coalition to achieve suffrage found themselves unable to unify for any other cause. As William Chafe notes about the escalating competition between the National Women's Party and the League of Women Voters during this period,

"By the end of the 1930s, the women's movement had stalled, its various factions expending more energy in seeking to destroy each other than in forging ahead to overcome a common enemy" (47). The female solidarity that was so important to the suffragists, to idealistic feminist characters like Frank and Margaret, and to working playwrights like Crothers and Morton was thus another casualty of winning the vote.

This rivalry among women is a major theme in a later post-suffrage play that, like *Mary the Third*, is sometimes seen as *anti*-feminist, even misogynist, because it depicts women contending with other women. Nonetheless, when read in historical context, Clare Boothe's 1936 play *The Women* can be seen as a materialist feminist critique of the cultural construction of gender among upper-class white women during this period. While Boothe's play is not nearly as innovative in its dramaturgy as is *Mary the Third*, it uses realism to parody the social mores of its characters' world and deconstruct the ideologies of gender-based power.[19] Furthermore, it suggests another reason women playwrights turned to realism. As Judith Barlow has noted about the conventionality of women's plays in this period, "Women who wanted their work accepted by producers, virtually all of whom were male, understood they must hew to the predominating cultural myths" (xiii). By satirizing those myths, however, and showing their deleterious effects on female characters, Boothe disclosed the ugly consequences of a world in which gender segregation is the norm, in which women are mere commodities, and in which women must always beware women.

The Women focuses on a group of Park Avenue socialites, wealthy women whose days are spent playing bridge, shopping, having their nails manicured, and undoing each other's marriages with malicious gossip. The plot revolves around yet another Mary, also known in this play as Mrs. Stephen Haines. Mary Haines's apparently happy marriage (reminiscent of Mary II's superficially serene one in *Mary the Third*) is shattered when she discovers (through the interference of her so-called "friends") that her husband is having a affair with a "man-trap" (37) named Crystal. Again like Crothers's Mary II, Mary Haines allows her friends to talk her into divorcing her husband, who then marries Crystal. After her divorce, Mary lives unhappily for two years, at which time she discovers Crystal's extramarital affair, tricks Crystal into divulging her infidelity, and ultimately wins Stephen back (we are led to assume) by revealing the truth to him.

On the surface, then, *The Women* looks suspiciously like the misogynist play its early critics (all male) perceived it to be. These reviewers described the play as "a kettle of venom" brewing with

"feline wit," featuring "the modern New York wife on the loose, spray-
ing poison over the immediate landscape" (Atkinson); as a comedy
marked by "vulgar commonness" and "sheer bad taste" (S. Young);
even as "a crime against the spirit" (Broun, cited in Boothe viii). Yet
beneath that surface and behind those central characters is the carefully drawn sketch of a historical era in which autonomous women
can barely subsist, in which women's activities are radically separate
from men's, and in which women's bodies are seen as merchandise
by women as well as by men. These conditions are satirized within
the play, suggesting that these superficial, selfish Park Avenue wives
are the products of their specific cultural context.

The most obvious attempt to document these specific material conditions is seen in the large cast. Of the forty-four characters, all female, only fourteen are wealthy, and only eight figure in the plot
involving Mary's divorce. The remaining characters are all working-
class women—the domestic servants, hairdressers, manicurists, and
sales clerks who wait on the Park Avenue wives, attend to their needs,
and make their futile leisure possible. These minor characters function as a sort of Greek chorus, commenting on the central action and
documenting the surrounding social conditions.

One topic that recurs in their conversations is the difficulty of earning a living; evidently working-class women of 1936 still faced the
same economic limitations that frustrated Miss Lulu Bett in 1920.
From the hairdressing shop to the business office, the women in this
play are all aware of their limited earning power. Miss Trimmerback,
for instance, a notary public, echoes the sentiments of Clara in *A
Man's World* when she expresses her envy of women who have husbands to support them. Regarding Crystal's impending marriage to
Stephen Haines, she says: "I wish I could get a man to foot my bills.
I'm sick and tired, cooking my own breakfast, sloshing through the
rain at 8 A.M., working like a dog. For what? Independence? A lot
of independence you have on a woman's wages" (117). This awareness
of women's economic inequality and their resulting dependence on
men is a recurring theme in the play, a litany chanted by the chorus
of working-class women. Lucy, a maid, remains married to an abusive
husband out of economic necessity; she explains, "Lord, a woman
can't get herself worked up to . . . a thing like [divorce] overnight. I
had a mind to do it once. I had the money, too. But I had to call it
off. . . . I found out I was in a family way" (136–37). Later, a maternity
hospital nurse rails at the complaining, wealthy Mrs. Potter:

Why, women like you don't know what a terrible time is. Try bearing a
baby and scrubbing floors. Try having one in a cold filthy kitchen, without

ether, without a change of linen, without decent food, without a cent to bring it up—and try getting up the next day with your insides falling out to cook your husband's———! (131)

Stories like these are reiterated throughout the play, by Mary's cook, by the servant Maggie, by the "cigarette girl," by the beauticians and models and sales clerks. While the stories and the characters' responses are often individualized, they are all based on the economic and personal limitations imposed by sexual stereotypes and differentiated gender roles. With these small interpolated tales of women's economic hardships, Boothe paints a vivid backdrop to the lives of her elite Park Avenue matrons, a backdrop in which men have all the earning power and women live in emotional isolation, dependent poverty, or purposeless leisure. By including these stories, Boothe calls into question the gender and class distinctions that lead to such inequities. And while Mary and her friends seem frivolous and nonproductive in contrast to the working-class characters, they too are clearly victims of their limited opportunities and their habituation to wealth.[20]

The settings of the play also manifest this unhealthy separation of gender roles. The twelve scenes all take place in domains conventionally associated with women: living rooms, kitchens, and boudoirs; beauty salons; fitting rooms; maternity hospitals; even, in the final scene, a powder room, that venue (mysterious to men) into which the women disappear in pairs. To some early reviewers, this staging seemed like an attempt to present life from a female point of view—in current parlance, to depict women's subjectivity. One such reviewer claimed that the play was "calculated to give the Men two of the most shockingly informative hours of their lives" ("The Women"). When looked at from a materialist feminist perspective, however, the settings all reveal how cut off these women are from any productive means of existence, how restricted they are from controlling their economic destinies. As Elenore Lester describes them, these leisure-class women, the most envied in the world, "actually lived in a kind of insecure purdah . . . [with] no assurance of a place in the world once they were discarded as sex objects" (42).

As a result of this separate female sphere that Boothe has constructed so carefully, we never see a man on stage. This absence does not mean, however, that men are inconsequential to the action. On the contrary: like the absent or silent women in Susan Glaspell's plays, the absent men in Boothe's play dominate the conversations of the women and impel all their actions, as the women struggle to avert the one great tragedy available to them: losing their man. The radical separation of men and women in this play reveals one subversive possibility of dramatic realism. As we saw in chapter 1, a realistic text will always contain the seeds of its own self-critique in its omissions and absences, its gaps and holes (Belsey 57). The gaps or holes in Clare Boothe's *The Women* are manifest in the absent men and the single-sex settings, where women are denied access to autonomy, to earning power, to reproductive freedom—in short, to any means of self-determination other than selling themselves to the highest bidder.

What *is* present on stage, then, is the female body, which in this play becomes a major market commodity, a woman's primary asset in obtaining that all-important male provider. From the opening scene, we overhear the women in the play worrying about dieting, exercising, avoiding wrinkles, staying young—not for health and fitness but to retain the interest of the wealthy men they need to support them. Several scenes foreground this obsession with appearance, by taking place in a beauty parlor, a fitting room, an exercise salon. Each of these scenes highlights the loss of personal control endured by women who have learned to see their own bodies as material resources.

In the beauty salon, for example, a character designated only as "Mud Mask" is warned: "Mustn't talk, ma'am. You'll crack yo'self" (27). This nameless woman is thus both disguised and silenced by her need to preserve a youthful appearance. In the exercise salon, Sylvia's attempt to claim ownership of her own body is denied by the exercise instructor: Sylvia complains, "Look, whose carcass is this? Yours or mine?" to which the instructor replies, "It's yours, Mrs. Fowler, but I'm paid to exercise it" (93–94), suggesting that the body in question is separate from identity—an animal, like a horse, to be exercised and groomed by a hired keeper. In the dressmaker's shop, three members of the sales staff watch Crystal trying on clothes and discuss her pursuit of Stephen Haines this way:

> *First fitter*: Look at that body. She's got him now.
> *Second salesgirl*: You can't trust any man. *That's* all they want.
> *Corset Model (Plaintively, hands on her lovely hips)*: What else have we got to give? (82).

In this world where her body is a woman's only resource, it is no wonder that even the independent Nancy, world traveler and author of several published books, views herself as "a frozen asset" because she is a virgin (11).

This obsession with the body as commodity climaxes in act 3, scene

1, which takes place in Crystal's (now Mrs. Stephen Haines's) ostentatious bathroom. The curtain rises on Crystal luxuriating in a black marble tub as she waits for a telephone call from her married lover. This depiction of an apparently naked woman on stage caused a sensation in 1936, but it is the logical endpoint of the play's emphasis on the female body as an object, be it a resource to be bartered, an asset to be improved, or an object of male desire or female envy. By presenting Crystal's naked body on stage and providing her with an explicitly sexual monologue as she speaks into the golden telephone, Boothe places the audience in a voyeuristic position—the same position occupied by the absent men of the play—and emphasizes Crystal's "to-be-looked-at-ness" (to borrow Laura Mulvey's phrase—11). Rey Chow has argued that "One of the chief sources of oppression for women lies in the way they have been consigned to visuality" (105). By using the conventions of realism to implicate the audience in this masculinist "consignment," Boothe literalizes the power of the outsider's gaze to dictate female function and govern female identity.

Given this stage world where the body is a commodity, where autonomy and self-definition are denied, and where female identity is imposed by physical appearance, by social role (i.e., "First Hairdresser") or by male acceptance (i.e., "Mrs. Stephen Haines"), it is no wonder that the women of the title are so full of frustrated self-loathing that they seem to drip venom at their entire gender—even at female fetuses, who, according to Sylvia, "always make you sicker . . . even before they're born" (13). When Mary's eleven-year-old daughter protests that she doesn't want to be a "lady" because ladies have nothing to do (49), we must agree that the girl has correctly observed the workings of Boothe's carefully documented stage world.

Little Mary's presence in this play is quite important. As a prepubescent girl, she carefully scrutinizes the performances of gender she witnesses in Mary and her friends. Her rejection of those performances as both limited and limiting suggests that she has not yet been fully indoctrinated into accepting the role for herself. In fact, Little Mary resents her developing figure, resisting the idea of inhabiting the adult female body that would mark her as merchandise and doom her to repeat the unappealing role of "lady." She also decries what she sees as typical female behavior, noting that girls "tattle" and that "ladies" have no fun (49). Finally, she pronounces Crystal's frilly bathroom—the most overcoded of all the "female" spaces in the play—as "perfectly ridiculous" (166). The young girl's disapproval of women's socially constructed roles and settings thus reveals gender to be a culturally determined performative act, a role Little Mary can refuse to enact once she has recognized it as scripted performance. By using Little Mary to emphasize the cultural construction of gender, Boothe underscores an important point about the women of her play. Boothe's Park Avenue wives are not manipulative *because* they are women; they are manipulative because, *as* women in their specific culture, they are powerless to control their own destinies. As Susan Carlson has shrewdly observed about them, "Trapped in a woman's world which exists only because it is necessary to the men's, the women cannot choose to be other than they are" (567).

I do not want to make extravagant claims for the feminism of the *The Women*. The play is, in part, a prisoner of its own satiric intent and conventional formula, ending as it does with the "happy" resolution of Mary's winning back her man and leaving us exactly where we began. Yet in depicting a world where women are denied access to economic opportunity, self-determination, and even self-definition, Boothe was clearly critiquing the material and historical conditions that left women so powerless. In an interview occasioned by the 1973 revival of the play, Boothe emphasized this point by stressing her own political activism for women's causes and estimating that her play, with its large all-female cast, was currently employing ninety percent of the actresses in nonmusical Broadway shows (Lester 44). Like Rachel Crothers, then, Boothe was sharply aware of the need for female solidarity in theatrical endeavors. Given this context, her depiction of a world of unhappy women striving against each other seems an unmistakable protest against the culture that produced them.

Expanding Contexts

Throughout this chapter, I have attempted to illustrate that both feminism and realism are flexible and changeable; as a result, the value of feminist realist plays must be measured within specific historical contexts. But the evolution of the women's suffrage movement in the United States, while the focal point of this discussion, was certainly not the only context in which playwrights like Crothers and Boothe were working. In the theatrical world of the 1910s to 1930s, as in the world at large, the denigration of women's work and the exclusion of women playwrights from access to production opportunities were widespread phenomena. In 1940, for example, George Jean Nathan explored the question of why "the ladies are . . . almost uniformly and abjectly inferior to men in the field of dramatic composition," explaining:

I do not wish to seem unchivalrous, but the fact remains that there isn't a woman playwright living today who seems to be able to confect a play that comes within hailing distance of the drama written by the more competent of her boy-friends. Aside from Lillian Hellman . . . the rank and file of the playwriting girls, in whatever nation you find them, are a sadly negligible lot. (427–28)

After dismissing, on various grounds, many of the playwrights discussed in this chapter (i.e., Crothers, Gale, Glaspell, Boothe, and others), Nathan continues: "The question poses itself. What is the trouble with the girls? Why can't they, apparently, cope with men in the writing of plays?" (429). Nathan's answers to his own question— that women write unconvincing male characters and that they lack objectivity—are astonishingly demeaning, but the simple fact that he felt compelled to pose the question and to publish his sexist answers speaks volumes about the theatrical and social contexts in which the female playwrights under discussion labored.[21] Clearly, these playwrights were as embattled as their characters.

Some playwrights reacted to this hostile climate by political activism within the theater community. Martha Morton, for example, frustrated at her exclusion on gender grounds from the all-male American Dramatists Club, responded by founding the competing Society of Dramatic Authors in 1907 (the forerunner of the present-day Dramatists' Guild), which was open to both female and male playwrights (Gipson 218–20). Others, like Crothers, turned to other women for support—as we have seen. By securing directing opportunities through her connections with star actresses, Crothers found ways to maintain artistic control over her own plays without sacrificing artistic integrity. Yet in an era when realism was considered the highest and most modern form of dramatic writing, many female playwrights used it simply as a way to have their voices heard. As Tania Modleski has explained this feminist appropriation of realism in other contexts:

[Mimesis is a] time-honored tactic among oppressed groups, who often appear to acquiesce in the oppressor's ideas about it, thus producing a double meaning: the same language or act simultaneously confirms the oppressor's stereotypes of the oppressed and offers a dissenting and empowering view for those in the know. (129)

Faced with an abusive climate and with limited access to stage production, feminist playwrights of this era had good reason to couch their feminist critiques in the most commonly accepted conventions of the day. But as Modleski reminds us, such appropriations of dominant discourse are also revisions of that discourse, creating a submerged polyvocality apparent to those who know to look beneath the realistic surface.

In chapter 4, we will examine some plays of the post-1960 era that exploit this polyvocal potential of realism fully and explicitly to express feminist visions. First, however, I want to explore another specific context from the early part of the century. In examining some feminist realist plays written by African-American women from 1916 to 1940—roughly the same period as that covered in this chapter—we can see how conditions of racial prejudice and segregation inflected the feminism of black women, giving rise to different contextual pressures and different reasons to write realistic plays.

3

Remembering the Disremembered:
Feminism, Realism, and the
Harlem Renaissance

H<small>ISTORIAN</small> Elsa Barkley Brown has recently noted the ultimate inseparability of race, class, and historical context in defining feminist issues. For Brown, these fundamental components of gender construction have been too long overlooked. She writes:

> we have still to recognize that being a woman is, in fact, not extractable from the context in which one is a woman—that is, race, class, time, and place. We have still to recognize that all women do not have the same gender. In other words, we have yet to accept the fact that one cannot write adequately about the lives of white women in the United States *in any context* without acknowledging the way in which race shaped their lives. (300)

Black feminist literary theorists were among the first to recognize the truth of Brown's statement, since the attention to intersecting identity positions that Brown endorses has long characterized the work of African-American women writers. Critics like Barbara Christian, Mae Henderson, Gloria T. Hull, Barbara Smith, and Valerie Smith represent just a few of the many voices insisting that "the meaning of blackness in this country [the United States] shapes profoundly the experience of gender" and that the study of these interlocking factors requires critical methods that "are necessarily flexible, holding in balance the . . . variables of race, gender, and class and destabilizing the centrality of any one" (V. Smith 47).

In this chapter, I focus on the feminist realism of four African-American playwrights who wrote from 1916 to 1940: Angelina Grimké, Mary P. Burrill, Georgia Douglas Johnson, and Shirley Graham. In order to understand both the political ideologies and dramatic forms of their plays, it is essential to explore those "unextractable" factors of era, race, and class that black feminist literary critics habitually investigate and that inevitably inflected the gender concerns of these four playwrights. The social upheavals in the United States and the cultural conflicts of the Harlem Renaissance all contributed significantly to the feminist realism of these four women's works. In an era when violent racial injustices (like lynching and suffrage battles) were widespread and insulting stereotypes of African Americans typified the popular stage, these female playwrights (like their male counterparts) used realistic drama as a means of protest and correction. Furthermore, as black women they shared an interest in reclaiming something of African-American women's unrecorded history, which they tried to recover and authenticate in their realistic plays.

Until very recently, these feminist playwrights were themselves part of the overlooked history of African-American women that their realism was (in part) designed to reclaim; as Henry Louis Gates, Jr., has noted, our knowledge of the work of early African-American women writers has been "broken and sporadic" (in Hull 1988, xi). It has been only in the past few years that scholars like Elizabeth Brown-Guillory, Gloria T. Hull, Jeanne-Marie A. Miller, and Kathy Perkins have begun recovering unpublished or out-of-print plays by black women and analyzing them from a black feminist point of view. As lately as 1988, for example, Cary Wintz proclaimed that women writers of the Harlem Renaissance "confined their politics to their writing, but even there one finds no overt commitment to feminism" (207).[1] Clearly this statement represents both a misunderstanding of contextual feminism and a disregard for the political activism that many of these playwrights engaged in. Grimké and Burrill, for instance, both wrote pro-birth control works and both fought for the passage of the Nineteenth Amendment (P. Young 5–6); Burrill also wrote for the NAACP-sponsored journal *The Liberator* (France 1979, 56). Georgia Douglas Johnson was active in the Anti-Lynch Movement (Stephens 1992, 332), and Shirley Graham protested discrimination against black soldiers during World War II (Perkins 210). Critical misjudgments like Wintz's emerge not only from the decades of neglect suffered by African-American women writers, however, but also from problems they confronted in their own times, as we shall see. Erlene Stetson aptly summed up the tensions and conflicts for women in the Harlem Renaissance when she described the era as "an especially rich period for considering Black women's literary relationships because its politics were expressed in an interlocking network of racial/social prejudice, patronage and reward, personal stance and audition, public gesture and spokesmanship" (245).

Given the importance of this "interlocking network" of political and historical contexts in understanding both the feminism of these playwrights and the dramatic forms of their plays, I turn now to a brief survey of the Harlem Renaissance before examining the texts in detail. In studying both the plays themselves and the multiple contexts that informed them, I hope to recapitulate some of what these black feminist playwrights were trying to do for their own ancestors and reclaim what Toni Morrison has called "the disremembered."

Drama in the Harlem Renaissance: Propaganda or Art?

The period from about 1919 to 1929, an era known variously as the Harlem Renaissance, the New Negro Renaissance, or the New Negro Movement, encompassed an immense flowering of African-American artistic expression. As I write in 1994, both the name of the period and the exact dates of its influence are under debate. "Harlem Renaissance" is the most familiar title, but scholars like Katana Hall have pointed out that this term devalues the contributions of such artists as Alain Locke and Georgia Douglas Johnson, who, like many other writers of the time, lived and worked outside New York. For this reason, and also because the term was coined by Locke in 1925 and used during the period (rather than applied in retrospect), Hall prefers the term "New Negro Renaissance" (28).[2] Other critics challenge the dates usually assigned, which are based on the end of World War I in 1919 and the stock market crash in 1929. Abraham Chapman, for instance, contends that certain defining elements of Harlem Renaissance literature were recognizable as early as 1917 in Claude McKay's poetry, while several other scholars suggest extending the endpoint to coincide with the Harlem riots in 1935 (Huggins) or even into the civil rights era of the 1960s.[3] Whatever the exact title and duration of the Renaissance, the decade of the 1920s saw the emergence of an African-American dramatic tradition that extended beyond the 1920s and Harlem and to which both women and men contributed.

It was also an era of great debate in African-American literary circles about the appropriate goals, methods, venues, audiences, and dramatic forms for a theater by and about black Americans. From the end of World War I and continuing through the 1930s, intellectuals like W. E. B. Du Bois and Alain Locke founded a number of competing black theatrical companies, while journals like *Crisis* and *Opportunity* sponsored playwriting competitions for black artists and published the sometimes heated debates between Du Bois and Locke about theater. One reason these intellectual leaders sought to create their own performance troupes and publishing opportunities was that Broadway remained largely closed to African-American dramatists. While Broadway producers of the period began to be interested in depictions of African-American life, they continued to foster primarily white visions of that life: twenty plays "with Negro themes" (Hatch 209) reached Broadway during the 1920s, but only five of them were written by African-American playwrights (all male), and among those five only Wallace Thurman's 1929 melodrama *Harlem*, written in collaboration with white author W. S. Rapp, achieved commercial success (Scott 438). Compounding this problem of access was the problem of image: many African-American characters in these white productions perpetuated the racist stereotypes of the minstrel tradition, depicting black men as lazy, comic, shuffling, and foolish, black women as one-dimensional mammies or sexual predators. These stereotypes both challenged racial pride and impeded the development of a true African-American theater; they were "grotesque caricatures of the Negro race, [which had] fixed in the public taste a dramatic stereotype of the race that has been almost fatal to a sincere and authentic Negro drama" (Gregory 155).

Another reason for creating alternative production and publication venues, however, was that these community leaders and theater practitioners were working to redefine theatrical practice in the specific context of African-American life. While some groups, like Anita Bush's Lafayette Players, wanted to perform plays unrelated to black experience, others, notably Du Bois and his Krigwa Players, wanted to produce propaganda plays to protest and so improve racial conditions. Others, like Locke and his Howard Players, fought for accurate stage depictions of black daily life as seen from a black perspective, while still others, like the Rose McClendon Players, attempted to dramatize the similarities between blacks and whites when placed in similar conditions (McKay 1987a, 617). A brief look at some of the foundational issues of these debates will provide necessary background for understanding the work of the African-American women whose plays are the focus of this chapter.

Writing in *Crisis* in 1926, W. E. B. Du Bois outlined a program for African-American theatrical practice that became something of a manifesto for the black theater companies of the period. He wrote:

The plays of a Negro theatre must be: 1. About us. That is, they must have plots which reveal Negro life as it is. 2. By us. That is, they must be written by Negro authors who understand from birth and continued association just what it means to be a Negro today. 3. For us. That is, the theatre must cater primarily to Negro audiences and be supported and sustained by their entertainment and approval. 4. Near us. The theatre must be in a Negro neighborhood near the mass of ordinary Negro people. (Du Bois 1926, 134)

While not many plays fit this definition in 1926, the principles Du Bois espoused in this statement—that black theatre be centered in black consciousness, penned by black writers, and performed in black community spaces for black audiences—were widely supported by African-American theatre artists of the time.

The controversies arose when these principles began to be put into practice, and the debate crystallized around the figures of Du Bois and Locke. Both men agreed that black art should explore black life. For Du Bois, however, all art was propaganda, and black art should be used to depict the barriers to economic and social advancement unfairly placed in the path of worthy African Americans. As Rebecca Cureau explains it, Du Bois "took the middle-class position that characterization of black life should project a proper image of the Negro" (78), a stance sometimes described as the "best-foot forward" school or the "genteel tradition" of African-American drama. In retrospect, it is clear that much of the impetus of the "best-foot-forward" school came from class bias on the part of Du Bois and his followers, who disparaged writers like Langston Hughes for their use of "low-life" characters (Cureau 85). Nonetheless, Du Bois at least recognized the social function of art and fostered it in his theatrical and critical enterprises. In order to prove to white audiences that African Americans deserved a chance at material success and social equality, African-American theater (according to Du Bois) should focus on "race plays" or "propaganda plays" that would protest racial prejudice and advance the social position of African Americans (Perkins 3).

Alain Locke vehemently disagreed. For him, individual expression—art for its own sake—was the only appropriate goal of creative endeavor. From our postmodern perspective, it may seem a naive maneuver on Locke's part to deny the ideological biases, the propaganda, inherent in all forms of creative expression. However, given the context of the Harlem Renaissance, Locke's aesthetic emphasis can be seen as providing an alternative to the African-American artist's bind of facing a double audience: a white audience with preconceived notions about blacks on stage and a black audience eager to see its own experiences reflected there.[4] As Locke wrote in a 1928 defense of his anti-propaganda position:

my chief objection to propaganda, apart from its besetting sin of monotony and disproportion, is that it perpetuates the position of group inferiority even in crying out against it. For it leaves and speaks under the shadow of a dominant majority who it harangues, cajoles, threatens or supplicates. It is too extroverted for balance or poise or inner dignity and self-respect. (in Huggins 312–13)

In fact, in pointing out that opposition to the status quo does not equal subversion of it, Locke's attitude anticipates the position taken by many current materialist feminists.[5] And together with Montgomery Gregory, his co-founder of the Howard Players, Locke developed an aesthetic alternative to the propaganda play promoted by Du Bois: the folk play.

As delineated by Gregory and Locke, the folk play depicted the "authentic life of the Negro masses of to-day" (Gregory 159) without emphasizing racial oppression. Focusing on the everyday experiences, customs, beliefs, traditions, and language of ordinary black people, the folk plays of the 1920s endorsed by Gregory and Locke went a step beyond the humorous dialect plays of the 1910s (such as those of Paul Laurence Dunbar) because they treated the whole range of human experience, from the trivial and comic to the serious and tragic (Miller 1990, 353). They were, in effect, an African-American-centered form of realism, written primarily for black audiences, and marked by an inherent belief in the mimetic power of the stage— even (or especially) when the plays were performed in community churches and schools instead of behind a full-sized proscenium arch.

The dangers of Locke's approach to drama have been pointed out many times, both by Du Bois and his followers (who worried about perpetuating racist stereotypes of African-American common people) and by critics today. Leslie Catherine Sanders, for instance, notes that the African-American folk play was quickly appropriated by white writers, in whose hands the characters became exotics (9); that many folk plays of rural life oversimplified the inherent problems (such as poverty) by imagining a false bucolic innocence (10); and that many of the characters did recapitulate traditional racist stereotypes (38).[6] Nonetheless, Locke and his associates made great strides in creating a black-centered stage reality, in assuming the presence of a black audience, in developing recognizably human black characters, and in fostering the work of many new African-American voices in the theater. Robert Fehrenbach has noted that in the 1920s "the Afro-American clearly had to defend the race from white friends and foes alike, to tell the Black side of the story, and to present the race more realistically in literature and drama, the very instruments by which it had so long been demeaned" (89). Locke's championing of folk plays went a long way toward reaching those goals.[7]

The public debate between Du Bois and Locke generated such heated controversy during the Renaissance that one recent critic has described it as a "cultural war . . . [fought] over accurate depictions of the African-American community" (Lubiano 1992, 263). And while there certainly were significant differences of opinion between the two intellectual leaders, from the vantage point of the 1990s one also sees remarkable similarities in what they were trying to accomplish. Perhaps most importantly, both wanted to replace demeaning stage stereotypes of African Americans with representations of human beings; as Jeanne-Marie A. Miller has explained, "Black humanity, for the most part, had to be proved to whites" (1982, 281). While class differences remained an issue (with Du Bois favoring characters of bourgeois aspirations and Locke promoting working-class characters in their own milieu), the importance of this shared project cannot be overestimated.

The other important similarity between the separate theatrical projects of Du Bois and Locke emerges from this prior desire to counteract stereotypes. Since both Du Bois and Locke favored what they saw as accurate portrayals of African Americans offstage, both obviously accepted the mimetic power of theatre to reflect reality in an unmediated way. As a result, the divergent traditions of propaganda plays and folk drama shared a reliance on stage realism, which offered the most direct method for portraying conditions as they were and for replacing Mammy and Uncle Tom with complex characters. Thus, while a few exceptional writers (like Marita Bonner, Jean Toomer, and Willis Richardson) were experimenting with expressionism and other stage innovations, most black playwrights relied upon realism to reach both a white audience that could redress racial inequities and a black audience that had rarely seen itself portrayed accurately or positively. For playwrights of this era, before post-structuralism undermined our faith in realism's mimetic abilities, realistic drama, by approximating as closely as possible the life experienced in African-American communities, could vividly protest the oppression of its members (in propaganda plays) and also celebrate black culture (in folk plays).

From Her Point of View: Women Playwrights

And how did women playwrights react to this vociferous debate over African-American theater? That question is difficult to answer, since their chances for commercial success were even more limited than those of their male counterparts, and as a result not all of their works have been preserved or recovered. Gloria Hull has examined some of the reasons that black women's opportunities for recognition were especially restricted during this period. Her research shows that many New York-based patrons and mentors of Harlem writers were homosexual men who favored the work of male writers; that much of Harlem's intellectual life took place in after-hours clubs, which respectable black women were not expected to frequent; and that poetry was the preferred genre of the publishing community, while many of the women were primarily writers of fiction (Hull 1987, 8–15). Those female writers based in Washington, D.C., may also have faced gender restrictions. While Kathy Perkins credits Locke and Gregory with supporting a number of women playwrights in their Howard University playwriting classes (7), Hull suggests that Locke was something of a misogynist who actively favored male students and excluded women from his intellectual circle (Hull 1987, 7–8).

Despite these added layers of difficulties, a number of African-American women contributed significantly to the theater of the Harlem Renaissance, although their exact number is difficult to determine. In "What Were They Saying?" Nellie McKay estimates that during the Harlem Renaissance eleven black women published twenty-one plays (as compared to only a half-dozen black male playwrights), but her estimate has already been shown to be low (Perkins). Furthermore, it does not include the many black women's plays that were never published but were performed in community schools, auditoriums, and churches (McKay 1987a, 625). These black female dramatists confronted all the playwriting tensions and conflicts of their male counterparts, with the additional problems of depicting black experience from their female viewpoints and of combating degrading sexual stereotypes as well as racial ones.

The already formidable problem of counteracting stereotypes, for example, was gravely exacerbated for black women. In her work on African-American women novelists, Barbara Christian has isolated four persistent stereotypes of black women: mammy, loose woman, tragic mulatta, and conjure woman (Christian 1980, 10–19). First developed during slavery to transfer responsibility for institutionalized rape from the white slave owners to their subjected female slaves, these stereotypes have lingered in the nation's consciousness and imagery, "mask[ing] the vulnerability of the female to sexual exploitation" (Wilkerson iv). These images have posed recurring problems for black women writers and performers. As actress Cynthia Belgrave has lamented: "If you're strong and stoical, you're a matriarch, and if you're weak and sensual, you're a whore. Of course there are no equitable variations in between" (in Brown-Guillory 1988, 107).[8] In a poignant 1925 essay on then-popular images of black women, Elise Johnson McDougald explained the psychological damage done to women who could not help but absorb the false but ubiquitous representations of them:

> even in New York, the general attitude of mind causes the Negro woman serious difficulty. She is conscious that what is left of chivalry is not directed at her. She realizes that the ideas of beauty, built up in the fine arts, have excluded her almost entirely. Instead, the grotesque Aunt Jemimas of the streetcar advertisements, proclaim only an ability to serve, without grace of loveliness. Nor does the drama catch her finest spirit. She is most often used to provoke the mirthless laugh of ridicule; or to portray feminine viciousness or vulgarity not peculiar to Negroes. This is the shadow over her. (370)

Given this cultural climate, both on and off the stage, it is clear that replacing stereotypical images of African-American women would be of paramount importance to these female playwrights. Realism, with its ability to present coherent and developing characters who are shaped by and respond to their environment, offered them a built-in opportunity to assert the creative humanity of black women.

While stereotypes of mammy and loose woman dominated representations of black women, the reality of African-American women's lives before the twentieth century had been all but effaced from American history, their unique experiences and perspectives left unrecorded and unremarked. There are, of course, multiple reasons for such oversight, ranging from poor record keeping by slave owners to a widespread politics of silence (what Darlene Hine has called a "culture of dissemblance"—915) among black women determined to protect their privacy and self-esteem in a culture where "true womanhood" meant being white. Given this secrecy and silence surrounding African-American women's shared and individual histories, writing plays to reconstruct their lives was both challenging and important. As Barbara Christian has pointed out, the concept of remembering and reevaluating the past "could not be at the center of a narrative's [or a play's] revisioning of history until the obvious fact that African-Americans did have a history and culture was firmly established in American society" (Christian 1990, 333); without such factual background information, writers would lack the details necessary to impart authenticity to their works and the audience would lack a context in which to read or view. For these black women playwrights of the Harlem Renaissance, therefore, a crucial first step in claiming the stage was to discover and depict the historical and cultural facts that black women had repressed or been denied access to.

For this task, like the tasks of depicting oppression and overturning stereotypes, African-American women playwrights turned to realism. While their numerous plays dramatize issues as varied as lynching, poor treatment of black war veterans, gender roles within the black community, and the debilitating effects of poverty, the explicitly feminist issues of reproductive freedom and motherhood appear repeatedly in their works and will form the focal point for my analysis of their plays. For even within the confines of this one narrow topic, examples abound of black female playwrights turning to realism to protest racial discrimination, to correct demeaning stereotypes, and to reclaim something of African-American women's unrecorded history.

Sisters Under the Skin: *Rachel* and *They That Sit in Darkness*

When Angelina Weld Grimké's play *Rachel* was first produced by the NAACP's Drama Committee in 1916, it became something of a cause célèbre in the African-American theatrical community. The program notes from the 1916 production proclaim the play as "the first attempt to use the stage for race propaganda in order to enlighten the American people relative to the lamentable condition of the millions of Colored citizens in this free republic" (in Fehrenbach 91). While a number of reviewers and NAACP members applauded the play's pioneering attempt to protest racial injustices, others saw its depiction of oppressed and beleaguered African Americans as both limiting and limited; in fact, it was this production of *Rachel* that caused Locke and Gregory to break away from the NAACP Drama Group and form the Howard Players (Sanders 23).

The plot of the play reveals Grimké's feminism as well as her commitment to promoting equality for African Americans. The story takes place behind the fourth wall of the Loving family parlor. A respectable, middle-class family consisting of a mother, a son Tom, and a daughter Rachel, the Lovings have come north after the lynching of the father and elder son, an incident that took place ten years prior to the action and of which Tom and Rachel know nothing at the start of the play.

The title character is a vivacious teenager when we first meet her, devoted to her family and her education. Her dominant characteristics are a love for·children (especially "the little black and brown babies"—143) and a fervent desire someday to marry and raise a large family of her own. As she matures into a young woman in the second and third acts, however, her ideals become blighted. The change in Rachel is prompted by a number of incidents: she discovers that her father and brother George were killed by a lynch mob; her brother Tom and his friend John Strong (with whom Rachel is in love) cannot find jobs equal to their college educations and must work as waiters to support their families; she meets a little black girl who has been so traumatized by the racism of her first-grade teacher and classmates that the child can no longer speak; and Rachel's young adopted son is physically bruised and spiritually wounded when a gang of white boys hurl rocks and racial slurs at him. Emotionally undone by the injuries to the men in her life and the children around her, Rachel refuses John's marriage proposal, vowing never to marry and bring more black children into the world only to suffer. The anguish her decision causes her is underscored when she crushes the roses John had given her, comparing them to the unborn children whom she figuratively kills.[9] An early working title for the play—*Blessed Are the Barren*—makes clear Grimké's sympathy for Rachel's choice.

Grimké's feminist concerns are apparent in a number of Rachel's actions. From the opening of the play Rachel is headstrong and independent, opposing the "ladylike" behavior that her mother tries to impose on her (140). Later, when John Strong determines that Rachel needs more fun in her life and decides to take her to the theater, Rachel retorts: "You talk as though I were a—a jelly-fish. You'll take me, how do you know *I'll* go? . . . Why, you talk as though my will counts for nothing. It's as if you're trying to master me. I think a domineering man is detestable" (157). And as Margaret Wilkerson has noted, Rachel's rejection of Strong's marriage proposal reveals Grimké's "striking sensitivity to the special way in which racism and sexism affect the black woman" when "a black man cannot protect her and her children from the assaults of a cruel world" (xvi).

That Grimké was cognizant of the particular ways racism and sexism affect black women is apparent from her unpublished writings about *Rachel*. In commenting on her motives for writing the play, Grimké defines white women as her target audience and motherhood as the hook by which she would enlist their support in black women's causes:

If anything can make all women sisters underneath their skins, it is motherhood. If then I could make the white women of this country see, feel, understand just what their prejudice and the prejudice of their fathers, brothers, husbands, sons were having on the souls of the colored mothers everywhere and upon the mothers that are to be, a great power to affect public opinion would be set free and the battle would be half won. (in Miller 1978, 517)

Motherhood is certainly *the* key issue of the play, and, in fact, a number of critics have complained that Grimké overloaded the play with excessive sentimentality on this topic. These commentators criticize Rachel's frequent effusions about babies and motherhood and the flowery language in which she habitually discusses them.[10] Given Grimké's goal of enlisting white women in black women's causes, however, I am inclined to agree with Judith Stephens, who sees Grimké as *intervening* in the code the play ostensibly espouses. Stephens writes:

In *Rachel,* Angelina Grimké threw the image of idealized motherhood back at white women in an attempt to make them see what meaning this so-called "revered institution" might hold for black women. . . . In writing *Rachel,* Grimké used the sentimental language of the [era's] dominant gender ideology, which idealized motherhood, but the play does not support or concede to that ideology. Instead, it breaks dominant gender ideology by raising the issue of race and asking white women to consider what black mothers must face. (1990, 62)

It would seem that Grimké anticipated the argument of Elsa Barkley Brown (with which I began this chapter) by recognizing that motherhood, like gender, is hardly a universal experience but is in part defined by race.

Despite Grimké's avowed interest in engaging a white female audience, a number of critics have asserted, probably correctly, that she also sought a black audience "that needed to see an image of its members . . . as they wished themselves to be" (Hatch 137; see also Hull 1987, 117–18). In order to protest the unfair treatment of blacks in a white-dominated society, Grimké consciously created characters to represent (in her words) "the best type of colored people" (in Miller 1978, 515). These characters are middle-class paragons, conscientious about family, work, school, and upward mobility; they speak proper English (Rachel even takes care to correct her adopted son's grammatical errors); in short, they are clear-cut examples of the "genteel" models advocated by Du Bois.

These genteel characters could be interpreted as just another form of stereotype, not a demeaning one, to be sure, but one guided by unchallenged bourgeois assumptions and middle-class aspirations. As James Hatch has remarked, "the author sees no conflict between middle class virtues and the beauties of being black" (138). But Grimké's challenge to the widespread images of black women takes on an added dimension in the character of Rachel, who reveals more complexity than a cardboard stereotype could bear. Rachel is, in Margaret Wilkerson's words, "the antithesis of the prevailing stereotypes," being "neither a superwoman nor of loose character; she is a tender, vulnerable person whom the evils of society overwhelm" (xvi). And as Helene Keyssar has noted, Rachel's competing desires regarding John and her future children signify not ambivalence on her part, but true polyphony, emphasizing dramatically the inherent conflicts in her role as an African-American woman. For Rachel, "abortion, as she conceives and enacts it [by destroying the symbolic roses], is the only act that will authenticate her double existence as a woman and a black person" (Keyssar 1989, 238). While some early critics of the play interpreted Rachel's refusal to marry as advocating race genocide (in Hull 1987, 121), Rachel's act is more one of autonomous self-definition. By rejecting the marriage she has so long desired, Rachel takes the feminist position of maintaining control of her body and choosing her reproductive destiny (McKay 1987b, 134). In this way, Rachel clearly transcends the then prevailing stereotypes of black women.

Grimké's probable interest in engaging two audiences—a white one that needed to be shown the conditions of oppression and a black one that needed to see positive stage images of itself—led her on both counts to employ the conventions of realism. In a letter written about *Rachel*, Grimké mentions reading the realistic plays of Henrik Ibsen and the naturalistic dramas of August Strindberg and Gerhart Hauptmann (Fehrenbach 95–96). Not surprisingly, she imported a number of their dramatic conventions into her own play. The most obvious realistic technique is her use of causal logic. As we saw above, stories from the past and incidents occurring in the present combine to form an unbreakable chain of events that restricts Rachel's options and leads inexorably to her rejection of motherhood. The structure of the play, as Fehrenbach has pointed out, complements the changes in Rachel: each act focuses on a specific example of racial prejudice, each of which is juxtaposed to and ruins some potential happiness of Rachel's (99).

But while Rachel may be the only fully realized character in the play, many of the other characters' actions are similarly motivated in ways that reveal the internal conflicts among the race, class, and gender roles with which they all contend and which Grimké attempted to portray realistically. Mrs. Loving's long narrative about her husband's death provides a good example. While this monologue has been criticized as impeding the flow of the action (Fehrenbach 101), it actually serves many purposes as an example of feminist realism in racial and historical context. Most obviously, the speech offers Rachel and Tom their first real glimpse of violence against blacks, and so provides them with their earliest motivation for subsequent despairing actions (like Rachel's rejection of marriage and Tom's abandoning his fruitless job search). And rather than providing an obstruction to the action, Mrs. Loving's long tale *is* the action; that is, the scene offers a realistic enactment of the African-American tradition of storytelling, of oral history in progress (a technique we will see more fully realized in Shirley Graham's play about slavery). In this way Grimké could document a persistent oral tradition and illustrate its effects. Finally, Mrs. Loving's reasons for breaking her silence about her husband's death expose the "culture of dissemblance" as ultimately damaging. When she realizes that Rachel and Tom both interpret her silence as concealing some shameful secret about their father, she recants her decision to protect them from the truth and shares the awful story. Recognizing that her children have been ashamed, she berates herself for being "criminally blind" to their misapprehension (147). In revealing the horrible truth of the lynchings, Mrs. Loving attempts to recover a racial and familial pride that she had allowed to be forgotten; she restores "the disremembered" to their important place in her family history.

In her later works—including an unpublished play called *Mara* and a short story called "The Closing Door"—Grimké continued her realistic depiction of genteel black characters and their conflicts over reproductive freedom. "The Closing Door" (which appeared in the 1919 *Birth Control Review*) depicts the despair of a distraught young woman who smothers her infant son when she hears that her brother has just been lynched. Like Rachel, she refuses her role as "an instrument," a breeder of children who will inevitably be abused. She laments being "a colored woman—doomed!—cursed!—put here!—willing or unwilling! . . . to bring children here—men children—for the sport—the lust—of mobs" (in Hull 1987, 129). While Gloria Hull has remarked that Grimké "concentrated almost exclusively on lynching in her drama and fiction" (1987, 131), I would argue that reproductive freedom and motherhood are similarly central concerns. Furthermore, I disagree with Hull's assessment of "The Closing Door" as "peculiar" or "wrong" in the context of a birth control journal. As we will see, abortion and infanticide were issues of recurring importance to the playwrights of the era as well as to the slave mothers and twentieth-century mothers that they depicted.

In fact, Grimké's version of black feminist realism, while partaking perhaps of more sentimentality and melodrama than current taste will accept as credible, did have a lasting impact on the black women playwrights who followed her. While "the stark realism and political nature" of *Rachel* startled many of Grimké's contemporaries (Scott 429), and while the debate over whether writing should be political or simply artistic continued to rage, *Rachel* defined playwriting as a powerful ideological tool for other black feminist playwrights of the Harlem Renaissance. In summing up Grimké's influence, Nellie McKay has written:

> black women playwrights in the years immediately following the debut of Grimké's play [followed] in her footsteps and [took] the relationship between art and identity seriously. As a result, they wrote a number of plays that presented images of black life opposed to the exotic ones that appeared in the commercial theatre of the time. In these they made no attempt to disguise their political motives and they spoke directly to the realistic problems that black people, especially black women, faced in their daily lives. (1987b, 134)

In Grimké's hands, the realistic propaganda play took on a distinctly feminist agenda appropriate to its time and to the conflicts within African-American communities. In this sense, she is the progenitor of a tradition that has continued throughout the century and includes Lorraine Hansberry's *A Raisin in the Sun* (the Younger family being direct descendants of the Lovings) and Alice Childress's *Wine in the Wilderness* (which I will discuss in the next chapter). She was also, as McKay notes above, a direct influence on many of the women playwrights of the Harlem Renaissance era.

Her influence can be seen as early as 1919, just three years after the original production of *Rachel,* when Grimké's friend and probable lover Mary P. Burrill published a realistic, pro-birth control play in the same 1919 issue of *The Birth Control Review* in which Grimké's "The Closing Door" appeared. Unlike Grimké, Burrill created characters who are neither genteel nor upwardly mobile. Instead, they are poor rural women trapped in an endless cycle of childbearing and poverty, unable to put their "best foot forward." What *They That Sit in Darkness* shares with *Rachel,* however, is a feminist interest in documenting the anguish of African-American motherhood, a protest agenda, and a realistic dramatic form.

Like *Rachel,* the play employs the fourth-wall convention, although the Jasper family living room of Burrill's one-act play is one of only two rooms in an overcrowded shack in the rural South. The action concerns two women: Malinda Jasper, who is the mother of ten children, and her seventeen-year-old daughter Lindy, who is preparing to leave for Tuskegee Institute on a grant. Using a sort of documentary realism, the play depicts the typical events of a day in Malinda's and Lindy's lives. Despite their hard work and dreams of a more comfortable future, they are unable to overcome the numbing poverty that restricts them. The stark and dingy setting, their weariness as they struggle over a washtub and with the many unruly younger children, the lack of milk for the baby and food for the others, and Malinda's apparent weakness (she has recently delivered her tenth baby) all vividly illustrate the destitution under which the family suffers and counteract the notion prevalent in the era (and lingering into our own) that poverty is somehow deserved or can be overcome by a willingness to work.

The climax of the play comes with the entrance of Elizabeth Shaw, a visiting nurse, who arrives to check on Malinda's heart condition.[11] Their brief conversation about birth control is central to the play. When Nurse Shaw naively counsels Malinda to avoid hard work and future pregnancies, the following dialogue ensues:

> *Mrs. Jasper*: But whut kin Ah do—de chillern *come!*
> *Miss Shaw*: You must be careful!
> *Mrs. Jasper*: *Be keerful!* Dat's all you nu'ses say! . . . Ah been keerful all Ah knows how but whut's it got me—ten chillern, eight livin' an' two daid! You got'a be tellin' me sumpin' better'n dat, Mis' Liz'beth!
> *Miss Shaw (fervently)*: I wish to God it were lawful for me to do so! My heart goes out to you poor people that sit in darkness, having, year after year, children that you are physically too weak to bring into the world—children that you are unable not only to educate but even to clothe and feed. Malinda, when I took my oath as a nurse, I swore to abide by the laws of the State, and the law forbids my telling you what you have a right to know! (71–72)

This brief exchange manifests many of the conflicts of the play. The contrast in the two women's dialects, for instance, illustrates realistically the differences in class and education that accompany their probable difference in race. Further, Miss Shaw believes in the letter of the law; she has accepted the privileges her race, education, job, and access to information have afforded her, and will not violate this power structure to help Malinda control her reproductive destiny or her life. Malinda, in contrast, knows that power (legal and otherwise) can only be used against her. For example, when her mentally deficient daughter Pinkie was sexually abused by a white employer who was never punished, Malinda learned firsthand that "cullud folks cain't do nothin' to white folks down heah!" (71). The fact that the state prevents health care professionals from providing information that would save lives—and that even Miss Shaw thinks they have a right to know—underscores the complex network of unseen authorities that conspire to maintain the darkness of impoverished lives. Nellie McKay has called *They That Sit in Darkness* unique in African-American drama because of its close focus on "the dilemma of poor, rural, uneducated black women—the most powerless of social groups" (1987b, 138). Miss Shaw's appearance and her refusal to use the power of her privilege to assist Malinda emphasize this point.

The plot, like that of *Rachel*, is structured according to a realistic causality. The refusal of Miss Shaw and the law to share information with Malinda leads inevitably to Malinda's death. That the cycle will be endlessly repeated as long as birth control information is withheld is abundantly clear in the fates of Malinda's eldest daughters. Pinkie and her illegitimate baby have already disappeared without a trace, and it is difficult to imagine a future for them any less grim than Malinda's. By the end of the play, Lindy's fate is likewise sealed. Realizing that she cannot go to college as planned but must take her mother's place as caretaker to the other children, Lindy relinquishes her dream of improving herself and her family's condition.

Burrill was also clearly attempting to refute racist and sexist stereotypes in her portrayal of the Jasper women. As Patricia Young has commented, the women in this play defy the traditional stereotypes of black women set forth by Christian and discussed above. However, as Young goes on to note, all three of the Jasper women are victims caught in society's net. For her, the play illustrates "the needless destruction of women's lives: compulsory child-bearing destroys Malinda's; forced labor and [white male] lust destroyed Pinkie's; and blighted dreams destroy Lindy's" (90). There are several ways to interpret these images of victimized black women. On the one hand, it is just such depictions of African Americans as limited and helpless, hemmed in on all sides and without potential for self-actualization, that Gregory and Locke were protesting in their criticism of "race" or "propaganda" plays. On the other hand, the Jasper women are neither passive to nor oblivious of their situation, but actively seek ways out of it: Malinda wants birth control information and Lindy wants an education. In fact, Burrill has created positive images of black women who seek to change their lives; their inability to overcome their victimization is clearly portrayed as society's fault, not theirs. Burrill emphasizes this point in her starkly naturalistic set, which illustrates the power of environment (both physical and social) to control destinies. Nellie McKay has cogently summed up this complex relationship between individual accountability and realistic social critique; she claims:

the issue is not one of a family's having more children than they can afford to raise comfortably, but of what inaccessibility to certain kinds of information means for social mobility, education, self-determination, health, infant and female mortality, and economic viability. The victimization of ignorance and poverty is in part the heritage of poor women's inability to control the size of their families in any practical way. . . . The blame is not on the individual, Burrill shows us, but on a system that withholds vital information and access from [voiceless people]. (1987b, 138–39)

With its realistic dialogue, naturalistic set, and the inevitable causal logic that leads to Malinda's death and Lindy's lost opportunity, Burrill used techniques of stage realism to denounce the law's enforcement of poverty and ignorance that, like the people they enchain, endlessly reproduce themselves.

These two propaganda plays—*Rachel* and *They That Sit in Darkness*—illustrate the capabilities of realism as a form of feminist social protest in the context of the 1910s. Grimké and Burrill used naturalistic settings, vernacular language, realistic characters, and linear causality in their plots to depict the conflicts over motherhood faced by African-American women of their era, hoping to use realism's mimetic power to question stereotypes and illustrate social injustices. While their characters differ markedly in economic class and in the forms of prejudice and oppression that affect them, both plays illustrate the strategic use of realism as a form of social criticism, as a way of documenting what *is* to suggest what should be.

Other women of the Harlem Renaissance followed their lead, writing numerous propaganda plays about current issues like lynching and suffrage.[12] Another group, however, chose to focus on African-American women of the past, writing history plays and dramatic recreations of the lost voices of their female ancestors. It is to some of those writers, and especially to plays about motherhood by Georgia Douglas Johnson and Shirley Graham, that I now turn.

Reclaiming Their Own Stories

Abena Busia has written movingly on the need for African-American women writers to reclaim the past; her words could also be applied to the work of some women playwrights of the Harlem Renaissance. She writes:

As black women we have recognized the need to rewrite or reclaim our own *her*stories, and to define ourselves. We are not reaffirming our presence or "actualizing" ourselves as if we have been absent, we know we never left; we are simply, but quite radically, reclaiming our own *stories,* which for so long have been told for us, and been told wrong. (1–2)

Many African-American playwrights during the Harlem Renaissance took this mission of recovering lost stories very seriously. Both male and female playwrights of the period wrote dramas about the achievements of African-American historical figures in an attempt to recover the past and to represent it from an African-American viewpoint. Randolph Edmonds's *Nat Turner* (1935), May Miller's *Harriet Tubman* (1935), and Langston Hughes's *Emperor of Haiti* (1936) are all prominent examples of this genre.

Of more interest from a feminist standpoint, however, are those realistic plays written to reclaim African-American women's history in a general way, by depicting the conditions of those women about whom specific facts are unknown, unrecorded, or simply repressed as unspeakable. In several striking cases, African-American women playwrights turned to a story that, as Toni Morrison comments in her novel *Beloved,* "was not a story to pass on" (Morrison 274). I refer to the story recounted in *Beloved* and depicted in several plays of the era, that of a mother's killing her child to protect it from a life of racial or sexual abuse.

Georgia Douglas Johnson's 1929 play *Safe* is a good example of this genre. Like Grimké's *Rachel* and "The Closing Door," *Safe* portrays a desperate woman seeking to protect her child from racism, this time in a small Southern town in 1893. The play encompasses a double action. On stage, the plot centers on Liza Pettigrew, happily married and about to give birth to her first child. Off stage, although discussed by the characters and in part overheard by the audience, an angry mob lynches seventeen-year-old Sam Hosea, a member of the Pettigrews' church and the sole support of his widowed mother, for slapping the face of a white man who had first struck him. These two events fuse when Sam is heard outside screaming "I don't want to die! Mother! Mother!" (29) and Liza's baby is born, identified as a son, and strangled by his distraught mother to keep him (in her words) "safe from the lynchers" (32).

As this summary reveals, *Safe* inherited both its propagandistic intent and its realistic depiction of racism from *Rachel* and *They That Sit in Darkness.* The play typifies American stage realism not only in its use of dialect, a picture-frame set, and causal action, but also in its illustration of the mutually influential relationship between public issues (the lynching) and private tensions (Liza's maternal fears).[13] Given the skillful interweaving of the political and the personal provided by the double action of the play, Judith Stephens's comment about the realistic structure of antilynch plays in general is particularly pertinent to *Safe:*

> The anti-lynch plays graphically depict lynching as *both* a violent crime *and* a pervasive influence in daily life. By giving their plays domestic settings and creating characters who are family members and neighbors, African American women recorded a view of lynching as a practice which impacted all aspects of life. (1992, 332)

By bringing the chilling results of lynching into the Pettigrews' peaceful living room, Johnson protested the way racial violence hovered menacingly over even the joyful aspects of African-American family life.

In addition to the propaganda message of this antilynch play, however, Johnson took a feminist step forward in depicting the way motherhood intertwined with racial oppression for African-American women. Kathy Perkins has explained how racial tensions for black women of the period were foregrounded by the responsibilities of motherhood. She writes that certain issues

> could only be expressed by a black woman. Neither the white nor the black male playwright could express the intense pain and fear a black woman experienced concerning her children—wondering, for instance, if the child she carried for nine months would be sold into slavery, or be a son who might one day be lynched. (2)

While I hesitate to endorse the seeming essentialism of Perkins's statement (which implies that the conditions of African-American motherhood are unimaginable to others), within *Safe* Liza's lament over Sam's impending doom does suggest the unique position of black mothers during this historical period. Echoing Rachel's apostrophe to the roses, Liza says of her expected baby: "What's little nigger boys born for anyhow? I sho hopes mine will be a girl. I don't want no boy baby to be hounded down and kicked 'round. No, I don't want to ever have no boy chile!" (28).

The extraordinary tensions of motherhood for African-American women have, in fact, continued to be a prominent theme in African-American women's plays throughout the twentieth century. As Helene Keyssar has noted, plays depicting black mothers' particular anxieties illustrate once again the inseparability of race and gender in defining feminist issues. Commenting on characters as diverse as Rachel in Grimké's play, Ruth in Lorraine Hansberry's *A Raisin in the Sun*, and Crystal in Ntozake Shange's *for colored girls*, Keyssar notes: "it is possible in many circumstances to ignore, unify, or diminish the multiple points of view inherent in being a black woman, but a hybrid consciousness reemerges insistently for each of these characters in the presence of the possibility or actuality of motherhood" (1989, 233). The same may certainly be said of Burrill's Malinda and Johnson's Liza as well. Whether this "hybrid consciousness" leads a loving character to reject motherhood, seek birth control, or murder her child, these plays all demonstrate that the mutually shaping influences of race, class, gender, and time period were clearly of recurring concern to the feminist playwrights of the Harlem Renaissance.

As Perkins's comment above further suggests, this conflict over motherhood is a particularly distressing legacy of slavery. When a child could be sold at an owner's whim, when a slave woman's behavior could be coerced by threats to her child, when a child is the result of rape, or when a child's inevitable slave status would only perpetuate the institution of slavery—all conditions that were not uncommon for slave women in the antebellum South (Hine and Wittenstein 295–96)—motherhood became a profoundly vexed issue. As a result of these gut-wrenching complexities, an emotionally overwrought mother might actually view infanticide as an act of love and protection, as Liza in *Safe* evidently did when faced with a lynch mob. Moving a step beyond lynching into the historical past, playwright and civil rights activist Shirley Graham explored the connection between child killing and slavery in her powerful 1940 drama, *It's Morning*.

Information about actual historical cases of infanticide among slaves is difficult to obtain. While historians like Eugene Genovese claim that slave abortions and infanticide were not a problem for slave owners because "the slaves . . . loved their children too much to do away with them" (497), oral histories and court records suggest that the infanticide committed by Margaret Garner, the historical slave woman on whom Morrison loosely based her protagonist Sethe in *Beloved*, was not unique. Bauer and Bauer, for instance, quote five examples of documented slave infanticides (416–18), as does Deborah White (87–88), with little apparent overlap between the two sets of cases.[14] While these few sources may not indicate a general trend— White makes the rather obvious point that infanticide was "atypical behavior" (88)—surviving slave narratives suggest that the enslaved mothers who killed their children acted out of love. The research of Darlene Hine and Kate Wittenstein suggests that "an understanding of the living death that awaited their children under slavery" (295) was a primary motivation.

But infanticide may simply have been the most extreme example of a widespread, and of course undocumented, female slave resistance to the institution of slavery. Hine and Wittenstein's work reveals that an extensive pattern of slave women in sexual rebellion may well have existed. Using actions ranging from sexual abstinence to abortion networks to infanticide, these women rejected "their vital economic function as breeders" (296), an opposition with major political and economic implications for the slave owners. After slavery was abolished, a politics of silence arose among black women regarding their past rebellious actions and their own sexuality, what Hine has called (as we saw earlier) "the culture of dissemblance." Events like infanticide, then, routinely left out of formal histories and seen in African-American oral tradition as "not a story to pass on," would clearly be of interest to a playwright bent on recovering African-American women's lost history and so "giv[ing] name to the nameless" (Lorde 1984, 37).

Graham's *It's Morning*, the most obvious example of this genre, is set in a slave cabin on the last day of December 1862.[15] Cissie, the slave mother of two children, has just received word that her beautiful and vivacious fourteen-year-old daughter, Millie, has been sold to a lascivious creditor. Cissie stumbles into the cabin where her friends sit and describes the man's touching Millie's breast, spitting on the floor, and laughing at the girl's terror. After Cissie's exit, Grannie Lou, the oldest slave on the plantation, offers two reminiscences to the disheartened group remaining. First she recalls Cissie's youth. To the astonishment of her current friends, the stolid Cissie was once as cheerful and lively as her daughter, until an overseer swore to "break huh will" (215)—and evidently did so by raping her repeatedly and humiliating her publicly. Grannie Lou then recounts the even older story of a queenly slave woman from Africa, noted for her strength in cutting down cane stalks, who lined up her three sons to watch the sunrise and beheaded them from behind—with one swoop of her cane knife—to prevent their being sold down river. Cissie overhears this last story and, at dawn on the next day (New Year's Day), kills Millie with a cane knife. The terrible story takes an ironic twist when the knock at the door that impelled Cissie's action turns out to be not the lustful creditor come to collect his prize, but a young Union soldier who informs the slaves that they are free. The play thus ends with Cissie's proffering Millie's limp body to the horrified Yankee boy who would have released her from bondage, suggesting that the sunrise framing him in the doorway, symbol of a new day dawning for the freed slaves, will never obliterate the ghastly atrocities on which slavery was built.

Despite this rather melodramatic symbolism at the end, the play, like *Rachel* and *They That Sit in Darkness*, depends on techniques of dramatic realism to counteract stereotypes. While Cissie's action can be seen as a mercy killing designed to spare Millie the life of degradation that Cissie herself has suffered, murdering her own child as a safeguard against sexual abuse effectively undermines Cissie's status as either nurturing mammy or sexual wanton. In re-creating slave life on stage, however, Graham's realism serves another purpose, one distinct in both purpose and technique from that used by Grimké and Burrill twenty years earlier or by Johnson in her version of the *Medea* plot. Instead of depicting present conditions to protest them, Graham's play dramatizes a past that has been suppressed. To accomplish this re-creation of the forgotten past, Graham fused the cause-and-effect logic, realistic setting, and upstanding characters typical of propaganda plays with the dialect, oral stories, and music that characterize folk plays. Because of this innovative embedding of African rhythms and culture within a traditional Aristotelian structure, Elizabeth Brown-Guillory has described *It's Morning* as "a major breakthrough in African-American drama" (1990, 82).

Graham's attention to faithfully representing African-American slave culture is apparent from the beginning of the playtext. In the opening stage directions, the playwright comments that the diverse dialects in *It's Morning* are intentionally not uniform, but are meant to reflect the various African languages from which slave dialects evolved as well as the changes in pitch and volume that African-Americans use to indicate changes in meaning (210). And by using realism's linear causality, Graham elucidates the tragic and long-lasting consequences of sexual abuse, which range in this play from spiritual damage to murder.

Yet because of the folk elements incorporated into this conventionally realistic framework, the play offers some hope for cultural survival beyond that suggested by the rising sun of the conclusion. By depicting oral history in action, *It's Morning* makes explicit the importance of keeping the past alive through storytelling. Both Cissie's past and the legend of the noble African woman are communicated to the slave women and to the audience through Grannie Lou's unofficial history, a spoken tale (much like Mrs. Loving's long-repressed tale of lynching in *Rachel*) related by one who claims she "ain't so ole dat Ah don' member" (216). Despite their lack of written documentation, however, Grannie's remembered truths are powerful: they explain Cissie's motives for killing Millie and provide a model (complete with choice of weapon) for the murder. To be sure, without Grannie Lou's oral history Cissie might never have taken her tragic action. However, in the context of the play, Grannie Lou's story emphasizes the heroism of the African mother and suggests the defiance and pride of black people who must use drastic measures to resist their enslavement

(Brown-Guillory 1990, 82). Furthermore, without such oral histories and without plays like this one, women like Cissie would be in the same straights as those Morrison described for her character Beloved: "Disremembered and unaccounted for, she cannot be lost because no one is looking for her" (274). Using a realistic stage format and elements of folk drama, Graham could record some of the content of African-American oral history, embody its interactive form, document its authority, and restore voice to long-silenced African-American women. Erlene Stetson has recently commented on the troublesome silences surrounding African-American women's history. She writes:

> For me, and I suspect for many other Black women researchers, the slavery period is personally the most painful and difficult to explore. The omissions, the neglect, and the deliberate distortions found in Black history in general are repeated a thousandfold in slave women's history. (244)

In realistically portraying some of that neglected history, Graham demonstrated the power of the past within the present and helped to pass on those neglected women's stories.

Transforming Images of Blackness

In a 1992 essay on contemporary representations of African Americans, bell hooks wrote:

> What can the future hold if our present entertainment is the spectacle of contemporary colonization, dehumanization, and disempowerment where the image serves as a murder weapon. Unless we transform images of blackness, of black people, our ways of looking and our ways of being seen, we cannot make radical interventions that will fundamentally alter our situation. (1992, 7)

In this statement, hooks suggests that controlling how one is represented is an essential step in promoting social change; it is a revolutionary act. Seen in this context, the four playwrights discussed in this chapter—Grimké, Burrill, Johnson, and Graham—can all be seen as feminist revolutionaries fighting to alter the ways African-Americans were seen and saw themselves reflected. Yet as we saw in chapter 1, for some feminists, these playwrights' reliance on stage realism invalidates their feminism and implicates them in the very cultural constructs they were trying to oppose. What these theorists sometimes overlook, I think, is that feminism is always contextual— a crucial issue in respecting the differences among women, as I hope this chapter on the Harlem Renaissance has clarified. Given the circumstances of a violently racist society, a black theatrical community in turmoil over how to define itself and its theater practice, and a shared commitment to women's issues specific to African-American communities and history, these four playwrights saw stage realism as an effective tool of resistance. Using realism's referential power, they could reach wide audiences (both black and white), depict existing racial and sexual persecution, protest injustice, counteract degrading stereotypes, and reclaim something of black women's unrecorded past.

Helene Keyssar's attention to the "hybrid consciousness" of African-American women (quoted in full above) suggests that employing a conventional tool of a repressive society—that is, using stage realism—may indicate neither a naiveté about representation on the parts of these playwrights nor a willingness to serve the status quo. Rather, one can see these dramatists as "cyborgs" (to borrow Donna Haraway's famous description of feminists), beings partially constructed by the culture they resist (as we all are) who use establishment tools for countercultural purposes. Haraway emphasizes that "cyborg" writing seizes all the methods of the patriarchy, particularly storytelling: "The [cyborg's] tools are often stories, retold stories, versions that reverse and displace the hierarchical dualism of naturalized identities. . . . Feminist cyborgs have the task of recoding communication and intelligence to subvert command and control" (217). In using conventional stage realism to depict positive images of blackness, to protest racial inequality, and to recreate legends that had been falsified, distorted, or forgotten, these feminist playwrights of the Harlem Renaissance were asserting their control over their own images; they were, in Haraway's terminology, "recoding" a system of communication. In viewing their realistic plays within the contexts for which they were created, we can participate in this activity—crucial, as hooks says, to overthrowing images that serve as "murder weapons"—of recognizing, understanding, respecting, and commemorating the feminist work of those who have been disremembered.

4

Refusing Containment

A story is always a question of desire. But whose desire is it that
speaks, and whom does that desire address?
                                        —de Lauretis 1984, 112

In chapter 2, I explored the ways realism could be used to represent
on stage the patriarchal systems of oppression that functioned offstage. Whether it be through the carefully orchestrated entrances
and exits in *The Eldest,* the dynamics of a repressive family unit in
Miss Lulu Bett, or the difficult choices faced by career women in *A
Man's World* and *The Flower Shop,* the realistic plays examined in
that chapter all document the confining cultural conditions in which
turn-of-the century women lived and against which they sometimes—
usually unsuccessfully—rebelled.

The plays I will discuss in this chapter document the social conditions of oppression as women playwrights see them fifty years later,
beginning in the mid-1960s and continuing to the present. A first,
dispiriting point these plays collectively make is that social restrictions upon women have not changed all that much since the Progressive Era. As my play analyses will demonstrate, family pressures,
class barriers, racial prejudices, limited economic opportunities, and
social and political limitations for women are still concerns uppermost
in these contemporary playwrights' dramatic explorations, regardless
of the historical time period (ranging from 1933 to the 1980s) in which
the plays themselves are set. Like the feminist realists of the 1910s,
'20s, and '30s, the playwrights discussed in this chapter all use the
closed structure and causal inevitability of realism to suggest the
social and cultural imprisonment of women in the (now postmodern)
world. In so doing, they partake of materialist feminism's project of
seeing women in social context and underscoring the roles of class,
race, and history in creating women's lives.

It is equally important to note, however, that these contemporary

feminist realists also depart from their early-twentieth-century counterparts in significant ways. Most obvious is their tendency to revise
realism, to expand its boundaries so as to include ideas and issues
that would be unavailable for exploration in a strictly Ibsenian realist
format. We saw in chapter 1 that realism is not the monolith for which
some critics have mistaken it. Rather, it has always been a flexible tool,
responsive to changing theatrical and social conventions. In some of
the plays I will discuss in this chapter, realistic structures such as
linearity and the fourth-wall barrier are interrupted by antimimetic
devices designed to express a character's memories or desires; in
others, realism's theatrical apparatus is emphasized in order to foreground the social systems of oppression that realism so uniquely represents. In short, the plays discussed here maintain the basic
framework of mimetic realism but also include experimental devices
that enlarge its horizons of concern.

Given the changing theatrical scene between the Progressive Era
and today, these modifications should not be surprising. As I noted
in chapter 1, the revived women's rights movement of the 1960s
emerged simultaneously with a new interest in innovative theater,
giving rise to playwrights who experimented with inherited forms
like realism (as well as to theorists who, because of the historical
confluence of the two forces, erroneously equate antimimesis with
political awareness). Eve Merriam described this renewed interest
in theatrical innovation as it occurred in the generation of women
playwrights that emerged with her in the 1960s and 1970s, explaining:
"First you had to write an Arthur Miller play, then you had to write an
absurd play. Now there is a new freedom—you can write empathetic
women characters" (in Moore xxix–xxx). This "new freedom" includes
the freedom to use traditional forms even while enlarging their
boundaries, the better to create those "empathetic" female characters
who refuse the confinements of patriarchal structures that realism
proposes.

But in this context of widening possibilities we should also notice
a third relevant development of the '60s: the explosion of feminist
theory that accompanied the new women's movement and avant-garde
theater. The feminist critique of realism that has emerged in the
past thirty years has been a direct result of this heightened feminist
awareness, this exploration of *everything*—from psychoanalytic theory to linguistics to cinema—from various feminist viewpoints. And
while I obviously question much of that feminist critique of realism,
many of the issues it raises are fundamental to current feminist thinking. In the late twentieth century, feminist (and other) theory itself
is a crucial component of the culture that realism purports to reflect.

One recurring concern of recent feminist theory will be of particular interest in exploring contemporary realist plays: the intertwined notions of subjectivity, narrativity, and desire. As suggested by the epigraph from Teresa de Lauretis with which this chapter began, feminists are becoming increasingly aware that female desires and feminist visions are rarely represented in drama and film. Of course, it is true that representing female desire, in and of itself, will not necessarily improve the social condition of women. In the first place, desire (like everything else about subjectivity) is increasingly understood to be a product of cultural interpellation, that is, to be at least partly constructed by dominant culture. And in the second place, as Peggy Phelan notes, "If representational visibility equals power, then almost-naked young white women should be running Western culture" (10), and clearly they are not. Nonetheless, the insertion of a desiring female subject into traditional structures (whether of language, literature, or drama) inevitably deforms the structure that originally repressed such subjectivity. Herein lies both the source of and the explanation for contemporary feminist playwrights' experimentation with realism.

The linguistic theories of Julia Kristeva provide a helpful analogue for understanding these processes. In "Revolution in Poetic Language," Kristeva suggests that the unified subject and orderly syntax of Platonic rationalism is always disrupted by desire. In Kristeva's linguistic model, signification is dependent on two processes: the semiotic (defined as a prelinguistic current of drives) and the symbolic (the logic and syntax of a coherent adult). Since all speaking subjects and all signifying practices are composed of both the semiotic and the symbolic, orderly symbolic systems are always already disrupted by the semiotic, a disruption that appears as a breach in or transgression of the symbolic order. And as Jeannie Forte has noted, these breaks in meaning allow "a possibility of authentic difference articulated as an alternative to the authoritative, Name-of-the-Father lingually-constructed society" (1988, 220–21).

In her later work, Kristeva goes so far as to associate the symbolic structures of linguistic communication with the phallus (1980, 165) and the semiotic, the "underside" of symbolic language, with the maternal. While I agree with Janelle Reinelt, who sees this formulation as "dangerously essentialistic" (1992, 387), the parallels to realistic dramatic structure, with its history of representing patriarchal domination of women, and the deformations of realist dramaturgy that emerge in the plays of some contemporary feminist-realist playwrights, are useful to explore. Kristeva notes:

> [I]n a culture where the speaking subjects are conceived of as masters of their speech, they have what is called a "phallic" position. The fragmentation of language in a text calls into question the very posture of this mastery. The writing that we have been discussing [i.e., texts with ruptures, blank spaces] confronts this phallic position either to traverse it or to deny it. (1980, 165)

In a realist dramatic text or performance, the ruptures to the phallic "master narrative" (Jameson 34) are represented by breaks in mimesis—flashbacks, split characters, direct address to the audience, and so on—that express the speaking subject's desires and indicate her refusal to be contained by the structures (social, theatrical) that encroach upon her. Using this combination of conventional realism and antimimetic devices, contemporary playwrights are collectively designing a new hybrid realism that speaks to both social oppression and individual subjectivity, even as it reveals that subjectivity (as we shall see) to be partly culturally constructed.

But Kristeva's example offers more than a paradigm, however apt, for understanding the complementary functions of realistic and antimimetic devices in contemporary women's plays. Kristeva also understands the political implications of her linguistic work, both on whole texts and on social formations in general, and her political insights are relevant to this study of realism. For Kristeva, poetic language—the expression of the semiotic through the symbolic—partakes of that symbolic ordering and thus "meets up with denotation and enunciation—verisimilitude and the subject—and, through them, the social" (1986, 110). As part of the dominant social order, both poetic language and mimesis, like the dramatic structures of oft-maligned realism,

> may appear as an argument complicitous with dogma—we are familiar with religion's use of them—but they may also set in motion what dogma represses. In so doing, they no longer act as instinctual floodgates within the enclosure of the sacred and become instead protestors against its posturing. And thus, its complexity unfolded by its practices, the signifying process joins social revolution. (1986, 112)

Given this inevitable connection of all signification to the patriarchal symbolic order, women writers who "flee everything considered 'phallic'" find themselves "abdicating any entry into history" (Kristeva 1980, 166) and thereby renouncing the possibility for insurrection.

Let us turn now to the exploration of four playwrights who chose *not* to abdicate a role in history, even if playing such a role demands some degree of participation in our culture's "master narratives." For while these playwrights all revise, to some degree, the form of realism they inherited, they do it in very different ways. Alice Childress's interest in Sean O'Casey—a playwright who used realism for radical political ends—led her to borrow a plot and character types from his plays, but to invest her lead female character with a voluble subjectivity that her model's clearly lacked. Barbara Lebow writes a traditional American family drama, yet disrupts the narrative with a female character's memories and desires that dismantle patriarchal authority and ultimately reconfigure the family itself. Marsha Norman and Wendy Kesselman actually foreground the restrictive properties of realism to emphasize female entrapment, but also show—both antimimetically and through realistic causality—the consequences of such repression on the individual psyche and the social foundation. Among them, these four playwrights offer a variety of feminist alternatives to conventional realism while making profound use of its inherent possibilities.

Revising the Masters: Alice Childress and the Social Construction of Identity

Alice Childress's *Wine in the Wilderness* (1969), unlike the other plays discussed later in this chapter, adheres to the formulas and conventions of dramatic realism without antimimetic exception. However, the play clearly offers a revision of the patriarchal, "Name-of-the-Father" content that such realistic structures are sometimes thought inevitably to uphold. In *Wine in the Wilderness*, Childress demonstrates that realism can be made to depict cultural context and expose its influence on individual identity—two clearly defined projects of materialist feminism. Furthermore, her play expresses a feminist vision, despite its roots in a conventional realism, since it focuses on a female character who refuses to be contained by others' definitions.

This revision of inherited realistic form can best be seen by comparing Childress's play to the work of Sean O'Casey, a self-identified materialist thinker, a master realist, and a playwright Childress openly admires. In a 1987 interview, Childress expressed her regard for the Irish playwright. Commenting on the importance of evoking the specific cultural context of a narrative, Childress remarked:

> I think there is something very particular about different races and religious backgrounds in America that has yet to be fully explored. . . . Some of the greatest plays have come from Sean O'Casey, *Irish* playwright, who wrote *about* the poor Irish, *for* the Irish. (in Betsko and Koenig 68)

The attraction an Irish playwright would have had for the African-American Childress is clear from her 1955 play *Trouble in Mind*, in which she equates the British rule imposed on Ireland with the cultural colonization of blacks by whites in twentieth-century America. In *Trouble in Mind*, Wiletta, an African-American actor, refuses to play the demeaning role of a "mammy" figure in a racist play. Abetted by the sympathy of an elderly Irish doorman who is proud that his ancestors fought for Irish home rule, Wiletta rejects her role in the potentially lucrative Broadway production, claiming, "I want to be an actress, I've always wanted to be an actress, and they ain't gonna do me the way they did the home rule!" (154). Wiletta's defiance of a stereotype that contradicts her sense of racial identity thus directly links British subjugation of the Irish people with white oppression of African Americans.

Reading Childress with this connection to home rule in mind, it becomes quite clear that O'Casey's *The Shadow of A Gunman* (1925) is the model for Childress's *Wine in the Wilderness* in terms of theme, setting, plot, characters, language, and final self-awareness of the central male character. *The Shadow of a Gunman* takes place in 1920s Dublin during the Sinn Fein rebellion against British rule of Ireland, and illustrates, in O'Casey's words, "the bewilderment and horror at one section of the community trying to murder and kill the other" (in Williams 1969, 148). The setting is a crowded, one-room tenement flat, residence of the would-be poet Donal Davoren. Davoren spends most of the day writing sentimental verse while ignoring the natural eloquence of his garrulous neighbors (whose frequent interruptions irritate him), priding himself on being "a pioneer in thought" rather than action, and studiously avoiding any connection to the personal and political life teeming around him. Convinced of his natural superiority to his fellow tenement dwellers, Davoren denounces them, declaiming: "Damn the people! They live in the abyss, the poet lives on the mountain-top; . . . The poet ever strives to save the people; the people ever strive to destroy the poet" (107). The irony of this statement becomes painfully clear at the play's end when Minnie Powell, a working-class neighbor who believes Davoren to be a rebel gunman in hiding, dies to protect him, leaving Davoren to moan his role as "poet and poltroon." As Raymond Williams has summed up the action of this play, "With real killing in the streets, the poverty and the pretence [sic] cross to make new inadvertent victims" (1969, 148).

Childress's *Wine in the Wilderness* is a very similar play, both structurally and thematically. Set in a one-room apartment in a Harlem tenement during a period of intraracial rioting in the 1960s, the play depicts the shift in self-awareness of Bill Jameson, an African-

American painter, who as the play begins is working on a three-part representation of black womanhood, from innocence (a portrait of a little girl) to experience (a "lost woman" or a "messed up chick," in Bill's parlance) to the jewel-studded, imperious, cold *Vogue* model who (for Bill) personifies wine in the wilderness. Like Davoren, Bill feels superior to those around him, criticizing the rioters for lacking a plan but refusing to take action himself. He takes Davoren's sense of superiority a step further, however, because he imagines his art as a corrective force, especially for black women. He hopes one day to exhibit his wine-in-the-wilderness triptych in a public place, perhaps a post office or a bank, "so the messed up chicks in the neighborhood can see what a woman ought to be" (389). As James Hatch has described him, Bill is one of E. Franklin Frazier's black bourgeoisie, educated but artificial, "preaching blackness, brotherhood, and love simply because it is in vogue" (737), decorating his apartment with African art while disparaging the African-American community around him.

Into this self-contained world enters Tommy Marie, a ghetto dweller whose home has been burned down in the riots and whom Bill's friends see as the perfect model for Bill's yet-to-be-painted "messed up chick." Like Minnie Powell in *The Shadow of a Gunman*, the uneducated, independent Tommy represents the undazzling tenement dwellers: she embodies their struggles, honesty, bravery, and eloquence, qualities lacking in the pretentious painter and unnoticed by him—at least, at first. Through his interactions with Tommy during the course of the play, Bill comes to recognize the emptiness of his artistic vision. This awareness comes, however, only after he and his friends misjudge, insult, and attempt to exploit Tommy, who suffers at their hands but, unlike Minnie Powell, survives. As in *Gunman*, in *Wine in the Wilderness* there is real killing in the streets, and poverty and pretense cross, but in Childress's play, Tommy Marie refuses to become another victim. Like Wiletta in *Trouble in Mind*, Tommy insists on defining herself and controlling how her representation is used; that is, she insists on defending her own home rule.

Tommy's struggle for home rule takes three distinct forms: she learns to challenge class assumptions, to expose racial bigotry, and to defy gender oppression. It is in the first of these three categories— class struggle—that Childress most clearly follows the O'Casey model: both plays show that assumptions about socioeconomic class status, whether true or false, can be used as implements of tyranny. In *The Shadow of a Gunman*, Minnie Powell is an uneducated, independent young woman who, in her words, has "had to push her way through life . . . without help from any one" (93) and who has developed, in O'Casey's words, "a force and assurance beyond her years" (88). To Davoren, however, she is only a pretty, flirtatious girl with the good taste to dress pleasingly, and while he is attracted to her, he laments her lack of education and allows his roommate to call her "an ignorant little bitch that thinks of nothin' but jazz dances" (108). Davoren condescends to her throughout their conversation, instructing her about the nature of poetry and poetic inspiration, and even fostering her romantic illusion that he is a gunman. In short, he cannot see Minnie's strength and heart beneath her working class speech and girlish appearance.

Tommy is similarly misinterpreted by Bill, who sees only a reflection of his middle-class assumptions in her appearance and behavior. Prepared to see the "messed up chick" his elitist friends Sonny and Cynthia have promised to bring him, Bill overlooks the fact that Tommy, like Minnie, has been "doin' for [herself]" all her life (397), and sees only her "messed up" appearance, the result of her home's being burned down in the riots. When he offers her a choice of alcoholic beverages and she chooses wine so as not to become quickly intoxicated (the others are drinking looted whiskey), Bill delightedly tells her, "That's all right, baby, you just a wine-o" (391). When he hears her name, Tommy, he jumps to the conclusion that her full name is the stereotypical Thomasina, which it is not. When Tommy doesn't recognize a portrait of Frederick Douglass, Bill lectures her on historical figures (Frederick Douglass, John Brown) and dismisses the contemporary leaders (Martin Luther King, Malcolm X) whom Tommy admires. Like Davoren, Bill wants no connection with the politics of the day. And just as Davoren's underestimation of Minnie ultimately produces powerful irony for the spectator, so does Bill's smugly maintained false impression of Tommy. Bill knows that the "messed-up chick" he plans to paint is a victim of hardship and suffering; he describes this abstract African-American woman as "The lost woman . . . what the society has made out of our women" (388). However, he fails to see—at least, until Tommy shocks him into awareness—either the strength and independence such women have developed or his own role in perpetuating their hardships. Through Tommy's eventual unmasking of Bill's pretensions, Childress reveals her own materialist roots, portraying, in her words, "have-nots in a *have* society" (1984, 112) and illustrating their dignity and strength in the face of condescension and contempt.

In addition to the class issues developed in both plays, both also explore the cultural construction of race, revealing self-definition in racial terms to be crucial to individual home rule. This linking of Irish and African-American racial identity has historical precedent, since both groups have suffered demeaning racial definitions imposed by dominant groups within their own homelands, and both groups have often been discussed in the same prejudicial language. In mid-nineteenth-century Britain, for example, Victorian scientists sometimes divided humanity into races according to physical features that, in their taxonomy, also represented differences in character. Their hierarchy of races located blue-eyed Teutons and Anglo-Saxons at the top, black peoples—especially "Hottentots"—at the bottom, with Celts and Jews somewhere in between (London Against Racism Campaign 55). Self-determination for the Irish would be impossible, according to this line of reasoning, because the Irish had certain affinities with "Africanoid" humans and so lacked understanding of rational liberty and self-government (Curtis 69–73). In 1886, for example, Lord Salisbury opposed home rule for Ireland by saying, "You would not confide free representative institutions to the Hottentots, for instance," and concluded that self-government worked well only for the "higher" races (in London Against Racism Campaign 57). Throughout the century English comparisons between Irish people and black people abounded, perhaps culminating with historian Edward Freeman's remark that "This would be a grand land if only every Irishman would kill a negro, and be hanged for it" (in Curtis 81).[1]

This Victorian hierarchy of races parallels the paternalistic arguments about racial inferiority that helped perpetuate the enslavement of black people in the United States through several centuries.[2] Since blacks were purported to be intellectually and morally inferior to whites and thus incapable of maintaining or governing themselves, and since anyone with even a drop of African-American blood was, by definition, black,[3] blackness in this country is quite clearly "a political and ethical construct" rather than a matter of skin color or cultural identification (West 25–26). Within this historical context, the notion of race is revealed as an artificial construct developed originally to protect property values. And in our still-racist, late-twentieth-century society, accepting blackness as a fixed and essentialized racial identity means being "subject to potential white supremacist abuse" (West 25).[4]

In exposing racial identity as a cultural construct designed to maintain an unequal balance of power, Childress again follows O'Casey's model, although she develops the theme more explicitly than he did. In *The Shadow of a Gunman* all the characters are Irish. Nonetheless, they spend a great deal of energy defining what "Irishness" actually comprises. From the opening scene of the play, Davoren and his roommate, Seumas Shields, criticize what they see as typical Irish character flaws. "The Irish people are still in the Stone Age," Shields complains when a neighbor wakes him by bellowing loudly (80). Later, when a business partner breaks an engagement, Shields laments, "Upon me soul, I'm beginning to believe that the Irish people aren't, never were, an' never will be fit for self-government" (84). While Shields's remarks are parodic, an ironic commentary on cultural stereotypes, they do suggest the way such stereotypes can be internalized and retain power even if home rule is won. And despite his comic pose regarding the various alleged forms of Irish incompetence, when the rioting comes to his own tenement, Shields reveals his dismay at the Irish civil strife: "I believe in the freedom of Ireland," he tells Davoren, "an' that England has no right to be here, but I draw the line when I hear the gunmen blowin' about dyin' for the people, when it's the people that are dyin' for the gunmen" (111). For Shields, then, the rebel gunmen are *not* Irish. Cultural identity for him thus depends on actions and words rather than on national origin; it is performative rather than a static identity position.

Childress's characters, like O'Casey's, share a racial heritage—in this case, African-Americanness. How they describe and enact that identity varies among them, however, suggesting that Childress shared O'Casey's materialist awareness that race is constructed for political ends. Moreover, the different definitions of blackness circulated among the characters form another source of oppression that, like class status, Tommy must recognize and renounce. As exemplified by their different political heroes (i.e., Frederick Douglass versus Malcolm X), Bill and Tommy disagree on what exactly it means to be black in America. For Bill, racial identity consists of decorating his apartment with African artifacts, reading books about African-American history, and fantasizing about Abyssinian maidens as exemplars of "perfect black womanhood" (387). When Tommy first enters and complains about the "niggers" that burned down her house, Bill insists that she use the term "Afro-Americans," explaining that "we can talk about each other a little better than that" (392). For Tommy, though, blackness is not art, history, or words, but lived experience and cultural heritage: it comprises family members who are Elks (originally a black organization, according to Tommy); membership in the African Methodist Episcopal Zion Church; family roots traced back to a specific Virginia plantation; and sharing what one has managed to retain after being victimized in a riot. At first, Tommy defers to Bill's notions and vocabulary, but when she learns that he had planned to use her as a model of black female degradation, she discredits his notion of African-American identity, crying:

If a black somebody is in a history book, or printed in a pitcher, or drawed on a paintin' . . . or if they're a statue, . . . dead, and outta the way, and can't talk back, then you dig 'em and full-a so much damn admiration and talk about "our" history. But when you run into us livin' and breathin' ones, with the life's blood still pumpin' through us, . . . then you comin' on 'bout we ain't never together. You hate us, that's what! You hate black me! (417)

For Tommy, race is a set of support structures designed to promote community and ease the effects of racism, and she distinguishes it from the false solidarity to which Bill and his friends give only lip service. Although for a time she wears the African robes that Bill provides for her, Tommy ultimately refuses to accept the trappings of blackness that, in the cases of Bill and his friends, signify nothing. In exposing Bill's concept of race as just another method for claiming authority, Childress reveals race as "a highly contested representation of power" (Higginbotham 253) that is "historically specific and inconsistent" (Lubiano 1991, 256). Although the playwright herself does not intrude into the seamless theatrical production of meaning—that is, she does not break the realistic frame—she does use Tommy to intervene in the constructions of race and class and so expose them as implements of social hierarchies.

But class and race are not the only factors by which Bill attempts to colonize Tommy when she enters his apartment. Gayle Austin has pointed out that "The sign of 'Woman' in this play bears the double cultural encoding of black in a white-dominant culture and female in a male-dominant one" (1990, 91), and Tommy suffers just as much from gender discrimination as she does from class prejudice or imposed racial definitions. That Bill thinks he can define ideal black female behavior is clear from his initial plans to use the triptych to show the neighborhood women "what a woman ought to be" (389). While Tommy poses for him, Bill tries to indoctrinate her on the trouble with African-American women: they eat too much, they don't know "a damn thing 'bout bein' feminine" (406), they are "too damn opinionated" (406), they want to "latch on" to a man (407), and, worst of all, they "all want to be great brains" instead of leaving "somethin' for a man to do" (405). But Bill's extravagant chauvinism cannot simply be chalked up to personal failing in this play. It is shared by Oldtimer, who prepares for Tommy's arrival by planning to "stomp her to death"; by Sonny, who orders Cynthia to cook for the others without even noticing her ironic response; and by Cynthia herself, who in a particularly disturbing scene instructs Tommy on how to attract a man. In Cynthia's reasoning, self-sufficiency "makes us [black women] lose our femininity. . . . It makes us hard" (399). She advises Tommy to stay in the background, to ask Bill's opinion before offering her own. For Cynthia, "what [black women] need is a little more sex appeal and a little less washing, cooking, and ironing" (400), and she ignores Tommy's rebuttal that if she doesn't do for herself, no one else will do for her (399). This conflict between two female characters over the nature of black womanhood underscores Childress's feminism as well as her commitment to exposing the cultural construction of identity positions.

In fact, both Cynthia and Tommy suffer from conflicting expectations of gender, class, and racial roles, and their very different physical appearances reveal that they are both trying to function within competing sign systems designed for different audiences. Cynthia, for example, wears her hair in a natural style, indicating (in the 1960s) acceptance of her African heritage and the beauty of blackness. Her clothing, however, is described as "tweedy" and "in quiet, good taste" (390), suggesting white American bourgeois values. Tommy, in contrast, wears a mis-matched skirt and sweater, signifying to Bill and company her poverty, her lack of taste, or both, but not the truth—that she is a victim of intraracial violence. Furthermore, she wears a cheap wig to hide her hair and because she is confused by the mixed cultural codes—"Do it this way, don't do it, leave it natural, straighten it, process, no process" (400)—that society transmits to black women of any class. In this way, Childress reveals that "sexism, racism, and classism are immutably connected to black women's oppression" (Brown-Guillory 1990, 106).

It is in depicting women's oppression that Childress most notably departs from O'Casey's dramatic model. She does this in several ways. First and most obviously, while O'Casey's Minnie and Childress's Tommy both function as catalysts for self-awareness in central male figures, Minnie acts out of ignorance (she believes Davoren is a revolutionary) and dies as a result. Tommy, on the other hand, not only survives, she lives to tell off her would-be exploiters and profit by the experience, walking out, as she says, "with much more than I brought in" (419). Through her interaction with Bill and the others, she comes to recognize the value of defining herself on her own terms. At the end of the play she tells Bill:

I don't have to wait for anybody's by-your-leave to be a "Wine In The Wilderness" woman. I can be if I wanta, . . . and I *am*. I am. I am. I'm not the one you made up and painted, the very pretty lady who can't talk back, . . . but I'm "Wine In The Wilderness" . . . alive and kickin'. (419)

Since Tommy does not share Minnie's enforced silence at the play's conclusion, the realistic closure that Childress inherited from

O'Casey is breached, the play deformed (as Kristeva would have it) by Tommy's outspoken desires—a feminist disruption of the master text. This disruption is powerful in Childress's play; as Gayle Austin notes of Tommy's impassioned speeches on her own behalf, "It is difficult to misinterpret a sign that speaks so forcefully of its signification" (1990, 91).

This shift in who controls Tommy's subjectivity and who defines what she represents signals Childress's second major departure from O'Casey. In *The Shadow of a Gunman*, Minnie forces Davoren to recognize his cowardice and impotence, but this is a purely personal shift in awareness. In contrast, Tommy pushes Bill to both a revised self-awareness and also a revitalized recognition of the political functions of art. He ends up envisioning a new triptych, not one designed to educate black women on their proper social roles, but one meant to celebrate the power and beauty that already exist in the African-American community. His new triptych features three new paintings: one of Oldtimer, representing "the guy who was here before there were scholarships and grants and stuff like that, the guy they kept outta the schools" (420); one of Cynthia and Sonny-Man, "Young Man and Woman, workin' together to do our thing" (421); and in the center Tommy as she is, a survivor of everything from riots and exploitation to misinterpretation and abuse. This time, Bill intends his painting to be displayed in his own community, so the neighborhood children can see the portrait and say, "Hey, don't she look like somebody we know?" (421). In short, Bill no longer attempts to impose a personal ideology on the representations he paints, recognizing now that meaning derives from social context.

This use of art as an agent of social change is, in part, what Alice Childress has done herself in *Wine in the Wilderness*. As a materialist like O'Casey but with a feminist perspective, Childress has created an artistic representation of a world where there is killing in the streets, where poverty and pretense meet, but where strong, self-sufficient women have a potent voice that can lead the way toward social change. Childress's play uncovers the characteristic assumption of the middle class that their beliefs are not conventions, but truths, and reveals the inclusions and exclusions that specific cultural conventions, racial definitions, and gender expectations ratify. The facts that her plot is linear and causally structured, that her setting is a domestic space, that her characters appear to be coherent, and that the action pretends to mimesis—in short, the fact that the play exemplifies well-crafted realism—does not diminish the materialist-feminist nature of the work or detract from its political message.

Revising the Family: Barbara Lebow's A Shayna Maidel

In her 1986 drama A *Shayna Maidel*, Barbara Lebow uses the conventions of realism to tell the story of a young Jewish woman named Rose White (formerly Rayzel Weiss), who, in New York in 1946, is struggling to maintain her independence from her tyrannical father, Mordechai Weiss. As the play begins, Rose learns that her sister Lusia, a Holocaust survivor, will soon arrive in New York. Because the two sisters were separated at an early age when Mordechai brought Rose to the United States (Lusia had scarlet fever, so she and her mother remained behind), they begin the play as strangers, struggling to understand each other. By the end of the play, however, they have shared their memories of their mother (who was killed in a death camp, and whom Rose remembers only dimly), worked together to find Lusia's husband Duvid, stood up to their father together, and so created the sisterly bonds that they never got to form as separated children. Despite the power of the Holocaust background and the pain of all Lusia has suffered, the play focuses on the family rather than the historical context. In the production notes the playwright warns that "The characters should be perceived by actors and director simply as members of a family who cannot communicate."

Because of its focus on the family unit, A *Shayna Maidel* may look, at first glance, as if it falls captive to all the dangers of realism against which some feminist critics warn us. It certainly falls into the category of Holocaust drama that, as Elinor Fuchs notes somewhat disparagingly, shows "catastrophic historical events as the private experience of individuals or families" rather than as a "collective catastrophe . . . summoned . . . in an historical, cultural, or metaphysical totality" (xii). However, the play engages in a critical revision of several issues seen as fundamental to realism and therefore antithetical to feminism: it challenges what the nuclear family consists of and how it should function, and it revises the dramatic structures of realism to permit alternative, "deforming" visions to emerge. Furthermore, in its alterations of inherited dramatic form the play provides room for Lusia's subjective visions, memories, and desires to exist on stage, sharing the set of Rose's apartment with the other, present and substantial characters. In this way the play extends the nuclear family that the play depicts, suggesting that the concept of the family is itself in crisis and must be re-evaluated and revised in light of cultural conditions.

The set provides the first example of Lebow's use of and alterations to realism. After a brief prologue depicting the birth of Mordechai in a Polish village in 1876, the rest of the play takes place in the domestic setting typical of realism: the kitchen, bedroom, and living room of Rose's apartment are all visible and all created in realistic detail. But from the opening scene of the present action, when Mordechai brings Rose the news of Lusia's imminent arrival, we see the differences between *this* realistic play and those that take place in a traditional, nuclear-family home. This apartment is Rose's private space, separate from her father and the home he shares with the Greenspans (who helped raise Rose). And while her father does exercise substantial control over Rose—he orders her to share her small apartment with Lusia, to take off two weeks from work to help Lusia acclimate herself to New York, to eat dinner at a restaurant after she has spent the day cooking a pot roast—it is Rose who controls what happens in her apartment between his visits. Mordechai may be an autocrat, but he does not fully control the space in which the play takes place. Obviously, the nuclear family has been disrupted by more than the war in Europe.

The explicit contrast between Rose and Lusia in their relationships with their father is perhaps the clearest indication that Lebow is questioning the efficacy of the nuclear family in this play. Rose, having been raised by the domineering Mordechai, is struggling to maintain her independence—some form of "home rule," as we saw in the case of Childress's Tommy. She has moved into her own apartment and Americanized her name, two actions that reveal her attempts to define her own subjectivity. Until Lusia arrives, however, Rose is only partly successful. Having been raised by a traditional father, she uses the stereotypically "female" method of silent subversion to resist Mordechai's control: she claims falsely to keep a kosher kitchen, hides evidence to the contrary when he arrives, and acquiesces pleasantly in his plans (such as a proposed visit to the Greenspans from which he excludes her) even when they run contrary to her own desires. In short, she does the best she can to define herself on her own terms while maintaining surface peace with Mordechai.

Lusia, who was raised by her mother apart from patriarchal control, responds to Mordechai very differently, although she remembers his autocratic ways. She tells Rose, "This I remember good about Papa. He gets so mad. He makes a big voice, everybody is . . . Nervous" (26). She also remembers that her mother was different, freer, after Mordechai left for the United States: "She's different without Papa here. She sings. And she never made jokes when he was around. I don't remember her laughing out loud" (31). In part because she saw these positive changes in her mother, and in part because, through her Holocaust experiences, Lusia has learned how to survive on her own, she resists Mordechai, albeit politely. When he demands that she accompany him on a visit, she acquiesces, as Rose would do. However, when he insists that she wear one of Rose's coats, she adamantly refuses, asserting, "I'm going with you like you want. I don't wear no coat" (58). Mordechai, "taken aback," nonetheless accedes to her wishes.

Lusia's primary subversion of Mordechai's self-interested control comes late in the play, when he reveals that he has acquired a letter from their deceased mother and has withheld it from Rose—to whom it is addressed—for several months. Angered by this evidence of his capricious control, Lusia reveals to Rose that Mordechai had been given the opportunity to bring Lusia and her mother to the United States before the Nazi invasion, but refused to borrow the money necessary to do so. This knowledge, along with the loving letter from her mother (which Rose asks Lusia, not her father, to translate), enables Rose to break free from her father's control. Her handing the letter to Lusia is the first independent action we see Rose take (her apartment and name change having been accomplished prior to the play's action). The play thus traces Rose's movement from isolation (her solitary apartment) to voluntary connection (with her sister and her mother), from ignorance of her past to an understanding of it. It also suggests that bonding to other women is crucial to female identity formation, but must be freely chosen, not enforced.

In addition to revising the patriarchal family structure thought to be inherent to realism, Lebow embeds antimimetic devices into the realistic framework of her play. Like most American plays, *A Shayna Maidel* disrupts the linearity and apparent seamlessness of realism to incorporate both the past and the future in the present time of the play.[5] Eight of the fifteen scenes in the play include either Lusia's fantasies about her future with Duvid or her memories of girlhood, incarceration, and eventual release. In these scenes, ghosts from the past walk through Rose's apartment. Their appearance is indicated by changes in lighting or music, but in the playwright's notes Lebow cautions, "Imagined characters should appear realistically within scenes, not be removed by scrims or other illusions." This "realistic" appearance of characters who exist only in Lusia's mind suggests several things. First, Lusia's memories, dreams, and desires are an ongoing component of her present; they are as important to her as Rose and Mordechai are, and as much a part of her daily life. By including them as active agents in the play, Lebow permits the audience to share in their reality. Second, Lusia's refusal to confine herself to the realistically portrayed present suggests the agency of her desires, especially when she says things like, "I am remembering . . . something . . . that is gonna happen" (53; ellipsis in original). Given Lusia's frequent entries into her remembered and imagined worlds (that is, into the semiotic level of her reality, made visible before us), a breach of patriarchal order—whether the symbolic level of communication that Kristeva invokes or the Name-of-the-Father authority demanded by Mordechai and suggested by the realistic format—becomes inevitable.

Lusia's subjective reality is not the only one included in this otherwise realistically constructed world, however. On one occasion, early in act 2, Rose is haunted by the sound of a child crying "Mama." After searching the apartment for a small intruder, she suddenly catches a glimpse of herself in the downstage "mirror"—that is, she "turns toward the audience to see herself" (59). Having done so, she realizes that the child is her repressed memory of her young self returning to her, that *she* is the one crying, even if her eyes are now dry. Not only does this small scene reveal that Rose's memories of and connection to her mother are being restored by her sister's presence, it suggests the difficulty she faces throughout the play in constructing identity independent of others. She can change her name and leave her father's home, but only by peering in the mirror of some other's gaze can she see who she is. In this way, the play reveals identity to be culturally constructed rather than independently chosen, even as it suggests the value of attempts—even futile attempts—to create identity out of one's subjective desires.

Given all this attention throughout the play to identity formation, subversions of the patriarchy, and subjective interventions into the "objective" world of realism, the ending of the play may seem a contradiction, a return to the status quo that the play has challenged. Lusia finds Duvid, who arrives at Rose's apartment. To cover the awkwardness of their reconciliation after so long and painful a separation, Lusia imagines a party in which her parents, her childhood friend Hanna, and her sister all partake, and which the audience witnesses. While this convivial community may be seen once again as Lusia's desire disrupting the coherent surface reality of her life, the re-establishment of family order that it proffers is reiterated a moment later as the fantasy party fades but Mordechai and Rose enter, and all four characters embrace. This apparent return to the familial status quo, like Mama's letter to Rose, led one critic to wax eloquent about "the durability of the family bond" presented by the play (Gussow C16).

Despite this apparent reconciliation of the family, however, significant changes have been made. Mother is permanently absent, due in large part to Mordechai's nonaction on her behalf. Lusia's psyche, represented antimimetically, is certainly fractured, and her resistance to her father's whims is not likely to decrease. Rose, too, has changed, with memories of her mother and strategies for defying her father newly at her disposal. Most importantly, as Vivian Patraka has suggested about other Holocaust dramas, patriarchy and fascism are revealed throughout *A Shayna Maidel* to be intimately connected (1987, 68), since in this play both are depicted as "inherently malevolent and prone to hostility" (Isser 139). While the ending may suggest temporary respite from this hostility, the Holocaust background, the repeated tyrannies of Mordechai, the subversive actions of Lusia, and the growing awareness of Rose all suggest that the ending is provisional, the status quo an uneasy and temporary respite from the reality the characters have endured and will continue to share.

In the next section of this chapter, I examine two plays that share certain themes and techniques with *A Shayna Maidel* and *Wine in the Wilderness:* they expose identity as a cultural construct, use realism to depict social pressures and cultural expectations, and depart from realism to reveal the psychological realities of damaged female characters as well as the desires repressed by social restrictions. These plays move a step beyond the adaptations used by Lebow in that they *emphasize* the restrictions of realism to mirror social restrictions on their characters. What Lebow has uniquely contributed to this discussion, though, is an investigation of the American patriarchy as capricious, violent, and detrimental to women and girls. In *A Shayna Maidel* Lebow has reconfigured the American family to show the terrors of patriarchal tyranny and the contrary importance of female bonding in the development of an ever-elusive female identity. *A Shayna Maidel* is therefore a radically feminist play—despite its realistic framework—in its critique of the sacred doctrines of patriarchal ideology.

Revising the Picture Frame: *Getting Out* and *My Sister in This House*

Marsha Norman's *Getting Out* (1978) and Wendy Kesselman's *My Sister in This House* (1982) provide the strongest examples of a modified realism well suited for expressing feminist visions: neither play succumbs to the potential reinscription of the status quo that some commentators (I think mistakenly) see in *A Shayna Maidel*, nor does either play adhere so strictly to the inherited form as does *Wine in the Wilderness*. Rather, Norman's and Kesselman's plays share not only a realistic format, but a *foregrounded* realism, in which the apparatus of stage realism—the proscenium arch, the details of set, and so on—are emphasized as theatrical metaphors for the cultural confinement of women. Within this restricted world, however, the agency of female characters' desires is represented antimimetically (as in Lebow's play), but with as much more attention to varying expressionistic techniques (from a divided protagonist to scenes presented out of sequence to pantomime) as to underscoring realism. Using this unique complex of intersecting dramatic forms, these two playwrights illustrate the cultural construction of social roles and individual subjectivity as well as the ultimate consequences—psychic for Norman and social for Kesselman—of living in a repressive environment.

Marsha Norman's *Getting Out* depicts the twenty-four hours following Arlene Holsclaw's release from a state prison. Although Arlene is legally free as the play begins, she is still surrounded by systems of enclosure. The set, which is divided into two parts, makes this point clear. The central performing area represents a cheap apartment, with conventional (if tawdry) accoutrements—bed, chair, sink, and so on—and the usual imaginary fourth wall. Around this realistic set, however, Norman erects yet another playing area, a catwalk of stairs and prison cells that completely surrounds the apartment. This playing area is both literal and metaphorical: it is used to enact remembered scenes from Arlene's prison days, but it also visually illustrates the restrictions placed on Arlene in the world outside the prison. By constructing a prison-like, interior proscenium arch to parallel the exterior arch of the stage, Norman has made visible in a theatrical context Arlene's continuing imprisonment in limited and limiting social roles.

The metaphor of theater as prison is extended in the opening speeches. Each of the two acts begins with prison announcements, broadcast throughout the theater by an unseen prison official. Because the house lights remain up during these announcements, the audience is included among the prisoners who listen and must comply with the instructions. We cannot sit comfortably in the darkness, watching as outsiders, but must share the prisoners' degrading lack of privacy and individuality.[6]

The content of the announcements suggests the many subtle ways that Arlene and her fellow inmates are restricted, even beyond the physical confinement represented by the boxed-in set. First the announcer lists a series of prohibitions: no library hours, no walking on the lawn, no using the picnic tables. Prison excludes freedom of choice. The announcer next reports that the prison exercise instructor, Mrs. Fischer, has given birth to a daughter. Her comment that Mrs. Fischer "thanks you for your cards and wants all her girls to know she had an eight-pound baby girl" reflects the prevailing paternalistic attitude toward the inmates, who are here equated linguistically with an infant. Then, after announcing three times that Frances Mills has a visitor, the broadcaster corrects herself: it is Frankie Hill, not Frances Mills, who has a visitor. This slip of the tongue reveals the loss of individual identity that accompanies the prisoners' loss of freedom.

Arlene's life outside the prison (at least on this first day) remains uncomfortably like the life inside suggested by these announcements. When she wants to remove the burglar-proof bars that line her apartment window, she is told that "The landlord owns the building. You gotta do what he says or he'll throw you out" (9). When Carl, her former pimp, arrives to entice her back to work for him, he scoffs at her plan to work at a legitimate job and spend her free time playing cards and watching television; "Sounds just like the dayroom in the fucking joint," he remarks (55). And when her neighbor Ruby, also a former prisoner, explains that life as a dishwasher is at least life outside a prison, Arlene retorts:

Outside? Honey, I'll either be in this apartment or inside some kitchen sweatin over the sink. Outside's where you get to do what you want, not where you gotta do some shit job jus so's you can eat worse than you did in prison. (59)

It is no wonder that Arlene feels as trapped outside a prison as she did inside one: her apartment and her limited options represent continued imprisonment, reflected visually in Norman's doubled proscenium arch.[7]

The chronological plot, familiar characters, and conventional dialogue of Arlene's day of release—all devices of traditional stage realism—also underscore her ongoing confinement. Each visitor to her apartment reminds Arlene of her history of oppression and of the present restrictions to her behavior. Benny, a former prison guard who has driven Arlene home, attempts to rape her, thereby recapitulating both her father's sexual abuse and the degrading voyeurism of the prison guards, who installed a two-way mirror in the inmates' shower. Carl, who accurately assesses Arlene's inability to earn a decent wage legally ("You come with me and you'll have money," he tells her. "You stay here, you won't have shit"—55) recalls the economic powerlessness that first drove Arlene to crime. Her mother, appearing ostensibly to help Arlene get settled in her apartment, refuses to invite Arlene home for Sunday dinner. Her explanation—

"I still got two kids at home. Don't want no bad example" (23)—
illustrates clearly Arlene's rejection by her family and by traditional
society at large. Just as the set emphasizes Arlene's continuing confinement, so the linear chain of the day's events suggests that her
options are limited and that she will be forever imprisoned by others'
expectations of her.

These recurring structures of confinement in *Getting Out* also reveal how little power Arlene has to construct her own identity. Questions of subjectivity, of how one defines oneself, arise throughout the
play, starting with the mature Arlene's rejection of the name "Arlie,"
a preference most of the other characters ignore. This question of
who controls Arlene's identity, her subjectivity, has been addressed
by several commentators. Madonne Miner argues convincingly that
the play offers no possibility for the creation of female subjectivity at
all, that it critiques three of "the most sacred tenets of capitalistic,
patriarchal ideology": that an individual may construct his/her own
identity; that identity is coherent; and that individuals can make
choices reflecting their desires (116–17). Jenny Spencer concurs, examining the male characters in the play and noting that "Arlene's
female identity is shaped, damaged, conditioned and reconstructed
by and *for* the representatives of patriarchal authority," making a
separation between self and sexual identity impossible for Arlene
(154). The repeated attention to the limited possibilities of Arlene's
already-restricted choices further emphasize what the plot and other
characters reveal: "Like inside, outside traps us behind bars—bars
composed not of iron but of ideology" (Miner 126).

Within the realistic set and chronological plot with which she demonstrates this cultural interpellation and restricted freedom, however,
Norman has experimented with dramatic form. These deviations from
realism show Arlene's interior reality and the emotional effects of her
lifetime of imprisonments. Most obvious is her creation of a separate,
younger Arlene—the wild, incorrigible "Arlie"—who, as John Simon
puts it, "rampages" through the prison scenes, in Arlene's memory,
and on stage for the audience (84). At the simplest level, Arlie represents Arlene's past. Although Arlie's words and actions are relegated
to the prison "surround" or are ignored by the characters who cannot
see her in the apartment, she and Arlene both face the same sources
of oppression, often suggested in parallel scenes of sexual, economic,
or familial exploitation.

Arlie is more than an innovative expository device, however. Since
she is played by a separate actor who often occupies the stage in
conjunction with the actor playing Arlene, Arlie represents a split in
Arlene, a rupture of personality that, like Lusia's, is the result of her

oppression—what Rosemary Curb might call "a mirroring of multiple selves in imprisoning cells" (1985, 308). In a provocative analysis of such fragmented female characters, Sue-Ellen Case has argued that a female character must necessarily undergo a double splintering to become a speaking subject. Case begins with Lacan's premise that all speaking subjects suffer a split between their sense of their own subjectivity and their position as a speaker in linguistic discourse. According to Case, female speakers undergo yet another rupturing of self between the subject position (a place in the symbolic order) and femaleness (that which the symbolic order represses). A character like Arlene is thus forced to enter the signifying system as a male-identified hooligan (like Arlie), but in order to mature and identify as a woman, she must "struggle with that earlier identification, both to overcome it and to retain its power" (Case 1989a, 132). This is precisely Arlene's predicament. Arlie may well "rampage" in Arlene's memory, but Arlene has had to develop a socially acceptable demeanor to escape incarceration without losing all her personal power. Arlie's presence on stage thus illustrates the repercussions for oppressed women of living in a society where even limited choice depends on painful adaptation.

Arlene is able to inhabit the subject position in the play as a result of another of Norman's structural experiments: the achronology of events. Arlie emerges on stage when scenes from the past disrupt the present day. The order of events presented mirrors Arlene's memory rather than an externally verifiable sequence of events or a reality that all the characters share. Arlene thus becomes a producer of meaning, not the cultural construct that the play's realistic elements and the other characters demand she be. As a result of Arlie's presence, we are able to witness the past events and external forces that drove Arlene to crime; recognize the psychological effects of abuse, restricted opportunities, and imprisonment embodied in Arlene's double consciousness; and share Arlene's past and present struggle to maintain some of Arlie's courage while developing a mature identity. While Arlie as she existed in the past may have been the male-identified ruffian determined to enter discourse, Arlie as she exists in Arlene's memory represents a field of untamed desires. Thus with the appearances onstage of this remembered Arlie, the semiotic enters and, once again, disrupts the orderly, symbolic level of the play's signification.

By the end of the play, however, Arlene does emerge as a mature, less divided character. Arlie, who sat center stage in the opening scene of the play, has been banished to the prison catwalk of Arlene's memory, even though the play ends with Arlene (now center stage herself) reminiscing about her younger avatar. Arlene is finally able to accept the conditions of her life and control them when possible, as we see when she firmly rejects both Benny and Carl. What has brought about this change in Arlene? *Getting Out* abounds in images of entrapment and offers no real chance for escape. Where has Arlene gathered her new strength?

The answer to this question is twofold. First, Arlene has seen the value of autonomy. Although she recognizes that she will not have extra money, fine friends, or the company of her family (even her son has been taken from her), she discovers that, on the "outside," "when you make your two nickels, you can keep both of em" (59). Even though the play, with its split subject, seriously questions the possibility of creating a single, stable identity that such autonomy may very well require, it is similar to *A Shayna Maidel* in positing value for the individual, however shifting and fragmented she may be, in attempting independence from the ties that bind.

A second source of strength for Arlene is her relationship with Ruby. Despite her initial rejection of her neighbor's overtures at friendship, Arlene comes to value the companionship and sympathy of a woman who, like her, has lived a lifetime of varied imprisonments, and who will not exploit or demean her as every other character in the play attempts to do. Lynda Hart has argued that Ruby provides the most important element of Arlene's rehabilitation, that Arlene needs "female nourishment" to integrate her two selves (1987, 74). Indeed, Ruby promotes Arlene's acceptance of her younger, wilder self, reminding her that "you can still love people that's gone" (75). As the play ends, Arlene accepts Ruby's supportive friendship. With Ruby's help, Arlene resolves to exercise those few options open to her and make the most of her meager economic opportunities. In this play, then, as in *A Shayna Maidel*, freely chosen female bonding provides (paradoxically) a path to the self.

It is true, as Helene Keyssar has pointed out, that a realistically constructed play like *Getting Out* can offer no solution or alternative to class- and gender-based hierarchies (1985, 150). However, because it infiltrates the narrative order of realism with antimimetic devices designed to reveal the costs and repercussions of such hierarchies, *Getting Out* avoids duplicating the patriarchal subjection of its main character (Worthen 1992, 183). Instead, *Getting Out* illustrates that a flexible realism can challenge the values encoded and disseminated by a patriarchal culture, assess the consequences of oppression by powerful cultural agents, and simultaneously support the alternative values—such as economic autonomy and female community—that feminism espouses.

Wendy Kesselman's *My Sister in This House* also uses an innovative combination of formal realism and experimental techniques to depict the harmful effects of restricting women's lives. In this play, based on the same true story that inspired Jean Genet's *The Maids*, the central characters are not literally imprisoned, but the forces that entrap them are just as potent and even more pervasive, and the consequences—for them as well as for their society—are even more disastrous.

The central characters are sisters, Christine and Lea Lutton, who work as servants in the home of Madame Danzard and her daughter Isabelle. The four women could live together in harmony, and Kesselman uses a number of parallel scenes to establish the correspondences of taste, habit, and experience between them (Hart 1989, 139; Mandl 249). Despite their similarities, however, the two sets of women inhabit different parts of the house, and the class distinction thereby preserved (and illustrated in the set) permanently segregates them. Like the set of *Getting Out*, that of *My Sister in This House* is a realistic representation of a divided world. One half of the stage depicts the elegant sitting/dining room of the Danzards; the other half, the kitchen where the Luttons work. Separating the two worlds is a staircase leading up to the tiny, unheated bedroom that Christine and Lea share. While their catwalk cell may not have the bars that Arlene's did, Christine and Lea are nonetheless imprisoned within its confines.

The basic plot, too, shares the fundamental realism of *Getting Out*. It comprises a linear sequence of causal events that lead inexorably to conflict between the two sets of characters, climax in the Luttons' murdering the Danzards, and resolution in Christine's death sentence and Lea's term in prison, where, metaphorically at least, she has always been.

Within this realistic set and plot, Kesselman, like Norman and Lebow, has experimented widely. In contrast to the other playwrights' techniques, however, which primarily illustrate the psychological effects of prisons and traps on Lusia and Arlene, Kesselman's theatrical devices and deviations from realism reiterate the restrictions of gender and class under which the Lutton sisters suffer, and predict their ultimate inability to escape confinement. For although Christine and Lea, like Lusia and Rose or Arlene and Ruby, create a shared life (especially in their lesbian relationship) and devise moments of autonomy, their day of release will never come.

Kesselman uses a number of visual symbols to suggest the Luttons' hopeless condition and to predict their inevitable rebellion. Madame Danzard's white glove (used to detect undusted spots) reveals the petty tyranny under which the Lutton sisters suffer; Christine's pink sweater (inappropriate for a servant) and the lacy undergarments she sews for Lea anticipate the challenge they ultimately launch against their oppressors. The most potent of these significant props, however, is the blanket that the Luttons' mother crocheted for the infant Lea. Maman, like Arlene's mother, is implicated in her daughters' oppression: she confined Christine in a dreaded local convent when she was a young child, despite the girl's repeated attempts to escape; she denied Christine her wish, years later, to remain at the convent and become a nun; and she put both girls to work as domestics as soon as they could earn money for her. At the beginning of the play, Maman's crocheted blanket functions as a security blanket for Lea, who is homesick, and as a source of resentment for Christine, who has never forgiven Maman for undermining all her personal choices and taking all her hard-earned money. After they break off relations with Maman, however, the sisters unravel the blanket, symbolically unraveling their ties to their greedy and manipulative parent. Nonetheless, escape is still impossible. As the stage directions reveal:

> As the blanket unravels faster and faster, they run around the room. They are constricted by the confines of the narrow room. They wind the wool around the bed, under the sink. They wind it around each other. (26)

Christine and Lea may feel that they have escaped their mother's domination, but the room in which she has placed them and the wool from her blanket keep them just as tightly locked in place as Maman herself ever did.

The most interesting of Kesselman's theatrical innovations is her extensive use of silence. Locked within the separate halves of the divided world they inhabit, the Luttons and Danzards never speak to each other until the final, climactic scene, the confrontation that leads to rage and murder. Their conversations remain strictly intra-familial, alternating or even overlapping from within their separate realms. During the few scenes in which members of both families are on stage together (and not on opposite sides of the staircase), the Luttons always remain silent. Some scenes are therefore enacted entirely in pantomime, as Lea is silently ordered to pick up the seed pearls dropped by Isabelle, or Madame's dusty white glove speaks eloquently to the Luttons of their tiny domestic failures.

These scenes of total silence illustrate dramatically the inability of the two families to communicate with each other. The characters never know of the similarities among themselves (although Isabelle and Lea, both younger and less rigid than Madame and Christine, do silently share chocolates and hair brushing, perhaps imagining the possibility of friendship). But the Danzards and the Luttons are in different social positions and do not, after all, share the same condition of voicelessness, as Kesselman dramatizes powerfully in scene 13. In this scene Madame and Isabelle direct Christine in altering Isabelle's dress without ever speaking to either servant. Although Christine continues to make the required adjustments throughout the scene, "*Never, during any point in the scene, is a word addressed to Christine or Lea*" (47). In fact, Madame Danzard refers to the silent Christine as "she," even in her presence, asserting firmly that the dress will be ready on Friday because "She hardly has anything to do" (47). Despite Madame's repeated criticism of Christine's skillful alterations, the Lutton sisters must remain silent under her instructions, waiting until they are alone together to complain of Madame's increasing injustices. Their inability to speak in Madame's presence signifies their powerlessness in a world inexorably divided by class status, and their frustration with their condition predicts the violence that will erupt when the women finally confront each other. For voiceless women imprisoned by an unjust society, antisocial action becomes inevitable.

That the ability to speak is equated with power in this play is made quite clear by the two scenes enacted in front of the proscenium arch, outside the Danzards' prison-house: scene 9, in which the Luttons have their picture taken by a photographer; and scene 16, in which they are sentenced for the murders of the Danzards. Although they are outside the divided house in these scenes, the Luttons are still controlled by powerful social forces, represented by the disembodied male voices of the photographer, the medical examiner, and the judge. Although these male characters are never seen, their very voices restrict, define, and finally determine the fates of Christine and Lea.

This power of speech to define and control is only hinted at by the photographer, to whom the sisters—dressed alike—seem to be identical twins, as lacking in individual identity as the inmates of the prison where Arlene was incarcerated. (In fact, the male voice-overs in this play function similarly to the voice-over prison announcements in *Getting Out*: they suggest the invisible yet inexorable systems of control that dominate the female characters, and they prevent audience detachment because of their disembodied, and therefore potentially ubiquitous, presence.) By the end of the play the sisters, like Arlene, are literally imprisoned, and although the judge orders them to explain the murders, to speak in their own defense, the Luttons have learned well that to speak is futile in a world where their voices will never be heard. Christine's final speech is a cry to see her sister—

a request which is, of course, denied. The play ends with the sisters standing "as if framed in a photograph," that is, pictured as society has mandated they appear: framed and silent.

Kesselman, however, has shown us another view of the Lutton sisters. By dramatizing the inescapable condition of servitude and oppression under which Christine and Lea suffer, Kesselman engages our sympathy for them, making their eventual murder of the Danzards even more appalling. The bodiless voice of the medical examiner describes the scene of the crime in "a flat, anonymous voice":

> a single eye was found, intact, complete with the optic nerve. The eye had been torn out without the aid of an instrument. . . . On the ground were fragments of bone and teeth. . . . The walls and doors were covered with splashes of blood reaching a height of seven feet. (64)

These images suggest that violence is the only possible result of inescapable repressions, that when subjectivity—a speaking voice—is denied, "Energy directed toward self-realization turns in on itself, transformed into its opposite: death" (Kilkelly 31). With her innovative combination of realism and experimentation, Kesselman has thus dramatized the conditions that impelled these murders, making audible throughout the play "that roar which lies on the other side of silence" (Eliot 135).

Materialist Feminism and Polyvocal Realism

The four plays discussed in this chapter have a number of things in common. First and most obvious, they all rely to a large extent on the structures of realism—its linearity, its detailed set and protective proscenium arch, its tendency toward resolving a problem and reaching closure. Using these techniques, Childress, Lebow, Norman, and Kesselman have all depicted historically situated female subjects governed by real social relations and emphasized the power of those social relations to define identity, curb choices, and in general restrict women. In this way they follow in the footsteps of the politically committed feminist-realists of the early decades of the twentieth century.

A second thing these four playwrights have in common, but which they do *not* share with most of their predecessors, is the inclusion of desires and drives—Kristeva's "semiotic"—as a thematic and structural counterpoint to those realistically presented social forces. Whether it be through antimimetically depicted subjectivity in Lebow and Norman or the social construction of identity in Childress and Kesselman, these four playwrights share in the project of disrupting realism, of showing *threats* to its power as well as the power itself. The primary difference between the female characters in these four plays and those of pre-1960s playwrights discussed in earlier chapters is that contemporary female characters refuse to be contained: they reject others' definitions as well as unjust social conditions. Tommy insists on home rule; Lusia denies the patriarchal authority of her father; Arlene embraces her "incorrigible" self in hopes of preserving autonomy; and Christine and Lea rebel violently against their oppressors. By depicting both oppressive historical conditions and women characters' contrary desires, and by using an innovative combination of mimetic and antimimetic devices to do so, Childress, Lebow, Norman, and Kesselman expose the conditions of patriarchal oppression and predict the seeds of its eventual destruction.

In developing this adapted realism, these and other contemporary women playwrights are creating a new, polyvocal realism that is both timely and appropriate for expressing contemporary feminist visions. At the present moment in feminist theoretical debate, one central conflict that seems to resist resolution is whether women are speaking subjects or cultural constructs. What these playwrights have done is show that their female characters are "at one and the same time inside *and* outside the ideology of gender, and conscious of being so, conscious of that twofold pull, of that division, that doubled vision" (de Lauretis 1987, 10). The varied realist structures that they have created to show this internal division is typical of much twentieth-century feminist nondramatic literature, a polyvocality that feminist literary critics have variously called "the movement between complicity and critique" (DuPlessis 33), a double-voiced discourse (Showalter 266), or a "palimpsestic" form (Gilbert and Gubar 1979, 72). In crafting this polyvocal dramatic form, these playwrights are contributing to the materialist feminist agenda, described as "dialectical" by Newton and Rosenfelt and offering "a way of seeing that prompts us to locate in the same situation the forces of oppression and the seed of resistance; to construct women in a given moment in history simultaneously as victims and agents" (xxii). By using this "dialectical" or "polyvocal" or "palimpsestic" form, contemporary feminist playwrights gain entry into public discourse without sacrificing their alternative visions.

This last point—that even innovative realist playwrights have access to production facilities and mainstream audiences—is one that should not be overlooked. To borrow again the words of Teresa de Lauretis (whose words also began this chapter), feminist revisions of representation and meaning cannot be accomplished "by destroying all representational coherence, by denying 'the hold' of the image in order to prevent identification and subject reflection" (1984, 67–68). By accepting the power of representational art—realism—to engage spectators, by recognizing the modifications possible within realist dramaturgy, and by accepting their roles as constructs of material culture even while they critique it, contemporary feminist realists have created a new and dynamic form of theater, capable of protesting what is and suggesting what might be.

Conclusion:
Appropriating the Master's Tools

As I write this conclusion in late summer 1994, I have just returned from overlapping national conferences sponsored by three different theater organizations: the Black Theatre Network (BTN), the Women and Theatre Program (WTP), and the Association for Theatre in Higher Education (ATHE). At all these venues the issue of realism was discussed and debated, with intelligent critiques launched from a variety of perspectives, feminist and otherwise. From Marlon Bailey at the BTN Conference, for example, I heard that realism is a colonial maneuver that limits what aspects of "reality" can be reflected on stage. For Bailey, true mimesis from an African-American point of view would have to include both the visible world (such as the parlor or kitchen we are accustomed to) and the invisible world (such as a character's ancestors—what white Western culture would probably deem "ghosts" not truly present in everyday reality). From this perspective, realism pretends to mimesis, but actually reflects only a selected segment of a complex, culturally specific, and not entirely visible "reality." Later in the week, at ATHE, I heard from Nathan Stucky that if art only *reflects* life, then it is *not* life. For Stucky, the only true realism comes from "natural performances," shows based on taped interviews that involve text, body, and voice in a "mediated presentation" (such as Anna Deveare Smith's *Fires in the Mirror*) rather than in the traditional "invented representation" of realist plays.

Even more pertinent to my own examination of realism from a feminist perspective was the ATHE panel entitled "Burning Down the House: Feminism and Realism," on which I participated. Joining me on the panel were two teachers and theater artists—Gayle Austin and Juli Burk—who have recently worked on separate feminist adaptations of Ibsen's *A Doll's House*. In her 1992 "theory play" *The Doll House Show*, playwright and director Gayle Austin juxtaposed scenes from Ibsen's original play with letters from Laura Kieler (the real-life model for Ibsen's Nora), monologues by feminist theorists who critique Ibsenian realism, and invented speeches by a living Barbie doll.

149

Juli Burk, who served as dramaturg for Split Britches' 1993 University of Hawaii-based production *Valley of the Doll's House*, described a show which presented scenes from Ibsen's play through three intertextual filters: Jacqueline Susann's *Valley of the Dolls*, the lesbian subjectivity of the two female actors who played Nora and Torvald, and the political realities and racial complexities of contemporary Hawaii. In both these productions, antimimetic interventions invited the emergence of multiple realities—such as the real-life effects of doll's house existence that we see in the fate of Laura Kieler, who was incarcerated as insane, or the white heterosexual privilege enjoyed by the Helmers. From these and other presentations about realism, I began to recognize even more completely than before what some of the challenges to realism have at stake.

Nonetheless, and despite the compelling theater produced by such resolutely antirealist performers as Anna Deveare Smith and Split Britches, I left the conferences with unshaken faith in conventional realism's capacity to express feminist visions. Just as the African-American or feminist interventions in realism discussed above *do* open up possibilities that realism may close off, realism can offer possibilities that the others do not—such as the ability to reach wide audiences. For while the theater educators who made up the bulk of the audience at my 1994 ATHE panel were uniformly excited by Austin's and Burk's innovative work, many of them wondered—both in group discussion after the presentations and in private conversation afterwards—how much of the feminist intervention was understood and appreciated by university (let alone community) audiences. Furthermore, while traditional realism may restrict the levels of "reality" that can be presented, a contemporary, modified realism (such as that practiced by Barbara Lebow or Marsha Norman—see chapter 4) can certainly serve the present and the past, the present-day characters and the ancestors, equally well.

It is important to recognize that feminist experimentation and feminist realism can and do exist simultaneously in the contemporary theater. The movement from realism to antirealism is not a linear progression, the evolution of an inferior dramatic form into a superior one. Yet this suggestion of evolution seems to be the subtext of many feminist critiques of realism, just as it underpins much feminist discussion of feminist critical praxis. Carol Neely has described this tendency to create a linear narrative out of feminist critical history. Describing our habit of dividing feminist criticism into three types— a strategy I myself used in chapter 1—Neely remarks that this classification technique

implies a thesis/antithesis/higher synthesis model in which feminist writing progresses toward increasing inclusiveness, integration, reconciliation,
and transcendence. These models create a kind of *Bildungsroman* for
feminist criticism; in its happy ending, feminist critics reintegrate their
life and work, revitalize the academy, reorder their students' priorities,
and transform the world . . . [However, these models overlook] a gap
between the insufficiency of feminist criticism—which I often find merely
pragmatic, narrowly prescriptive, unjustifiably romantic, or impenetrably
theoretical—and the many, vigorous, uncategorizable examples of feminist criticism that proliferate chaotically, energetically, illuminatingly
everywhere. (77–78)

By creating a similar linear narrative to discuss the development of
feminist drama through its so-called liberal, radical, and materialist
phases, critics may be missing the "chaotic, energetic" and multifari-
ous forms of drama—including realism—that feminist theater artists
practice, in different contexts and for different reasons. I find it extremely ironic that some feminist critics assess dramatic changes in
this linear fashion when what they object to in realism is its confining linearity.

In fact, it is not unusual to find feminist playwrights shifting dramatic form from play to play, taking advantage of theater's sundry
resources in various ways, depending on what they want to say, how
they want to say it, and to whom it is addressed—all factors, as we
saw throughout this book, that influence a playwright's choice of dramatic form. Their careers, like the development of feminist drama,
do not always take linear trajectories from realism to something "better"—as we shall see in the following example.

The Case of Adrienne Kennedy

I began this book with the case of Maria Irene Fornes to illustrate
the difficulties in defining any one playwright as either feminist or
realist. Just as Fornes's work exemplifies the thorny problems of
definition, so does Kennedy's career to date discredit the notion that
feminist playwriting is evolving from realism (sometimes associated
with an "outdated" liberal feminism—see chapter 1) to a more complex, sophisticated feminist experimentalism.

Kennedy's pre-1990 plays have made her a model of the
postmodern-feminist dramatic practitioner, according to many influential feminist critics. These early plays—especially *Funnyhouse of
a Negro* (1964) and *The Owl Answers* (1965)—take place in spaces
not bound by the walls of rooms or by the limitations of linear time.
They shift constantly from setting to setting, from present time to

history, from external reality to surreal dream world. In this way, the plays reflect prismatically the experiences of the central character, in each case a young woman suffering the dislocations of her mixed racial heritage, her uncertain parentage, and the burden of collective human history as well as her individual experiences. To emphasize the fragmentation of this recurring central character, Kennedy typically splits her stage persona. In *Funnyhouse,* "Negro-Sarah" is visited by the Duchess of Hapsburg, Queen Victoria, Jesus, and Patrice Lumumba, all identified in the cast list as "One of herselves" (1). In *The Owl Answers,* the protagonist is identified as "SHE who is CLARA PASSMORE who is the VIRGIN MARY who is the BASTARD who is the OWL" (25), and each of these avatars appropriates Clara's voice and vision. In these ways, Kennedy expresses in dramatic form the myriad psychological ruptures of being African American in a white-dominated society and female in a patriarchal culture.

Although Kennedy's plays did not immediately attract much critical attention, in recent years feminist critics have applauded her dramatization of the external pressures on and internal instabilities of contemporary women, especially black women. So for Elin Diamond, Kennedy's plays participate in feminism's "oldest, and still most valuable, project":

> to demystify the male gender bias of that stable subject, to borrow deconstruction's strategic subversion of humanist concepts, such as the masculine cogito that traditionally stands in for God the Father. (1992, 133)

Rosemary Curb "remains fascinated with the political accuracy of Kennedy's art," of plays that "no doubt fail the liberal feminist's search for role models of women winning," but nonetheless "foreground gender [and] the inextricable matrix that it forms with race and class" (1992, 154). And for Jeanie Forte, "Kennedy's work vividly illustrates Adrienne Rich's 'politics of location,' the necessity for naming one's position in history, which she says must start, for women, with the politics of the body" (1992, 164). Central to all these feminist assessments is an appreciation for Kennedy's innovative dramaturgy, described by Forte as "fragmented, decentered, nonlinear, marked by marginality and alterity, begging for comprehension and simultaneously defying it, haunting a search for and identity in a world where all such categories have been rendered mobile, elusive" (1992, 159).

Given such high (and certainly deserved) feminist praise for Kennedy's antimimetic dramas, what are we to make of her more recent work? In the 1990s, Kennedy has reversed the apparent direction of feminist playwriting, moving *toward* a more conventional realism rather than away from it. In *The Ohio State Murders* (first produced 1992), Kennedy shifts from the troubled "psychic collage" characteristic of her previous work to a form that is "Relatively conventional, more of an 'external monologue,'" with a protagonist who is "remarkably intact" (Cummings 1992, 32–33). The play presents the monologue of Suzanne Alexander, a rare Kennedy protagonist with a surname and a single, stable identity. Suzanne, a famous writer who is visiting the university she once attended, has been asked to speak on the sources of the violent imagery in her work. The play takes place in the library stacks where Suzanne is working on her presentation, and shifts back and forth in time as her attempt to locate the sources of violence in her writing stimulates her memories. Despite the flashbacks, however, the play proceeds in a linear fashion, with the adult Suzanne presenting memories that proceed fitfully but nonetheless chronologically. The memories themselves tell of the murders of Suzanne's twin daughters as infants, and are structured as a rather conventional murder mystery.

Why this movement from a feminist-approved polyvocality toward realism? When asked this question directly, Kennedy replied, "I don't understand why *OSM* came out like that" (letter to the author, July 1994). Despite this disclaimer, her published comments on the play reveal her awareness that realism might offer some new possibilities. Kennedy writes:

> I learned a lot from writing *The Ohio State Murders* because that was the very first time I put something in the exact time that it had happened, and then added my imagination to the story and the subtext. . . .
> I've discovered over the years that very often I'm trying to make up things when real things are far more powerful; they're begging to be used. (1994, 189–90)

This comment suggests a reversal of her usual emphasis. By grounding the play in the specific time and place of conventional realism and in those "real things . . . begging to be used," Kennedy found her imagination *freer* to create than if she had struggled from the start to imagine a situation.

The subject matter of the play also suggests why *The Ohio State Murders* emerged in a more realistic format than had been usual for Kennedy. The play asks Suzanne to cast a line into the past, to seek past sources for the images she writes; as Nicole King has noted, the play focuses not on psychological experience, as Kennedy's early plays do, but on causes and consequences. Illuminating causes and consequences is, of course, a staple of linear realism, emphasizing the cultural and hermeneutic codes of meaning that (as I explained in chapter 1) define the realist project. By setting the play in "the exact time it happened" and structuring the action according to the chronological progression of Suzanne's remembered past, Kennedy appropriated realism's retrospective analysis for feminist purposes of her own, telling a horrific tale of sexual abuse and racial discrimination. The play ends as Suzanne speaks publicly of her dead daughters for the first time, using her reawakened memories to achieve a new understanding of the sources of her own imagery. In short, the play ends with a realistic resolution: a new awareness on the part of a central protagonist.

The existence of this play suggests that Kennedy, a feminist exemplar (according to many feminist critics), is willing to use a variety of available dramatic forms, choosing the one for each play that best liberates her creativity and tells the story of female experience that she wants to tell. The movement from realism to experimental dramatic forms that seems to characterize contemporary feminist dramatic practice is evidently neither inevitable nor immutable. Moreover, Kennedy is not alone among active feminist playwrights in choosing to work in a variety of dramatic forms, including realism.

Valetta Anderson, an Atlanta-based playwright, chose conventional realism for her 1991 drama *She'll Find Her Way Home*. Conceived as the first part of a trilogy, the play is set in Mississippi in the 1870s and tells the story of Martha Robb, a light-skinned, young, African-American woman who must choose between two suitors: the equally light-skinned Thomas, who hopes to take Martha to Dakota where they can pass as white and so avoid the widespread persecution of former slaves; and the African-looking Isaiah, a socially conscious young man who is committed to working for racial equality and of whom her mother approves. When asked why she chose realism for this play, Anderson replied:

> I began *She'll Find Her Way Home* with the goal that it and the rest of the trilogy would be such stage hits that they culminate as a block-buster, television mini-series. This goal resulted in the traditional story-line of a "well made" play. . . . *She'll Find Her Way Home* is also the intertwining of two love stories, the love between a mother and her daughter, and the love between that daughter and her future husband. So the story itself flowed within conventional timelines and arrived at conventional audience expectations. That's realism to me. (letter to the author, August 1994)

Anderson's comments reveal two things about the feminist possibilities of stage realism. First, it is the form most likely to reach wide commercial audiences—those who watch "blockbuster, television mini-series." Second, it remains an appropriate form for love stories and other domestic dramas, spheres of experience that feminists should be cautious not to discredit in their eagerness to move beyond traditional representations of women's often thwarted lives.

Nonetheless, in working on *Virgins in Paradise*—the still-in-process sequel to *She'll Find Her Way Home*—Anderson found that she could not answer the questions she hoped to explore—questions about the white former owners of Isaiah's family and the interactions between owners and slaves—in conventional realism. She writes, "Mary [Isaiah's mother] insisted on moving through time to put her experiences within a context that makes sense in relation to today" (letter to the author, August 1994). Furthermore, she wanted to "strip Eurocentric values and viewpoints from Mary's experiences," and a chorus of ancestors and temporal juxtapositions have seemed the best methods to date. However, Anderson admits to being torn about her formal choices in this play. "My intent is still that these plays reach the widest black audience possible, which still seems to be through the medium of t.v.," she writes. And further, she mentions that the form of the play is the thing that emerges *last* in her creative process; she writes to tell a story from a particular point of view, not from any "conscious intent to use a particular form." About the antimimetic form of the present version of *Virgins in Paradise*, Anderson writes:

> I am not suggesting that my goals could not be accomplished within the rise and fall of a well written "well-made," realistic play. And maybe, once I get the whole play out, and take a step back, I'll be able to synthesize this emotional, psychic and herstorical turn . . . (letter to the author, August 1994)

Taken as a whole, Anderson's plays and her comments on playwriting suggest that realism is one among many forms that can be fruitfully appropriated for feminist purposes, and that, in fact, there are some significant advantages to doing so.

Another contemporary feminist playwright who shares this view is St. Louis-based Joan Lipkin, whose successfully produced plays include *Some of My Best Friends Are* (1989) and *He's Having Her Baby* (1990), both musical comedies (music and lyrics by Tom Clear) that take on the subjects of gay rights and reproductive rights, respectively. Her more recent work, however—such as *Small Domestic Acts* (1992)—turns away from the musical revue format. Iris Smith, who interviewed Lipkin for *TDR*, describes this change:

> Lipkin finds herself thinking more about the audiences who are the reasons for her plays. . . . Lipkin's activism is [now] directed less toward

avant garde-influenced confrontation than it is toward a dialogue mixing the weight of public speech with the ease of private conversation. (98)

Once again, we see a self-proclaimed feminist playwright turning toward more naturalistic production styles in order to engage a wider audience. And while *Small Domestic Acts* cannot be classified as a realist play (the characters are aware of and directly address the audience throughout the play, for instance), the play uses audience collaboration to revise the realistic contract I described in chapter 1 and which the characters invoke constantly. While Lipkin insists on "renegotiat[ing] what is a conventional spectator position" (I. Smith 117), she also asserts, "I believe in storyline. I think the audience likes a good yarn" (I. Smith 123). Although Lipkin believes that "most traditional realism creates a fixed and *dishonest* world in which the audience is held captive," she also admits, "Clearly, I incorporate some elements of realism into my work" (I. Smith 123). Equally clearly from Lipkin's remarks, realism is one of many theatrical forms available to playwrights today, and feminist playwrights can take advantage of this variety.

Crossroads and Tools

Lipkin's comments, like Anderson's and like the case of Adrienne Kennedy, illustrate that realism is currently at a crossroads in contemporary American theater, a crossroads that intersects with contemporary feminist theory. Realism can reach wide audiences, but it is in some ways false to postmodern experience. It can depict domestic conditions and developing love relationships, but it does not typically include characters who are not a part of shared, visible, external reality, and does not lend itself to alternative configurations of gender relationships or families. It can reveal the past sources of present conditions, but not the psychic instability of characters who have been shattered by life in a repressive culture. And yet it endures.

I choose this image of crossroads not only to imply realism's intersection with feminist and postmodern thinking, but also to illustrate that realism has been somewhere and is going somewhere; it is a dynamic dramatic medium with a history and a future that I hope more feminist critics can appreciate and embrace. For in its century-long use, realism has intersected not only with representatives of repressive hierarchy (the low road, if you will); it has also crossed paths with myriad feminist playwrights (such as those discussed throughout this book) who found historically specific feminist reasons to use realistic dramatic form.

I best understand realism in the way that John McGrath (in chapter 1) and Donna Haraway (in chapter 3) discuss it: as a tool, an implement or weapon that can be put to a wide variety of ideological uses. In particular, Haraway argues that a cyborg writer (that is, any writer—like a feminist—who exists within and is shaped by distinct but overlapping cultures) must seize all the tools at her disposal to remake the world as coalition, not hegemony (Haraway 217). In Haraway's vision, such a reshaping of experience would avoid reproducing the "telos of the whole" (198) that restrictive or dualistic or totalizing theories (like patriarchy, or perhaps even like prescriptive feminisms) insist on. This vision of the future provides a powerful incentive to re-think the feminist potential of realism.

In fact, some of the very contemporary feminist thinkers who decried realism a decade ago are beginning to revise their assessments. Jill Dolan, for example, has recently noted that while realism's limitations have been successfully documented and usefully theorized, realist plays continue to be produced, especially by marginalized communities and historically under-represented groups who need to see their experiences reflected and validated on stage (1994, 26). In answer to her own questions about the continued use of realism by such groups, Dolan concludes that "returning to realism frequently to check its status and meaning seems inevitable" (1994, 27). Central to Dolan's understanding that realism may be useful in certain historical contexts is her awareness that criticism, too, is a product of its time. She locates the feminist critique of realism as a phenomenon of the 1980s, a time when materialist feminists' borrowing from Marxist critical methods "sent a generation of feminist theater and performance scholars to write about avant-garde and experimental performance" (1994, 26) rather than about play texts or traditional forms. Just as that critical maneuver reflected the then-current state of feminist theory, so too is the continued use of realism in different cultural contexts (especially but not exclusively for marginalized groups) a legitimate endeavor for feminist theater artists today.

Janelle Reinelt has made a similar revisionist move in her recent essay on the Brecht/Lukács debates over realism. While her previous work has concentrated, as she notes herself, on "the Brechtian foregrounding of gender construction" in certain feminist plays, she admits that "a strong case could also be made for the meticulous realism of character, dialogue, and environment *within* the particular scenes of these plays" (1994, 134). Her most recent thinking suggests that feminist dramaturgy can embrace both realism and Brechtian devices in "a hybrid feminist style which combines features of both traditions, epic and realist" (1994, 123). Reinelt's assessment echoes my own discussion of a "hybrid realism" in chapter 4.

Revisionings such as Dolan's and Reinelt's bode well for the continued feminist exploration of the possibilities of stage realism. And since contemporary feminist playwrights from Maria Irene Fornes to Adrienne Kennedy continue at least to dabble in realism, it is time to acknowledge that realism exists simultaneously with more avant-garde forms of contemporary theater. Realism is not the shabby remnant of a shameful past, but a fully functional mechanism of feminist social intervention.

Notes

1. Realism and the Feminist Critique

1. It is clear from Keyssar's recent work that she uses the term "traditional" to embrace all "Western dramaturgical strategies," including modern stage realism (1991, 92).

2. See her interview with Scott Cummings (1985, 55), or the interview with Liz Hughes and Trudy Scott quoted in Dolan 1988, 141, n. 29.

3. Roland Barthes, S/Z 18–20. I have chosen to use Barthes's terminology here because his work has had a great impact on a number of materialist feminist critics of realism, as we shall see later in this chapter.

4. Catherine Belsey, for example, revises Barthes's codes in her discussion of the inevitable gaps and omissions in realism's purported seamlessness. I discuss her position in more detail later in this chapter.

5. See, for example, W. B. Worthen (1992, 14 and throughout) and Brenda Murphy (46–49).

6. See Catherine Belsey, esp. 53, for a discussion of realism's dependence on closure.

7. For more detailed analyses of these three forms of feminist drama, see Gayle Austin 1990, 4–6; Sue-Ellen Case 1988, chaps. 4 and 5; Jill Dolan 1988, 4–18, also chaps. 5 and 6; Michelene Wandor 1986, chap. 8.

8. For a more theoretical analysis of the limitations of this liberal feminist project, see Ebert 92–95.

9. I realize that my description of cultural feminism is oversimplified and risks eliding the differences within the cultural feminist movements. I am consciously grouping together many different practitioners of radical and cultural feminism under this rubric because of their shared assumptions toward stage realism. For a more diverse overview of their project, see Linda Alcoff, 298–304.

10. In 1986, Linda Walsh Jenkins estimated that more than 150 feminist theater groups have produced work in the United States since the 1960s, with many new groups taking the place of those who die out (Chinoy and Jenkins 276). This phenomenon is exemplified in my native Philadelphia, where the only resident feminist theater ensemble, Daughter Productions, folded from lack of funding in 1990, but a new group, the Women's Theatre Ensemble, produced its first show in 1992.

11. This notion of a uniquely female way of knowing is controversial in feminist circles. Two major proponents of this position are Carol Gilligan and Nancy Chodorow. For a good overview of their work and the responses to it, see Fraser and Nicholson 26–34.

12. A good summary of playwrights' comments on developing a "female aesthetic" appears in Chinoy and Jenkins 349–52. See also the interviews with female playwrights in Betsko and Koenig, where the topic of a separate female aesthetic is consistently addressed.

13. For a good summary of, and response to, anti-essentialist thinking, see de Lauretis 1990. See also Judith Butler 1990a, chap. 1; Christina Crosby; and Iris Marion Young.

14. Lynda Hart, presentation on a panel entitled "Looking at Seeing," Women and Theatre Conference, Atlanta, 31 July 1992.

15. As Sue-Ellen Case has argued, this constitutes a sort of *negative* feminism, since "alterity . . . simply configures a distance from the dominant" (1990, 12).

16. Teresa Ebert (103), Michelene Wandor (1986, 184), and Chris Weedon (172) have all argued convincingly that ideology resides not in formal properties but in political uses of forms.

17. See, for example, Belsey, 51–57; Dolan 1988, 84; Diamond 1988, 87 and 1989, 61; Forte 1989, 115–17; Reinelt 1986, 154.

18. A number of important scholars have recently written full-length books that address the centrality of the audience in meaning production. See, for example, Bennett 1990, Blau, Dolan 1994, and Worthen 1992. Articles on this topic also abound.

19. The discussion of the "male gaze" has been borrowed from film studies, notably Mulvey's influential 1975 article, the works of Teresa de Lauretis (esp. 1984), and those of E. Ann Kaplan. As Susan Bennett points out, though the cinematic viewing situation is not identical to the theatrical one (1990, 80–81), the two are similar enough to warrant analysis of the disembodied viewing gaze in theater studies, too. For some good examples of theatrical applications, see Case 1988, 118–24; Dolan 1988, 12–17.

20. Semiotic studies of theater and film abound. See, for example, Alter (esp. 93–95 on the polyvocality of theater); Bennett 1990, 72–91; Case 1988, 112–27; Elam; Pavis; Silverman.

21. Judith Barlow made this observation in the discussion following an ATHE panel on "The Value of Realism to Feminist Drama: A Debate in Transition," Seattle, 9 August 1991. Barlow and I were joined on the panel by Sheila Stowell and Mary L. Cutler.

22. See Gillian Swanson's analysis of the determining factors of race, class, and gender in formulating a spectator's response.

23. Sheila Stowell (1992b) argues this point convincingly.

24. Vanden Heuvel 1989, 587. He is quoting Demastes 120.

25. Judith Fetterley's extremely influential book on American literature, *The Resisting Reader,* is the basis for much of the criticism that suggests reading against the ideology of a text or performance. For some good examples of feminist drama theorists who have revised this literary technique for use in analyzing theater, see Austin 1990, 21–37 and Bennett 1990, 60–61 and 84–91.

26. For further discussion of this issue of power in representation, see Butler 1992 and Weedon, 13–21.

27. See, for example, the pioneering work of Judith Butler 1990a and Teresa de Lauretis 1987.

28. See, for example, Jill Dolan, 1988, 84; Jeanie Forte 1989, 115–16; Michael Vanden Heuvel 1992, 48; and W. B. Worthen 1992. Even Sheila Stowell, who argues against what she sees as overgeneralization in Belsey's work (1992a, 86), assumes that Belsey is disparaging realism instead of offering us a new way to read it.

29. See Diamond 1988 and Reinelt 1986 for two prominent examples.

30. For a sampling of critics who persuasively propose such alternatives to realism, see Case 1989b and 1990; Davy; Dolan 1988, 99–117; and Forte 1988.

31. Much has been written about the troubled production history of *A Doll's*

NOTES TO CHAPTER 2

House and especially about public outrage over the conclusion; see Errol Durbach (13–23) for a good summary. See Dukore for discussion of the English revisions, both serious and parodic, that resulted from the outrage over Nora's "unnatural" abandonment of her children.

32. William Demastes has noted that today's theater audiences have been "trained" in realism by television and cinema (30).

33. Penny Boumelha has also seen this twofold possibility for feminist readings of realist texts. She argues: "Realist texts can be read by and for feminism, not in a flatly mimetic sense but as they enact in both their coherences and their incoherences the struggle between their representation and its own limits and incompletions" (82).

34. For further discussion of the modified realism of Miller and Williams, see Schroeder.

35. See the introduction to *Plays by and about Women* by Sullivan and Hatch for discussion of *Overtones* as expressionistic (ix).

36. A number of contemporary women playwrights have experimented with divided subjects. In addition to Norman, see, for example, Cherríe Moraga's *Giving Up the Ghost*, Ruth Wolff's *The Abdication*, and Sharon Pollock's *Blood Relations*. Sue-Ellen Case provides an interesting reading of this feminist appropriation of a Lacanian model (1989a, 128–34).

37. See, for example, several recent anthologies of feminist essays that focus on keeping the conflicts within feminism productive. Hirsch and Keller's *Conflicts in Feminism* is a good starting point, as is Butler and Scott's *Feminists Theorize the Political*. Warhol and Price's *Feminisms* offers an excellent sampling of the diversity among feminist literary criticism.

2. Domestic Spaces, Women's Rights, and Realism: 1910s–1930s

1. The notion that American realism has always been entangled with expressionism and other antimimetic forms is also explored in Schroeder, esp. 24–28.

2. In her 1985 essay on "The Compatibility of Traditional Dramatic Form and Feminist Expression," Judith Stephens, like Cole, argues that *Miss Lulu Bett* is a feminist play because of the choices Lulu makes in defining herself. What I hope to add to this discussion is a materialist-feminist analysis of the economic and social forces Gale critiques as impingements on Lulu's developing agency.

3. Jill Dolan, for example, in discussing Marsha Norman's *'night, Mother*, has observed that the play is "like most traditional American dramas" in its "focus on individual suffering" and its "unwillingness to discuss [a central character's] dilemma in terms of a wider social context" (1988, 36–37). For Dolan, these flaws make Norman's play "weak as a political statement and inadequate from a materialist feminist perspective" (36). While Dolan's comments may have some validity in describing Norman's play, her contentions have too often been generalized by feminist drama theorists and used as reasons to dismiss *all* realist texts, as we saw in some detail in chapter 1.

4. This premise is evidently based on historical fact. The published version of the play begins with the following quotation from a "press clipping": "The war brides were cheered with enthusiasm and the churches were crowded when the wedding parties spoke the ceremony in concert" (3).

5. See, for example, Doris E. Abramson, Judith Barlow, Helen Krich Chinoy, Cynthia Cole, Sharon Friedman, Lois Gottlieb, Deborah S. Kolb, Brenda Murphy, and Cynthia Sutherland.

6. Crothers's paralleling the feminist movement in her dramatic works has been noted by various scholars, especially Deborah Kolb (150); and Lois Gottlieb 1979, 149 and 1987, 138.

7. See, for example, Barlow xv; Flexner 245; Gottlieb 1979 throughout.

8. Page numbers refer to the unpublished manuscript in the University of Pennsylvania rare book room. Each act is paginated separately. Although the play has never been published, it received several productions in the 1910s (both on Broadway and by a repertory company, which performed the play at the Bedford State Reformatory for Girls). See Gottlieb 1979, 157.

9. For interesting analyses of *A Man's World* as a feminist statement on the double standard, its emphasis on the need for women to be economically independent from men, and its depiction of the interaction between private spaces and public issues, see Abramson, Cole, Friedman, Gottlieb 1979, and Murphy.

10. In *A Stage of Their Own*, Stowell writes: "There is no doubt that suffrage drama was written as part of a consciously organised scheme to propagate political doctrine and advocate social and cultural changes which would contribute to the dismantling of a system based upon patriarchal oppression. To that extent it is unabashedly feminist propaganda, and anticipates in some remarkable ways the self-consciously 'women's theatre' that emerged in the 1960s" (43). Among the similarities between suffrage drama and 1960s feminist theater she notes that both movements were "political and didactic"; both strove to demonstrate to women "the ramifications of their social, political, cultural and economic inequality" and so incite them to fight for change; both spoke primarily to the converted; and she cites Janet Brown (140) as noting that both forms used techniques of sex-role reversal, historical role models, satire of sex roles, and the direct portrayal of women's oppression (67).

11. In "Apropos of Women and the American Theatre," Rachel France argues that the developments in suffrage drama paralleled the changes within the suffrage movement itself. Gilman's play bears out her contention, since in 1911 one important method of involving women in the movement was to point out the effect of public policy on what many women continued to see as their only appropriate bailiwick—the home (Lebsock).

12. The stage directions note that the play takes place in "A parlor, porch or garden, belonging to Mrs. Carroll" (144). In any of these cases, Mrs. Carroll's domestic space has been given over to public discourse.

13. The review of Frank's book as unusually strong for a woman writer was ironically paralleled by some of the early reviews of Crothers's play. Walter Eaton, for example, wrote that *A Man's World* was "an interesting and at times moving play, frankly and honestly written from a woman's point of view, but it just misses the masculinity of structure . . . necessary to make it dramatic literature" (156). Crothers's own material was clearly culled from her own life experiences, and in some cases, such as this one, actually predicted them.

14. Michelene Wandor has commented on this use of realism to introduce mainstream theater audiences to controversial new ideas. She writes: "Historically, artistic movements which seek to represent the experiences of oppressed groups reach initially for a realistic and immediately recognisable clarity. . . . Such realism has a radical impact when the content is new, when the selection of ordinary everyday elements in life are shaped into a work of art" (1980, 11).

15. See Estelle B. Freedman for an interesting overview of these various historical accounts of post-1920 feminism.

16. O'Neill's interest in the suffrage movement at all is rather curious, given his opinion of the suffragists. He writes that these "Militants lived a richly colored

emotional life. Like children, zealots, and romantics, they were either way up or way down, but whether high or low they were always intense, doctrinaire, and assertive" (274).

17. Cott's argument for re-evaluating 1920s feminism is actually quite compelling. She begins by noting that those historians who see feminism as faltering in the 1920s usually overestimate the value of winning the vote. For her, "Concentrating on suffrage and the electoral arena means viewing women's politics through the conventional lens where male behavior sets the norm" (153). To change the lens, she continues, "the organizational and political roles of women's voluntary associations— which, far from declining, multiplied in membership—must be considered within politics rather than outside politics" (155). In fact, Cott sees very little difference in women's grassroots politics before and after suffrage, with women's groups of both periods marked by multiple and divided interests, and with volunteerism and membership in women's groups at a constant level. When seen this way, "The level of organization among American women [after 1920] appears to compare very favorably with that before" (166).

While Cott's argument is convincing, it is nonetheless true that public perception of women's political activities changed once the militant suffragist was no longer a visible and powerful emblem for widespread social reform. As William Chafe has noted, the Nineteenth Amendment did little to change women's political power (43) or economic opportunities (78), and the young women of the 1920s were largely apathetic to women's rights (103). So while Cott is undoubtedly correct is viewing women's voluntary associations as evidence of significant political organization, without the banner of suffrage to unite them, women's groups had much less visibility after 1920 than they had before 1920.

18. See, for one example, the review of the play in the *New York Times*, 6 February 1923, 14:2.

19. As Judy Little has argued, "parody can be used as 'an exposé to destroy'" the power systems of another (20). Boothe is using social satire in just this parodic way: to expose and demolish male-created hierarchies of power.

20. Boothe's wealthy women are not unlike a character described in the Florence Kiper review with which I began this chapter. Writing about Augustus Thomas's 1913 play *A Man Thinks* (written in direct response to Crothers's *A Man's World*), Kiper observes: when the main character's wife "announces her undying love for the husband who has just bullied and insulted her, one is not amazed at all, remembering that for the woman dependent on luxury it is a business to cherish and to conserve her provider" (924). In all the ways that they, too, manipulate others to "conserve [their] providers," Boothe's characters show how little progress even privileged women had made in achieving equality in the first three decades of the twentieth century.

21. Nathan's discussion of women playwrights' "weaknesses" is chauvinistic to a point almost beyond belief. About their male characters, he writes: "when they tackle male characters, they go completely to pot. . . . [W]omen playwrights may know their own sex, although even here there has never lived a female playwright who knew women as deeply, fully, and articulately as male playwrights have amply proved they knew them, but they seem to know next to nothing about men. They see men as either romantic heroes or as childlike and blundering oafs, either as intellectual and emotional giants or as goats and blockheads" (429–30). About their lack of "objectivity," he continues: "It seems to be impossible for a woman playwright to stand aloof and apart from her central woman character and not identify herself,

in however slight a degree, with her" (430). I would like to comment further on these remarks, but I am speechless.

3. Remembering the Disremembered: Feminism, Realism, and the Harlem Renaissance

1. I should note in passing that Wintz devotes only three pages of his 232-page book on the Harlem Renaissance to the contributions of women artists, and most of those three pages merely summarize Gloria T. Hull's excellent work in *Color, Sex, and Poetry*. His history of the period is a prime example of the critical neglect of black women that some of the playwrights he overlooks were attempting to redress.

2. None of the prevailing descriptive terms for this African-American cultural phenomenon is very precise. I feel uncomfortable using "Harlem Renaissance" for the reasons Hall outlines: several of the playwrights I will discuss here lived and worked outside New York, and the term was not one of self-definition used at the time. Still, "New Negro Renaissance," a term applied by Alain Locke during the 1920s, implies, for me, an endorsement of Locke's aesthetic agenda, to which some of the playwrights I will discuss did not ascribe. I have finally settled on "Harlem Renaissance" simply because it is conventional and quickly recognizable.

3. See John Hope Franklin; the introduction to Singh, Shiker, and Baldwin; the introduction to Kramer; Plum; and Wintz.

4. W. E. B. Du Bois brilliantly explained this "double-consciousness" or "twoness" of the African American living in a white-dominated culture in *The Souls of Black Folk* (1989, 5). For discussion of this sense of being viewed by two different audiences as it pertains to black artists and actors, see James Weldon Johnson (477) and Clarence Muse (cited in Thompson 29–30).

5. See, for example, Case 1990, 12.

6. bell hooks makes a point about imperialist paradigms of black identity that helps explain Sanders's point here. For hooks, the notion of "authentic" black experience is essentializing and demeaning, positing an image of the "primitive" African American and "seeing as 'natural' those expressions of black life which conformed to a pre-existing pattern or stereotype" (1990, 29).

7. Helene Keyssar has examined folk drama (especially the Russian folk drama described by Mikhail Bakhtin) as being somewhat more complex and dialogic than that described (at least overtly) by Locke and Gregory. While she does not specifically comment on the folk drama of the Harlem Renaissance, Keyssar makes the important point that much current feminist and African-American drama partakes of the very qualities Bakhtin applauded in folk drama. She says: "As Bakhtin implies about folk drama, the voices we hear in many black American dramas and feminist dramas are the voices of marginal folk, voices that are both in conflict with dominant ideological positions and resistant among themselves to the reductions of uniformity" (1991, 95). What this statement suggests to me is that perhaps Locke and Gregory were more "propagandistic" in their artistic endeavors than they acknowledged, using folk characters and situations as a site of resistance to dominant cultural images.

8. For a fascinating analysis of how degrading stereotypes of black women conceal unequal power relations, and especially of how these hidden power relationships affected the outcome of the Clarence Thomas confirmation hearings, see Lubiano 1992.

9. Rachel laments the inevitable destruction of black children as she grinds the rosebuds under her feet, making explicit the comparison between the two. Jean-Marie Miller sees Rachel's action as a symbolic infanticide, the murder of her unborn

children (1978, 521); Helene Keyssar concurs, calling the action a symbolic "abortion" (1989, 238).

10. See, for example, Hatch 138; Fehrenbach 97; and Hull's summary of this response, 1987, 123.

11. Elizabeth Shaw is not racially defined in the play text. It is tempting to read her as white simply because of her education and class status. But as Sandra Richards has pointed out to me, presumably some black women trained at institutions like Tuskegee worked as public health nurses in the South. Furthermore, Richards notes that Burrill may have envisioned a black nurse to avoid presenting a mixed-race cast in a segregated society (letter to the author, 8 September 1994). Nonetheless, I see Elizabeth Shaw as white for two reasons. First, Shaw's unwillingness to provide Malinda with the information she needs reveals complicity with the white power structure and suggests her membership in it. Second, her reference to Malinda and her impoverished peers as "you people" connotes her sense of their distinct otherness, a distinction reinforced by Malinda's calling her "Miss Elizabeth" (reminiscent of antebellum plantation conventions) while the nurse calls Malinda by her first name. Whatever Miss Shaw's race, however, class differences certainly obtain, and class overrides both race and gender in determining Miss Shaw's behavior.

12. At a 1992 panel on Anti-Lynch Plays by Women (Association for Theatre in Higher Education Conference, Atlanta, August 1992), Judith Stephens handed out a list-in-progress of anti-lynch plays. On this subject alone, she has to date uncovered eleven plays by black women written from 1916 to 1933. Clearly the notion that African-American women artists of the Harlem Renaissance were not political in their writings (see Wintz, cited above) is erroneous.

13. Matthew Roudané has recently edited a collection of essays illustrating the intersection of public and private as endemic to American drama. See *Public Issues, Private Tensions: Contemporary American Drama*.

14. For the details of documented cases of slave infanticide in the United States, see Bauer and Bauer 416–18; Botkin 154; Hine and Wittenstein 291–95; Lerner 38, 61–62; and White 87–89.

15. Throughout this discussion, I refer to the version of *It's Morning* printed in Perkins's anthology *Black Female Playwrights* and housed (according to Perkins's bibliography) in the Fisk University Library special collection, Nashville, Tennessee. A different version of the same play with the slightly different title *It's Mornin'* appears in Elizabeth Brown-Guillory's anthology *Wines in the Wilderness*. While Brown-Guillory cites no manuscript, she evidently bases her version of the play on the 1940 Yale University Theatre production (83). In the Yale version, the storyline, many of the characters, and many of the speeches are identical to those in the Fisk version. However, the Yale version dramatizes two things that occur offstage in the version under discussion: the visit of the slave owner, Mrs. Tilden, to Cissie's cabin; and the New Year's party Cissie gives so that Millie may enjoy one final day of happiness.

Brown-Guillory's comments on the play as quoted in my text refer to the Yale version. However, they refer to elements (like Grannie Lou's status as voodoo woman and Graham's use of music) common to both plays and are therefore relevant to the version under discussion.

4. Refusing Containment

1. I am grateful to Susan Bennett for sharing the hard-to-obtain pamphlet from the London Against Racism Campaign with me.

2. See the excellent summary of nineteenth-century United States scientific racism in Gould, esp. 39–72.

3. See Davis, esp. 4–5, for discussion and definition of the "one-drop" rule.

4. In addition to West's incisive discussion of race as a cultural construct, see Crenshaw; hooks 1990; and Lubiano 1992.

5. For a detailed analysis of how American realism incorporates the past into the present, see my *The Presence of the Past in Modern American Drama*.

6. On this point I obviously disagree with Keyssar, who sees Norman's play as voyeuristic (1985, chap. 7). See also Murray 376–88, who discusses in some detail the ways the play encourages audience complicity with Arlie's behavior and values.

7. A number of other commentators on the play have noted that, for Arlene, getting out is not much different from being in. See Hart 1987, 70; Miner 126–27; Murray 384.

Bibliography

Abramson, Doris. 1990. Rachel Crothers: Broadway feminist. In *Modern American drama: The female canon*, edited by June Schlueter, 55–65. Rutherford, N.J.: Fairleigh Dickinson University Press.

Alcoff, Linda. 1989. Cultural feminism versus post-structuralism: The identity crisis in feminist theory. In *Feminist theory in practice and process*, edited by Micheline R. Malson, Jean F. O'Barr, Sarah Westphal-Wihl, and Mary Wyer, 295–326. Chicago: University of Chicago Press.

Alter, Jean. 1990. *A sociosemiotic theory of the theatre*. Philadelphia: University of Pennsylvania Press.

Anderson, Valetta. 1991. *She'll find her way home*. Unpublished manuscript.

Atkinson, Brooks. 1936. Review of *The Women*. New York Times 28 December, 13.

Auerbach, Eric. 1953. *Mimesis: The representation of reality in Western literature*. Translated by Willard R. Trask. Princeton: Princeton University Press.

Austin, Gayle. 1989. The madwoman in the spotlight: Plays of Maria Irene Fornes. In *Making a spectacle: Feminist essays on contemporary women's theatre*, edited by Lynda Hart, 76–85. Ann Arbor: University of Michigan Press.

———. 1990. *Feminist theories for dramatic criticism*. Ann Arbor: University of Michigan.

———. 1994. *The doll house show:* Feminist theory in the house of Ibsen. Paper presented at Association for Theatre in Higher Education Conference, 27 July, Chicago.

Bailey, Marlon. 1994. Paper presented at Black Theatre Network Conference, 26 July, Chicago.

Barlow, Judith E. 1985, ed. In *Plays by American women: 1900–1930*. New York: Applause.

Barthes, Roland. 1974. *S/Z*. Translated by Richard Miller. New York: Farrar, Straus, & Giroux.

Bassnett-McGuire, Susan E. 1984. Towards a theory of women's theatre. In *Semiotics of drama and theatre*, edited by Herta Schmid and Aloyisius van Kesteren, 445–66. Philadelphia: John Benjamins.

Bauer, Raymond M., and Alice H. Bauer. 1942. Day to day resistance to slavery. *Journal of Negro History* 27 (October): 388–419.

Baym, Nina. 1991. The madwoman and her languages: Why I don't do feminist theory. In *Feminisms: An anthology of literary criticism*, edited by Robyn R. Warhol and Diane Price Herndl. New Brunswick, N.J.: Rutgers University Press.

Becker, Susan. 1983. International feminism between the wars: The National Women's Party versus the League of Women Voters. In *Decades of discontent: The women's movement, 1920–1940*, edited by Lois Scharf and Joan M. Jensen, 223–42. Westport, Conn.: Greenwood Press.

167

Belsey, Catherine. 1985. Constructing the subject: Deconstructing the text. In *Feminist criticism and social change: Sex, class and race in literature and culture*, edited by Judith Newton and Deborah Rosenfelt, 45–64. New York: Methuen.

Bennett, Susan. 1990. *Theatre audiences: A theory of production and reception*. London: Routledge.

———. 1993. Subject to the tourist gaze. *TDR* Spring, 9–13.

Betsko, Kathleen, and Rachel Koenig, eds. 1987. *Interviews with contemporary women playwrights*. New York: Beech Tree Books.

Blau, Herbert. 1990. *The Audience*. Baltimore: Johns Hopkins University Press.

Boothe, Clare. 1937. *The women*. New York: Random House.

Botkin, B. A., ed. [1945] 1989. *Lay my burden down: A folk history of slavery*. Athens: University of Georgia Press.

Boumelha, Penny. 1988. Realism and the ends of feminism. In *Grafts: Feminist cultural criticism*, edited by Susan Sheridan, 77–91. London: Verso.

Brater, Enoch. 1990. After the absurd: Rethinking realism and a few other isms. In *Around the absurd: Essays on modern and postmodern drama*, 293–301. Ann Arbor: University of Michigan Press.

———, ed. 1989. *Feminine focus: The new women playwrights*. New York: Oxford University Press.

Brown, Elsa Barkley. 1992. "What has happened here": The politics of difference in women's history and feminist politics. *Feminist Studies* 18 (Summer): 295–312.

Brown, Janet. 1979. *Feminist drama: Definition and critical analysis*. Metuchen, N.J.: Scarecrow.

Brown-Guillory, Elizabeth. 1988. *Their place on stage: Black women playwrights in America*. New York: Praeger.

———, ed. 1990. *Wines in the wilderness: Plays by African American women from the Harlem Renaissance to the present*. New York: Greenwood Press.

Burk, Juli Thompson. 1994. Split Britches and the lesbian subject in Henrik's hallowed halls. Paper presented at Association for Theatre in Higher Education Conference, 27 July, Chicago.

Burrill, Mary P. [1919] 1989. *They that sit in darkness*. In *Black female playwrights: An anthology of plays before 1950*, edited by Kathy A. Perkins, 67–74. Bloomington: University of Indiana Press.

Busia, Abena P. B. 1988. Words whispered over voids: A context for black women's rebellious voices in the novel of the African diaspora. In *Studies in Black American Literature*, vol. 3. *Black feminist criticism and critical theory*, edited by Joe Weixelman and Houston A. Baker, Jr. Greenwood, Fla.: Penkevill Publishing Company.

Butler, Judith. 1988. Performative acts and gender constitution: An essay in phenomenology and feminist theory. *Theatre Journal* 40, no. 4: 519–31.

———. 1990a. *Gender trouble: Feminism and the subversion of identity*. New York: Routledge.

———. 1990b. Gender trouble, feminist theory, and psychoanalytic discourse. In *Feminism/postmodernism*, edited by Linda J. Nicholson, 324–40. New York: Routledge.

———. 1992. Contingent foundations: Feminism and the question of "postmodernism." In *Feminists theorize the political*, edited by Judith Butler and Joan W. Scott, 3–21. New York: Routledge.

Butler, Judith, and Joan W. Scott, eds. 1992. *Feminists theorize the political.* New York: Routledge.

Carlson, Susan. 1984. Comic textures and female communities 1937 and 1977: Clare Boothe and Wendy Wasserstein. *Modern Drama* 27 (December): 564–73.

Case, Sue-Ellen. 1988. *Feminism and theatre.* New York: Methuen.

———. 1989a. From split subject to split britches. *Feminine focus: The new women playwrights,* edited by Enoch Brater, 126–46. New York: Oxford University Press.

———. 1989b. Toward a butch-femme aesthetic. In *Making a spectacle: feminist essays on contemporary women's theatre,* edited by Lynda Hart, 282–99. Ann Arbor: University of Michigan Press.

———, ed. 1990. *Performing feminisms: Feminist critical theory and theatre.* Baltimore: Johns Hopkins University Press.

Chafe, William H. 1991. *The paradox of change: American women in the twentieth century.* New York: Oxford University Press.

Chapman, Abraham. 1967. The Harlem Renaissance in literary history. *CLA Journal* 11 (September): 38–58.

Childress, Alice. [1969] 1973. *Wine in the wilderness.* In *Plays by and about women,* edited by Victoria Sullivan and James Hatch, 379–421. New York: Random House.

———. 1971. *Trouble in mind: A comedy-drama in two acts.* In *Black theater: A 20th century collection of the work of its best playwrights,* edited by Lindsay Patterson, 137–74. New York: Dodd, Mead & Co.

———. 1984. A candle in a gale wind. In *Black women writers (1950–1980): A critical evaluation,* edited by Mari Evans, 111–16. New York: Doubleday.

Chinoy, Helen Krich. 1982. Suppressed desires: Women in the theatre. In *Women, the arts, and the 1920s in Paris and New York,* edited by Kenneth W. Wheeler and Virginia Lee Lussier, 126–32. New Brunswick, N.J.: Transaction Books.

Chinoy, Helen Krich, and Linda Walsh Jenkins, eds. [1981] 1987. *Women in American theatre.* Revised and expanded edition. New York: Theatre Communications Group.

Chodorow, Nancy. 1978. *The reproduction of mothering: Psychoanalysis and the sociology of gender.* Berkeley: University of California Press.

Chow, Rey. 1992. Postmodern automatons. In *Feminists theorize the political,* edited by Judith Butler and Joan W. Scott, 101–17. New York: Routledge.

Christian, Barbara. 1980. *Black women novelists: The development of a tradition, 1892–1976.* Westport, Conn.: Greenwood Press.

———. 1990. "Somebody forgot to tell somebody something": African-American women's historical novels. In *Wild women in the whirlwind: Afra-American culture and the contemporary literary renaissance,* edited by Joanne M. Braxton and Andrée Nicola McLaughlin, 326–41. New Brunswick, N.J.: Rutgers University Press.

Cole, Carole L. 1991. *The search for power: Drama by American women, 1909–1929.* Ph.D. Diss., Purdue University.

Cott, Nancy F. 1990. Across the great divide: Women in politics before and after 1920. In *Women, politics, and change,* edited by Louise A. Tilly and Patricia Gurin, 153–76. New York: Russell Sage Foundation.

Crenshaw, Kimberlé. 1992. Whose story is it, anyway? Feminist and anti-racist appropriations of Anita Hill. In *Race-ing justice, en-gendering power,* edited by Toni Morrison, 402–40. New York: Pantheon.

Crosby, Christina. 1992. Dealing with differences. In *Feminists theorize the political*, edited by Judith Butler and Joan W. Scott, 130–43. New York: Routledge.

Crothers, Rachel. 1913. *Ourselves*. Unpublished manuscript. Rare Book Collection, University of Pennsylvania Library.

―――. [1915] 1985. *A man's world*. In *Plays by American women: 1900–1930*, edited by Judith E. Barlow, 1–69. New York: Applause.

―――. 1923. *Mary the third. Three plays by Rachel Crothers*. New York: Brentano's.

―――. [1928] 1967. The construction of a play. In *The art of playwriting: Lectures delivered at the University of Pennsylvania*, 115–34. Freeport, N.Y.: Books for Libraries Press.

Cummings, Scott T. 1985. Seeing with clarity: The visions of Maria Irene Fornes. *Theater* 17 (Winter): 51–56.

―――. 1992. Adrienne Kennedy: Her mythology of one emanates a mysterious but universal truth. *American Theatre* 9 (June): 32–33.

Curb, Rosemary. 1980. An unfashionable tragedy of American racism: Alice Childress's *Wedding band. Melus* 7.4: 57–68.

―――. 1985. Re/cognition, re/presentation, re/creation in woman-conscious drama: The seer, the seen, the scene, the obscene. *Theatre Journal* 37 (October): 302–16.

―――. 1992. (Hetero)Sexual terrors in Adrienne Kennedy's early plays. In *Intersecting boundaries: The theatre of Adrienne Kennedy*, edited by Paul K. Bryant-Jackson and Lois More Overbeck, 142–56. Minneapolis: University of Minnesota Press.

Cureau, Rebecca T. 1982. Toward an aesthetic of Black folk expression. In *Alain Locke: Reflections on a modern Renaissance man*, edited by Russel J. Linneman, 77–90. Baton Rouge: Louisiana State University Press.

Curtis, L. P., Jr. 1968. *Anglo-Saxons and Celts: A study of anti–Irish prejudice in Victorian England*. Bridgeport, Conn.: Conference on British Studies.

Davis, F. James. 1991. *Who is black? one nation's definition*. University Park: Pennsylvania University State Press.

Davy, Kate. 1986. Constructing the spectator: Reception, context, and address in lesbian performance. *Performing Arts Journal* 10, no. 2: 43–52.

de Lauretis, Teresa. 1984. *Alice doesn't: Feminism, semiotics, cinema*. Bloomington: Indiana University Press.

―――. 1987. *Technologies of gender: Essays on theory, film, and fiction*. Bloomington: Indiana University Press.

―――. 1990. Upping the anti (sic) in feminist theory. In *Conflicts in feminism*, edited by Marianne Hirsch and Evelyn Fox Keller, 255–70. New York: Routledge.

Demastes, William W. 1988. *Beyond naturalism: A new realism in American theatre*. New York: Greenwood Press.

Diamond, Elin. 1988. Brechtian theory/feminist theory: Toward a gestic feminist criticism. *TDR* 32 (Spring): 82–94.

―――. 1989. Mimesis, mimicry, and the true-real. *Modern Drama* 32, no. 1: 58–72.

―――. 1992. Mimesis in syncopated time: Reading Adrienne Kennedy. In *Intersecting boundaries: The theatre of Adrienne Kennedy*, edited by Paul K. Bryant-Jackson and Lois More Overbeck, 131–41. Minneapolis: University of Minnesota Press.

Dolan, Jill. 1988. *The feminist spectator as critic.* Ann Arbor: University of Michigan Institute Research Press.

———. 1990. "Lesbian" subjectivity in realism: Dragging at the margins of structure and ideology. In *Performing feminisms: Feminist critical theory and theatre*, edited by Sue-Ellen Case, 40–53. Baltimore: Johns Hopkins University Press.

———. 1994. *Presence and desire.* Ann Arbor: University of Michigan Press.

Donovan, Josephine. 1987. Toward a women's poetics. In *Feminist issues in literary scholarship*, edited by Shari Benstock, 98–109. Bloomington: Indiana University Press.

Du Bois, W. E. B. [1903] 1989. *The souls of black folk.* New York: Penguin.

———. 1926. Krigwa little theatre movement. *Crisis* 32: 134–36.

Dukore, Bernard F. 1990. Karl Marx's youngest daughter and *A doll's house. Theatre Journal* 42 (October): 1990.

DuPlessis, Rachel Blau. 1985. *Writing beyond the ending: Narrative strategies of twentieth-century women writers.* Bloomington: Indiana University Press.

Durbach, Errol. 1991. *A doll's house: Ibsen's myth of transformation.* Boston: Twayne.

Eaton, Walter Prichard. 1910. *At the New Theatre and others: The American stage: Its problems and performances.* Boston: Small, Maynard.

Ebert, Teresa L. 1992. Gender and the everyday: Toward a postmodern materialist feminist theory of mimesis. In *"Turning the century": Feminist theory in the 1990s*, edited by Glynnis Carr, 90–122. *Bucknell Review.* Lewisburg, Pa.: Bucknell University Press.

Elam, Keir. 1980. *The semiotics of theatre and drama.* London: Methuen.

Eliot, George. 1977. *Middlemarch.* New York: Norton.

Fehrenbach, Robert J. 1990. An early twentieth-century problem play of life in black America: Angelina Grimké's *Rachel.* In *Wild women in the whirlwind: Afra-American culture and the contemporary literary renaissance*, edited by Joanne M. Braxton and Andrée Nicola McLaughlin, 89–106. New Brunswick, N.J.: Rutgers University Press.

Felski, Rita. 1989. *Beyond feminist aesthetics: Feminist literature and social change.* Cambridge, Mass.: Harvard University Press.

Ferber, Edna. 1979. *The eldest.* In *A century of plays by American women*, edited by Rachel France, 67–73. New York: Richards Rosen Press.

Fetterley, Judith. 1978. *The resisting reader: A feminist approach to American fiction.* Bloomington: Indiana University Press.

Flexner, Eleanor. 1938. *American playwrights, 1918–1938: The theatre retreats from reality.* New York: Simon & Schuster.

Forte, Jeanie. 1988. Women's performance art: Feminism and postmodernism. *Theatre Journal* 40, no. 2: 217–37.

———. 1989. Realism, narrative, and the feminist playwright—a problem of reception. *Modern Drama* 32, no. 1: 115–27.

———. 1992. Kennedy's body politic: The mulatta, menses, and the medusa. In *Intersecting boundaries: The theatre of Adrienne Kennedy*, edited by Paul K. Bryant-Jackson and Lois More Overbeck, 157–69. Minneapolis: University of Minnesota Press.

France, Rachel. 1993. Apropos of women and the American theatre: The suffrage play. *Theatre History Studies* 13: 33–46.

————, ed. 1979. *A century of plays by American women.* New York: Richards Rosen Press.

Franklin, John Hope. 1980. *From slavery to freedom: A history of Negro Americans.* 5th ed. New York: Knopf.

Fraser, Nancy, and Linda J. Nicholson. 1990. Social criticism without philosophy: An encounter between feminism and postmodernism. In *Feminism/postmodernism*, edited by Linda J. Nicholson, 19–38. New York: Routledge.

Freedman, Estelle B. 1983. The new woman: Changing views of women in the 1920s. In *Decades of discontent: The women's movement, 1920–1940*, edited by Lois Scharf and Joan M. Jensen, 21–44. Westport, Conn.: Greenwood Press.

Friedl, Bettina. 1987. Introduction. In *On to victory: Propaganda plays of the woman suffrage movement*, edited by Bettina Friedl, 1–42. Boston: Northeastern University Press.

Friedman, Sharon. 1984. Feminism as theme in twentieth-century American women's drama. *American Studies* 25, no. 2: 69–89.

Fuchs, Elinor, ed. 1987. *Plays of the holocaust.* New York: Theatre Communications Group.

Gainor, J. Ellen. forthcoming. The Provincetown Players' experiments with realism. In *American dramatic realism: (In)validating a culture*, edited by William W. Demastes. Tuscaloosa: University of Alabama Press.

Gale, Zona. [1921] 1985. *Miss Lulu Bett.* In *Plays by American women: 1900–1930*, edited by Judith E. Barlow, 87–161. New York: Applause.

Gallop, Jane, and Carolyn Burke. 1980. Psychoanalysis and feminism in France. In *The future of difference*, edited by Hester Einstein and Alice Jardine. Boston: G. K. Hall.

Gardiner, Judith Kegan. 1987. Gender, values, and Lessing's cats. In *Feminist issues in literary scholarship*, edited by Shari Benstock, 110–23. Bloomington: Indiana University Press.

Gassner, John. 1956. *Form and idea in modern theatre.* New York: Dryden.

Genovese, Eugene. 1972. *Roll, Jordan, roll: The world the slaves made.* New York: Random House.

Gilbert, Sandra M., and Susan Gubar. 1979. *The madwoman in the attic: The woman writer and the nineteenth-century literary imagination.* New Haven: Yale University Press.

————. 1987. *No man's land: The place of the woman writer in the twentieth century.* New Haven: Yale University Press.

Gilligan, Carol. 1982. *In a different voice: Psychological theory and women's development.* Cambridge, Mass.: Harvard University Press.

Gilman, Charlotte Perkins. [1911] 1987. *Something to vote for: A one act play.* In *On to victory: Propaganda plays of the woman suffrage movement*, edited by Bettina Friedl, 143–61. Boston: Northeastern University Press.

Gipson, Rosemary. 1982. Martha Morton: America's first professional woman playwright. *Theatre Survey* 23: 1982.

Gottlieb, Lois. 1975. Obstacles to feminism in the early plays of Rachel Crothers. *University of Michigan Papers in Women's Studies* 1, no. 4: 71–84.

————. 1979. *Rachel Crothers.* Boston: Twayne.

————. 1981. Looking to women: Rachel Crothers and the feminist heroine. In

Women in American theatre, revised and expanded edition, edited by Helen Krich Chinoy and Linda Walsh Jenkins, 137–45. New York: Theatre Communications Group.

Gould, Stephen Jay. 1981. *The mismeasure of man*. New York: Norton.

Graham, Shirley. 1989. *It's morning*. In *Black female playwrights: An anthology of plays before 1950*, edited by Kathy A. Perkins, 211–24. Bloomington: University of Indiana Press.

Gregory, Montgomery. [1925] 1968. The drama of Negro life. In *The new Negro: An interpretation*, edited by Alain Locke, 153–60. New York: Arno.

Grimké, Angelina Weld. [1920] 1974. *Rachel*. In *Black theater, U.S.A.: Forty-five plays by black Americans, 1847–1974*, edited by James V. Hatch, 137–72. New York: Macmillan.

Gussow, Mel. 1987. Theatre: "Shayna maidel" *New York Times* October 30, C16.

Hall, Katana Lazet. 1990. *Reclaiming the legacy: An Afracentric analysis of selected plays by African American wimmin playwrights, 1916–1930*. Ph.D. Diss., Bowling Green State University.

Haraway, Donna. 1990. A manifesto for cyborgs: Science, technology, and social feminism in the 1980s. In *Feminism/postmodernism*, edited by Linda J. Nicholson, 190–233. New York: Routledge.

Hart, Lynda. 1987. Doing time: Hunger for power in Marsha Norman's plays. *Southern Quarterly* Spring, 67–79.

———. 1989. "They don't even look like maids any more": Wendy Kesselman's *My sister in this house*. Edited by Lynda Hart. In *Making a spectacle: Feminist essays on contemporary women's theatre*, 131–46. Ann Arbor: University of Michigan.

Hatch, James V., ed. 1974. *Black theater, U.S.A.: Forty-five plays by black Americans, 1847–1974*. New York: Macmillan.

Henderson, Mae Gwendolyn. 1989. Speaking in tongues: Dialogics, dialectics, and the black woman writer's literary tradition. In *Changing our own words: Essays on criticism, theory, and writing by black women*, edited by Cheryl A. Wall, 16–37. New Brunswick, N.J.: Rutgers University Press.

Higginbotham, Evelyn Brooks. 1992. African-American women's history and the metalanguage of race. *Signs* 17 (Winter): 251–74.

Hine, Darlene Clark. 1989. Rape and the inner lives of black women in the Middle West: Preliminary thoughts on the culture of dissemblance. *Signs* 14 (Summer): 912–20.

Hine, Darlene, and Kate Wittenstein. 1981. Female slave resistance: The economics of sex. In *The black woman cross-culturally*, edited by Filomina Chioma Steady, 289–99. Cambridge, Mass.: Schenkman.

Hirsch, Marianne, and Evelyn Fox Keller, eds. 1990. *Conflicts in feminism*. New York: Routledge.

hooks, bell. 1990. *Yearning: Race, gender, and cultural politics*. Boston: South End Press.

———. 1992. *Black looks: Race and representation*. Boston: South End Press.

Huggins, Nathan Irvin, ed. 1976. *Voices from the Harlem Renaissance*. New York: Oxford University Press.

Hull, Gloria T. 1984. Alice Dunbar-Nelson: A personal and literary perspective. In *Between women: Biographers, novelists, critics, teachers, and artists write about their work on women*, edited by Carol Ascher, Louise DeSalvo, and Sara Ruddick, 105–12. Boston: Beacon Press.

———. 1987. *Color, sex, and poetry: Three women writers of the Harlem Renaissance*. Bloomington: Indiana University Press.

———, ed. 1988. *The works of Alice Dunbar-Nelson*. New York: Oxford University Press.

Isser, E. R. 1990. Toward a feminist perspective in American holocaust drama. *Studies in the Humanities* 17, no. 2: 139–48.

Jacobus, Lee A., ed. 1989. *The Bedford introduction to drama*. New York: St. Martin's Press.

Jameson, Fredric. 1981. *The political unconscious: Narrative as a socially symbolic act*. Ithaca: Cornell University Press.

Jenkins, Linda Walsh. 1984. Locating the language of gender experience. *Women and Performance* 2, no. 1: 5–20.

Jensen, Joan M. 1983. All pink sisters: The War Department and the feminist movement in the 1920s. In *Decades of discontent: The women's movement, 1920–1940*, edited by Lois Scharf and Joan M. Jensen, 199–222. Westport, Conn.: Greenwood Press.

Johnson, Georgia Douglas. 1990. *Safe*. In *Wines in the wilderness: Plays by African American Women from the Harlem Renaissance to the present*, edited by Elizabeth Brown-Guillory, 26–32. New York: Praeger.

Johnson, James Weldon. 1928. The dilemma of the Negro author. *The American Mercury* December, 477.

Kaplan, Amy. 1988. *The social construction of American realism*. Chicago: University of Chicago Press.

Kaplan, E. Ann. 1983. *Women and film: Both sides of the camera*. New York: Methuen.

Kennedy, Adrienne. [1962] 1988a. Funnyhouse of a Negro. In *Adrienne Kennedy: In one act*, 1–23. Minneapolis: University of Minnesota Press.

———. [1962] 1988b. The owl answers. In *Adrienne Kennedy: In one act*, 25–45. Minneapolis: University of Minnesota Press.

———. 1994. Introduction to *The dramatic circle*. In *Moon marked and touched by sun: Plays by African-American women*, edited by Sydné Mahone, 189–91. New York: Theatre Communications Group.

Kesselman, Wendy. 1982. *My sister in this house*. New York: Doubleday.

Keyssar, Helene. 1985. *Feminist theatre: An introduction to the plays of contemporary British and American women*. New York: Grove Press.

———. 1989. Rites and responsibilities: The drama of black American women. In *Feminine focus: The new women playwrights*, edited by Enoch Brater, 226–40. New York: Oxford University Press.

———. 1991. Drama and the dialogic imagination: *The Heidi chronicles* and *Fefu and her friends*. *Modern Drama* 34 (March): 88–106.

Kilkelly, Ann Gavere. 1986. Who's in the house? *Women and Performance* 3, no. 1: 29–34.

King, Nicole. 1993. Unimaginable bodies in *The Ohio State Murders*. Presented at Association for Theatre in Higher Education Conference, 6 August, Atlanta.

Kiper, Florence. 1914. Some American plays from the feminist viewpoint. *Forum* 51: 921–31.

Kolb, Deborah S. 1975. The rise and fall of the New Woman in American drama. *Educational Theatre Journal* 27 (May): 149–60.

Koppen, Randi S. 1992. "The furtive event": Theorizing feminist spectatorship. *Modern Drama* 35 (September): 378–94.

Kramer, Victor A., ed. 1987. *The Harlem Renaissance re-examined.* New York: AMS Press.

Kristeva, Julia. [1974] 1980. Oscillation between power and denial. Translated by Marilyn A. August. In *New French feminisms: An anthology,* edited by Elaine Marks and Isabelle de Courtivron, 165–67. New York: Schocken Books.

———. [1974] 1986. Revolution in poetic language. Edited and translated by Toril Moi. In *The Kristeva reader,* 89–136. New York: Columbia University Press.

Kuhn, John G. 1968. Maria Irene Fornes. In *Contemporary dramatists,* edited by D. L. Kirkpatrick. Chicago: St. James Press.

Leavitt, Dinah Luise. 1980. *Feminist theatre groups.* Jefferson, N.C.: McFarland.

Lebow, Barbara. 1985. *A shayna maidel.* New York: New American Library.

Lebsock, Suzanne. 1990. Woman and American politics, 1880–1920. In *Women, politics, and change,* edited by Louise A. Tilly and Patricia Gurin, 35–62. New York: Russell Sage Foundation.

Lerner, Gerda, ed. 1973. *Black women in white America: A documentary history.* New York: Random House.

Lester, Elenore. 1973. The women: Older but not wiser. Review. *Ms.* August, 42–45.

Little, Judy. 1991. Humoring the sentence: Women's dialogic comedy. In *Women's comic visions,* edited by June Schoen, 19–32. Detroit: Wayne State University Press.

Locke, Alain. [1925] 1968. The new Negro. In *The new Negro: An interpretation,* edited by Alain Locke, 3–16. New York: Arno.

London Against Racism Campaign. 1984. *Nothing but the same old story: The roots of anti–Irish racism.* London: Information on Ireland.

Lorde, Audre. 1981. The master's tools will never dismantle the master's house. In *This bridge called my back: Writings by radical women of color,* edited by Cherríe Moraga and Gloria Anzaldúa, 98–101. New York: Kitchen Table Press.

———. 1984. Poetry is not a luxury. In *Sister outsider.* Trumansburg, N.Y.: Crossing Press.

Lubiano, Wahneema. 1991. But compared to what? reading realism, representation, and essentialism in *School daze, Do the right thing,* and the Spike Lee discourse. *Black American Literature Forum* 25 (Summer): 253–82.

———. 1992. Black ladies, welfare queens, and state minstrels: Ideological war by narrative means. In *Race-ing justice, en-gendering power: Essays on Anita Hill, Clarence Thomas, and the construction of social reality,* edited by Toni Morrison, 323–63. New York: Pantheon.

McDougald, Elise Johnson. [1925] 1968. The task of Negro womanhood. In *The new Negro: An interpretation,* edited by Alain Locke, 369–82. New York: Arno.

McGrath, John. 1979. The theory and practice of political theatre. *Theatre Quarterly* 9, no. 35: 43–54.

McKay, Nellie. 1987a. Black theater and drama in the 1920s: Years of growing pains. *Massachusetts Review* 28 (Winter): 615–26.

———. 1987b. "What were they saying?": Black women playwrights of the Harlem

Renaissance. In *The Harlem Renaissance re-examined*, edited by Victor A. Kramer, 129–48. New York: AMS Press.

Mandl, Bette. 1990. Disturbing women: Wendy Kesselman's *My sister in this house*. In *Modern American drama: The female canon*, edited by June Schlueter, 246–53. Rutherford, N.J.: Fairleigh Dickinson University Press.

Marranca, Bonnie. 1984. The real life of Maria Irene Fornes. *Performing Arts Journal* 8, no. 1: 29–34.

Miller, Arthur. [1957] 1981. Introduction. In *Collected plays*. New York: Viking Press.

Miller, Jeanne-Marie A. 1978. Angelina Weld Grimké: Playwright and poet. *CLA Journal* 21 (June): 513–24.

———. 1982. Black women playwrights from Grimké to Shange: Selected synopses of their works. In *But some of us are brave*, edited by Gloria T. Hull, Patricia Bell Scott, and Barbara Smith, 280–96. Old Westbury, N.Y.: Feminist Press.

———. 1990. Georgia Douglas Johnson and May Miller: Forgotten playwrights of the New Negro Renaissance. *CLA Journal* 33 (June): 349–66.

Miner, Madonne. 1985. "What's these bars doin' here?"—the impossibility of *Getting out*. *Theatre Annual* 40: 115–36.

Modleski, Tania. 1986. Feminism and the power of interpretation: Some critical readings. In *Feminist studies/critical studies*, edited by Teresa de Lauretis, 121–38. Bloomington: Indiana University Press.

Moore, Honor, ed. 1977. *The new women's theatre: Ten plays by contemporary American women*. New York: Random House.

Moraga, Cherríe. 1986. *Giving up the ghost*. Los Angeles: West End Press.

Morrison, Toni. 1987. *Beloved*. New York: Knopf.

Mulvey, Laura. 1975. Visual pleasure and narrative cinema. *Screen* 16 (Autumn): 6–18.

Murphy, Brenda. 1987. *American realism and American drama, 1880–1940*. Cambridge: Cambridge University Press.

Murray, Timothy. 1983. Patriarchal panopticism, or the seduction of a bad joke: *Getting out* in theory. *Theatre Journal* 35, no. 3: 376–88.

Nathan, George Jean. 1940. *Encyclopedia of the theatre*. New York: Knopf.

Neely, Carol Thomas. 1985. Feminist criticism in motion. In *For alma mater: Theory and practice in feminist scholarship*, edited by Paula A. Treichler, Cheris Kramarae, and Beth Stafford, 69–90. Urbana: University of Illinois Press.

Newton, Judith, and Deborah Rosenfelt. 1985. Toward a materialist-feminist criticism. Introduction. In *Feminist criticism and social change: Sex, class and race in literature and culture*, edited by Judith Newton and Deborah Rosenfelt, xv–xxxix. New York: Methuen.

Norman, Marsha. 1978. *Getting out*. New York: Doubleday.

O'Casey, Sean. [1925] 1972. *The shadow of a gunman*. In *Three plays*, 75–130. London: Macmillan.

O'Neill, William L. 1969. *Everyone was brave: The rise and fall of feminism in America*. Chicago: Quadrangle Books.

Patraka, Vivian M. 1987. Contemporary drama, fascism, and the holocaust. *Theatre Journal* 39 (March): 65–77.

———. 1989. Lillian Hellman's *Watch on the Rhine*: Realism, gender, and historical crisis. *Modern Drama* 32 (March): 128–45.

Patterson, Ada. 1909. A chat with the dean of America's women playwrights. *Theatre Magazine* 10: 126–30.

Pavis, Patrice. 1982. *Languages of the stage.* New York: Performing Arts Journal.

Perkins, Kathy A., ed. 1989. *Black female playwrights: An anthology of plays before 1950.* Bloomington: Indiana University Press.

Pevitts, Beverley Byers. 1987. Fefu and her friends. In *Women in American theatre,* edited by Helen Krich Chinoy and Linda Walsh Jenkins, 317–21. New York: Theatre Communications Group.

Phelan, Peggy. 1993. *Unmarked: The politics of performance.* London: Routledge.

Plum, Jay. 1992. Rose McClendon and the black units of the Federal Theatre Project: A lost contribution. *Theatre Survey* 33 (November): 144–53.

Pruette, Lorine. [1924] 1972. *Women and leisure: A study of social waste.* American women: images and realities. New York: Arno.

Quigley, Austin E. 1985. *The modern stage and other worlds.* New York: Methuen.

Reinelt, Janelle. 1986. Beyond Brecht: Britain's new feminist drama. *Theatre Journal* 38 (May): 154–63.

———. 1989a. The politics of form: Realism, melodrama and Pam Gems' *Camille. Women and Performance* 4, no. 2: 96–103.

———. 1989b. Realism, narrative, and the feminist playwright—a problem of reception. *Modern Drama* 32 (March): 115–27.

———. 1994. A feminist reconsideration of the Brecht/Lukács debates. *Women and Performance* 7, no. 1: 123–39.

Reinelt, Janelle G., and Joseph R. Roach, eds. 1992. *Critical theory and performance.* Ann Arbor: University of Michigan Press.

Reinhardt, Nancy. 1981. New directions for feminist criticism in theatre and the related arts. In *A feminist perspective in the academy: The difference it makes,* edited by Elizabeth Langland and Walter Gove, 25–51. Chicago: University of Chicago Press.

Roudané, Matthew, ed. 1993. *Public issues, private tensions: Contemporary American drama.* New York: AMS Press.

Sanders, Leslie Catherine. 1988. *The development of black theatre in America: From shadows to selves.* Baton Rouge: Louisiana State University Press.

Schroeder, Patricia R. 1989. *The presence of the past in modern American drama.* Rutherford, N.J.: Fairleigh Dickinson University Press.

Scott, Freda L. 1985. Black drama and the Harlem Renaissance. *Theatre Journal* 37 (December): 426–39.

Shaw, Bernard. 1898. *Plays: Pleasant and unpleasant.* Chicago: Herbert S. Stone & Co.

Showalter, Elaine. 1985. Feminist criticism in the wilderness. In *The new feminist criticism: Essays on women, literature, and theory,* edited by Elaine Showalter, 243–70. New York: Pantheon.

Silverman, Kaja. 1983. *The subject of semiotics.* New York: Oxford University Press.

Simon, John. 1979. Theatre chronicle: Kopit, Norman, and Shepard. *Hudson Review* 32: 77–88.

Singh, Amritjit, William Shiker, and Stanley Baldwin, eds. 1989. *The Harlem Renaissance: Revaluations.* New York: Garland.

Smith, Iris. 1994. "Who speaks and who is spoken for?" An interview with playwright Joan Lipkin. *TDR* 38, no. 3 (Fall): 96–127.

Smith, Valerie. 1989. Black feminist theory and the representation of the "Other." In *Changing our own words: Essays on criticism, theory, and writing by black women*, edited by Cheryl A. Wall, 38–57. New Brunswick, N.J.: Rutgers University Press.

Sontag, Susan. 1986. Preface. In *Maria Irene Fornes Plays*, 7–10. New York: Performing Arts Journal Publications.

Spencer, Jenny. 1989. Marsha Norman's *she-tragedies*. In *Making a spectacle: Feminist essays on contemporary women's theatre*, edited by Lynda Hart, 147–65. Ann Arbor: University of Michigan Press.

Spivak, Gayatri Chakravorty. 1988. Can the subaltern speak? In *Marxism and the interpretation of culture*, edited by Cary Nelson and Lawrence Grossberg, 271–313. Urbana: University of Illinois Press.

Stephens, Judith L. 1985. The compatability of traditional dramatic form and feminist expression. *Theatre Annual*: 7–23.

———. 1988. From positive image to disruptive apparatus: Feminist perspectives in American plays and dramatic criticism. *Pennsylvania Speech Communications Annual* 44: 59–67.

———. 1990. The anti-lynch play: Toward an interracial feminist dialogue in theatre. *Journal of American Drama and Theatre* 2, no. 3: 59–69.

———. 1992. Anti-lynch plays by African American women: Race, gender, and social protest in American drama. *African American Review* 26 (Summer): 329–39.

Stetson, Erlene. 1984. Silence: Access and aspiration. In *Between women: Biographers, novelists, critics, teachers, and artists write about their work on women*, edited by Carol Ascher, Louise DeSalvo, and Sara Ruddick, 237–51. Boston: Beacon Press.

Stowell, Sheila. 1992a. Rehabilitating realism. *Journal of Dramatic Theory and Criticism* 6, no. 2: 81–88.

———. 1992b. *A stage of their own: Feminist playwrights of the suffrage era*. Ann Arbor: University of Michigan Press.

Stucky, Nathan. 1994. Re/performance and mimesis: Constructing a theatrical reality. Paper presented at Association for Theatre in Higher Education Conference, 28 July, Chicago.

Sullivan, Victoria, and James Hatch, eds. 1973. *Plays by and about women*. New York: Random House.

Sutherland, Cynthia. 1978. American women playwrights as mediators of the "woman problem." *Modern Drama* 21 (September): 319–36.

Swanson, Gillian. 1986. Rethinking representation. *Screen* 27 (September-October): 16–28.

Thompson, Sister M. Francesca, O.S.F. 1980. The Lafayette Players, 1917–1932. In *The theatre of black Americans, vol. 2*, edited by Errol Hill, 13–32. Englewood Cliffs, N.J.: Prentice-Hall.

Vanden Heuvel, Michael. 1989. Ransacking realism: The plays of American new realism. *Contemporary Literature* 30 (Winter): 583–88.

———. 1992. Complementary spaces: Realism, performance, and a new dialogics of theatre. *Theatre Journal* 44 (March): 47–58.

Wandor, Michelene. 1980. Introduction. In *Strike while the iron is hot: Three plays on sexual politics*, edited by Michelene Wandor, 5–15. London: Journeyman Press.

———. 1986. *Carry on, understudies: Theatre and sexual politics.* London: Routledge.

Warhol, Robyn R., and Diane Price Herndl, eds. 1991. *Feminisms: An anthology of literary theory and criticism.* New Brunswick, N.J.: Rutgers University Press.

Weedon, Chris. 1987. *Feminist practice and poststructuralist theory.* Oxford: Basil Blackwell.

Wentworth, Marion Craig. 1912. *The flower shop.* Boston: The Gorham Press.

———. 1915. *War brides.* New York: Century.

West, Cornel. 1993. *Race matters.* Boston: Beacon Press.

Wetzsteon, Ross. 1986. Irene Fornes: The elements of style. Review. *Village Voice* 29 April, 42–45.

White, Deborah Gray. 1985. *Ar'n't I a woman?: Female slaves in the plantation South.* New York: Norton.

Wilkerson, Margaret B., ed. 1986. *9 plays by black women.* New York: Penguin.

Williams, Raymond. 1969. *Drama from Ibsen to Brecht.* New York: Oxford University Press.

———. 1977. *Marxism and literature.* Oxford: Oxford University Press.

Wintz, Cary D. 1988. *Black culture and the Harlem Renaissance.* Houston: Rice University Press.

Wolff, Ruth. 1977. *The Abdication.* In *The new women's theatre,* edited by Honor Moore. New York: Vintage.

The women. 1937. Review. *Time* 4 January, 30.

Worthen, W. B. 1989. *Still playing games: Ideology and performance in the theater of Maria Irene Fornes.* In *Feminine focus: The new women playwrights,* edited by Enoch Brater, 167–209. New York: Oxford University Press.

———. 1992. *Modern drama and the rhetoric of theater.* Berkeley: University of California Press.

———., ed. 1993. *The HBJ anthology of drama.* Fort Worth: Harcourt Brace Jovanovich.

Young, Iris Marion. 1990. The ideal of community and the politics of difference. In *Feminism/postmodernism,* edited by Linda J. Nicholson, 300–23. New York: Routledge.

Young, Patricia Alzatia. 1986. *Female pioneers in Afro-American drama: Angelina Weld Grimké, Georgia Douglas Johnson, Alice Dunbar-Nelson, and Mary Powell Burrill.* Ph.D. Diss., Bowling Green State University.

Young, Stark. 1937. Not a review. *New Republic* 7 April, 263.

Index

Abramson, Doris E., 73, 162n.9
Alcoff, Linda, 159n.9
Alter, Jean, 28, 118
Anderson, Valetta, 154–56. Plays: *She'll Find Her Way Home*, 154–55; *Virgins in Paradise*, 155
Anti-lynch plays. *See* lynching
Antimimesis, 25
Atkinson, Brooks, 88
Audience: Anderson on, 154–55; double (mixed race), 97–101, 105–7; and Fornes, 38; in *Getting Out*, 138; Grimké on, 105–7; Lipkin on, 155–56; mainstream, 37–38, 43, 148; in *My Sister in This House*, 145; nineteenth-century, 36; and realism, 17–19, 27–30, 37–38, 150; in *A Shayna Maidel*, 135–36
Auerbach, Eric, 16
Austin, Gayle: on Childress, 130, 132; on Fornes, 16, 40; *The Doll House Show*, 149–50

Bailey, Marlon, 149
Bakhtin, Mikhail, 164n.7
Barlow, Judith, 55, 85, 87, 160n.21
Barthes, Roland, 17, 33, 159n.3
Bassnett-McGuire, Susan E., 21, 38
Bates, Kathy, 28
Bauer, Raymond M. and Alice H., 115
Baym, Nina, 42
Becker, Susan, 46, 79
Belgrave, Cynthia, 102
Beloved (Morrison), 113, 115, 118
Belsey, Catherine, 33–34, 90, 159n.4,
Bennett, Susan, 10, 30, 160n.19
Betsko, Kathleen, 16, 23, 38, 124
Björnson, Björnstjerne, 45
Boothe, Clare: *The Women* 88–92
Bonner, Marita, 101
Boumelha, Penny, 53, 161n.33
Brater, Enoch, 41

Brecht, Bertolt, 27, 30, 35, 157
Brieux, Eugène, 45
Broun, Heywood, 88
Brown, Elsa Barkley, 95, 106
Brown-Guillory, Elizabeth, 117–18, 165n.15
Burk, Juli, 149–50
Burrill, Mary P., 95, 96, 115, 117, 118; *They That Sit in Darkness*, 109–12
Busia, Abena P. B., 112
Butler, Judith, 32, 34–35, 42, 65

Carlson, Susan, 92
Case, Sue-Ellen: on alterity, 160n.15; on realism, 27, 29, 48; on split subjects, 141, 161n.36
Chafe, William H., 46, 56, 70–71, 79–80, 86, 163n.17
Chapman, Abraham, 97
Childress, Alice, 124–33. Plays: *Trouble in Mind*, 125–26; *Wine in the Wilderness*, 124–32
Chodorow, Nancy, 159n.11
Chow, Rey, 91
Christian, Barbara 95, 102, 103, 111
Closure: Belsey on, 33; Fornes on, 34; feminist critique of, 32; in *The Flower Shop*, 76–78; in *A Man's World*, 76; in *Miss Lulu Bett*, 53–55; and realism, 19–20
Cole, Carole L., 55, 57, 78, 79, 82
Commire, Anne, 23
Cott, Nancy, 46, 79, 163n.17
Crothers, Rachel, 48; on women, 61, 79. Plays: *A Man's World*, 71–78, 79; *Mary the Third*, 48, 81–97; *Ourselves*, 62–68, 70, 79
Cultural feminism, 15, 23–25, 31
Cummings, Scott T., 153, 159n.2
Curb, Rosemary, 23, 64, 141, 147, 152
Cureau, Rebecca, 99

181

Curtis, L. P., Jr., 128
Cyborg, 119, 157

de Lauretis, 120, 122, 148–49, 160 n.19
Demastes, William W., 17, 19, 36, 41, 161 n.32
Diamond, Elin, 27, 35, 152
Dissemblance, culture of, 103, 108, 116
Dolan, Jill: on audience, 29; on Fornes, 15–17; on mimesis, 23, 32; on realism, 27, 157–58, 161 n.3
Domestic setting: entrapment in, 51–70; in Mary the Third, 81–85; in realism, 27, 29, 48–49; reversal of, in A Man's World, 72
Donovan, Josephine, 22
Double-voiced discourse. See Polyvocality
Du Bois, W. E. B., 40, 97–101, 106, 164 n.4
DuPlessis, Rachel Blau, 148

Eaton, Walter Prichard, 162 n.13
Ebert, Teresa L., 25, 34, 39
Edmonds, Randolph, 113
Eldest, The (Ferber), 51–54, 111, 120
Eliot, George, 146

Ferber, Edna: The Eldest, 51–54, 111, 120
Fehrenbach, Robert J., 100, 104, 107, 108
Felski, Rita, 20, 25, 38, 41, 45
Feminism. See Cultural feminism; Liberal feminism; Materialist feminism
Feminist drama: problems of defining, 16
Fetterley, Judith, 160 n.25
Flexner, Eleanor, 65
Flower Shop, The (Wentworth), 71–79
Fornes, Maria Irene: on closure, 34; on experimental dramatic forms, 38; Fefu and Her Friends 40; and feminism, 15–16; and hybrid dramatic forms, 15–18, 40; and realism, 15–18, 158
Forte, Jeanie, 32–33, 42, 122, 152
France, Rachel, 96, 162 n.11
Fraser, Nancy, 159 n.11
Frazier, E. Franklin, 126
Freeman, Edward, 128
Friedl, Bettina, 46

Friedman, Sharon, 47, 72, 81
Fuchs, Elinor, 39, 133

Gainor, J. Ellen, 47
Gale, Zona: Miss Lulu Bett, 53–57, 72
Gallop, Jane, 31
Gardiner, Judith Kegan, 42
Gassner, John, 19
Gates, Henry Louis, 96
Gems, Pam, 19
Genet, Jean, 143
Genovese, Eugene, 115
Gerstenberg, Alice: Overtones, 40, 48
Getting Out (Norman), 137–42
Gilbert, Sandra M., 40, 49–50, 71, 148
Gilligan, Carol, 159 n.11
Gilman, Charlotte Perkins: Something to Vote For, 68–70
Gipson, Rosemary, 93
Glaspell, Susan, 49, 89
Gottlieb, Lois, 64, 67, 72, 74, 81
Graham, Shirley, 95; It's Morning, 115–18; and motherhood, 112, 115–17; and oral history, 108, 117–18; and political activism, 96
Gregory, Montgomery, 98, 100, 102, 104, 111
Grimké, Angelina Weld: and double audience, 105–7; and feminism, 95–96, 104–5; on motherhood, 105–7; and oral history, 107–8; Rachel 104–9; and realism, 112
Gubar, Susan, 40, 41, 49–50, 71, 148
Gussow, Mel, 136

Hall, Katana, 97, 164 n.2
Hansberry, Lorraine, 109, 114
Haraway, Donna, 119, 157
Harlem Renaissance, 95–103, 164 n.2
Hart, Lynda, 24, 142, 143
Hatch, James V., 98, 106, 126
Hauptmann, Gerhart, 107
Hellman, Lillian, 49, 93
Henderson, Mae, 95
Higginbotham, Evelyn Brooks, 130
Hine, Darlene Clark, 103, 115, 116
Holocaust drama, 133–34, 137
hooks, bell, 118–19, 164 n.6
Huggins, Nathan Irvin, 97, 100
Hughes, Langston, 99, 113
Hull, Gloria T., 95–96, 102, 106–8, 164 n.1

Hybrid consciousness (of African-American women), 115, 119
Hybrid dramatic forms, 16, 17, 40, 123, 157–58

Ibsen, Henrik, 18, 37, 45, 76, 107, 149–50
Infanticide, 108, 113–14, 115–17
It's Morning (Graham), 115–18
Isser, E. R., 137

Jacobus, Lee, 18
Jameson, Fredric, 39, 123, 125
Jenkins, Linda Walsh, 23, 159n.10, 159n.12
Jensen, Joan M., 80
Johnson, Georgia Douglas: and political activism, 96; *Safe* 113–15

Kaplan, Amy, 18, 36–37, 51
Kaplan, E. Ann, 160n.19
Kendall, 38
Kennedy, Adrienne, 151–54; *The Ohio State Murders*, 152–54.
Kesselman, Wendy: *My Sister in This House*, 143–47
Keyssar, Helene: on folk drama, 164n.7; on Fornes, 15–16, 142, 159n.1; on *Getting Out*, 142, 165n.9, 166n.6; on hybrid consciousness, 114–15, 199; on *Rachel*, 107, 165n.9; on realism, 19; on women's plays, 23
Kilkelly, Ann Gavere, 146
King, Nicole, 153
Kiper, Florence, 44–45, 47–49, 61, 64, 76, 163n.20
Koenig, Rachel, 16, 23, 38, 124
Kolb, Deborah S., 46, 64, 80
Koppen, Randi S., 28
Kristeva, Julia, 122–23, 132, 136, 147
Kuhn, John G., 15

Lacan, Jacques, 141
Leavitt, Dinah Luise, 42
Lebow, Barbara, *A Shayna Maidel*, 133–37
Lebsock, Suzanne, 46, 70
Lester, Elenore, 89, 92
Liberal feminism, 21, 37, 152
Little, 163n.19
Lipkin, Joan: *Small Domestic Acts*, 155–56

Locke, Alain, 97–102, 104, 111, 164n.2
London Against Racism Campaign, 128, 165n.1
Lorde, Audre, 43, 116
Lubiano, Wahneema, 101, 130
Lynching: as feminist issue, 104, 114; in Grimké, 104–8; in Johnson, 113–14; plays protesting, 113–14

McDougald, Elise Johnson, 103
McGrath, John, 42, 157
McKay, Nellie, 98: on Grimké, 107, 109; on *They That Sit in Darkness*, 111–12; on women playwrights of the Harlem Renaissance, 102
Mainardi, Pat, 42
Mandl, Bette, 143
Man's World, A (Crothers), 71–78, 79
Marranca, Bonnie, 15, 17, 41
Mary the Third (Crothers), 48, 81–97
Materialist feminism, 21, 25–34, 39, 57, 120, 124, 127, 157; in Childress, 124–32; in *Ourselves*, 64; polyvocality and, 147–48; in *The Women* 87–89
Medea, 117
Melodrama, 18, 19, 36–37, 47
Merriam, Eve, 121
Miller, Arthur, 18, 19, 29, 40
Miller, Jeanne-Marie A., 96, 100, 101, 164n.9
Miller, May, 113
Mimesis: Diamond on, 35; Ebert on, 39; feminist critiques of, 20–35; Modleski on, 93; power of, 35, 47; as protest of status quo, 50–51; and realism, 16
Miner, Madonne, 140
Miss Lulu Bett (Gale), 53–57, 72
Modleski, Tania, 93
Moore, Honor, 121
Morrison, Toni, 97; *Beloved*, 113, 115, 118
Morton, Martha, 71, 87, 93
Motherhood, 104–18
Mulvey, Laura, 91, 160n.19
Murphy, Brenda, 36, 76
Murray, Timothy, 166n.6
My Sister in This House (Kesselman), 143–47

Nathan, George Jean, 92–93, 163n.21
Naturalism, 18–19, 45; influence on

Grimké, 107; in *They That Sit in Darkness*, 111–12
Neely, Carol Thomas, 150
Newton, Judith, 26, 148
Nineteenth amendment. *See* Woman suffrage
Norman, Marsha: *Getting Out* 40, 137–42

O'Casey, Sean, 124; *The Shadow of A Gunman*, 125–32
The Ohio State Murders (Kennedy), 152–54.
O'Neill, William L., 46, 79, 80, 162 n. 16
Oral history: in Graham, 108, 117–18; in Grimké, 107–8
Ourselves (Crothers), 62–68, 70, 79
Overtones (Gerstenberg), 40, 48

Patraka, Vivian M., 27, 137
Patterson, Ada, 71
Perkins, Kathy A., 68, 96, 99, 102, 114, 115
Pevitts, Beverly Byers, 16
Phelan, Peggy, 122
Polyvocality: and feminism, 42; in Kennedy, 152–53; and realism, 93–94, 147–48; in theater, 28; in women's texts, 39–40
Poststructuralism: critiques of realism, 26–27, 31, 33
Prison: in *Getting Out*, 29, 40, 138–43; realism as, 25–27; as setting, 29
Proscenium, 27, 40
Pruette, Lorine, 46, 80

Quigley, Austin E., 20

Rabe, David, 29
Rachel (Grimké), 104–9
Radical feminism. *See* Cultural feminism
Realistic contract, 17–18, 156
Realism: adaptability of, 40–41, 121, 123, 147–50, 156; Belsey on, 33–34; definitions of, 15–20; feminist challenges to, 21–35; as history of representation, 38–39; liberal feminism and, 21, 37; materialist feminist uses of, 120; as parody, 87; polyvocality of, 40; reevaluations of, 35–36, 149–50; 157–58; as social critique, 36–37, 40–41, 45–

47, 51; used to counteract stereotypes, 101–4, 116–17; used to reclaim history, 113, 117–18
Reinelt, Janelle, 16, 19, 68–69, 122, 157–58
Reinhardt, Nancy 22
Reproductive choice, 104, 107, 108, 110
Resolution, 17–18, 22, 148
Richards, Sandra, 165 n. 11
Robins, Elizabeth, 28
Rosenfelt, Deborah, 148

Safe (Johnson), 113–15
Sanders, Leslie Catherine, 100, 104
Schroeder, Patricia R., 161 n. 1
Scott, Freda L., 98, 109
The Shadow of A Gunman (O'Casey), 125–32
Shange, Ntozake, 114
Shaw, Bernard, 19, 36, 45, 49
Shayna Maidel, A, 133, 135, 136, 137, 142
She'll Find Her Way Home (Anderson), 154–55
Shepard, Sam, 29
Sherman, Martin, 29
Showalter, Elaine, 39, 40, 148
Silence, 144–46. *See also* Dissemblance, culture of
Simon, John, 140
Small Domestic Acts (Lipkin), 155–56
Smith, Anna Deveare, 149, 150
Smith, Barbara, 95,
Smith, Iris, 155, 156
Smith, Valerie, 95
Something to Vote For (Gilman), 68–70
Sontag, Susan, 16
Spectator. *See* Audience
Spencer, Jenny, 140
Spivak, Gayatri Chakravorty, 10
Split Britches, 149–50
Stephens, Judith: on anti-lynch plays, 113, 114, 165 n. 12; on Fornes, 15, 16; on *Miss Lulu Bett*, 53, 161 n. 2; on *Rachel*, 106; on realistic conventions, 41, 42
Stereotypes: of African-American women 102–3; of African Americans, 96, 98, 100–101; counteracting with realism, 101, 104; in *It's Morning*, 116–17; in *Rachel*, 106–7; in *They That Sit in*

Darkness, 111; in *Trouble in Mind*, 125

Stetson, Erlene, 96, 118

Storytelling. *See* oral history

Stowell, Sheila: on aesthetic forms, 41; on audiences, 28, 29; on Belsey, 160 n.28; on realism, 20, 28, 29, 36, 37, 41, 47; on *Something to Vote For*, 68; on suffrage drama, 162 n.10

Strindberg, August, 37, 45, 48, 107

Stucky, Nathan, 149

Suffrage plays, 47; *Something to Vote For*, 68–70

Suffragists. *See* woman suffrage

Sutherland, Cynthia, 46, 55, 61, 68, 80

Swanson, Gillian, 160 n.22

They That Sit in Darkness (Burrill), 109–12,

Trouble in Mind (Childress), 125–26

Tyler, Royall, 28

Vanden Heuvel, Michael, 29, 33, 36

Verisimilitude, 47, 123

Virgins in Paradise (Anderson), 155

Vote. *See* Woman suffrage

Wandor, Michelene, 21, 24, 162 n.14

War Brides (Wentworth), 57–60

Weedon, Chris, 38

Wentworth, Marion Craig: *The Flower Shop* 71–79; *War Brides,* 57–60

West, Cornel, 128

Wetzsteon, Ross, 15, 18, 34

White, Deborah Gray, 115

Wilkerson, Margaret B., 102, 105, 107

Williams, Raymond, 26, 37, 125

Williams, Tennessee, 40

Wine in the Wilderness (Childress), 124–32

Wintz, Cary D., 96, 164 n.1

Wittenstein, Kate, 115

Woman suffrage: aftermath of movement, 46, 79, 80, 86–87; as dramatic theme 44, 47, 56, 59, 68–70; women's political activities and, 45–46

The Women (Boothe), 88–92

Worthen, W. B., 15, 16, 19, 41, 47, 142

Young, Patricia Alzatia, 96, 111

Young, Stark, 88